The Coordination of the European Union

The Coordination of the European Union

Exploring the Capacities of Networked Governance

Andrew Jordan and Adriaan Schout

UNIVERSITY PRESS

OXFORD
UNIVERSITY PRESS

Great Clarendon Street, Oxford OX2 6DP

Oxford University Press is a department of the University of Oxford.
It furthers the University's objective of excellence in research, scholarship,
and education by publishing worldwide in

Oxford New York

Auckland Cape Town Dar es Salaam Hong Kong Karachi
Kuala Lumpur Madrid Melbourne Mexico City Nairobi
New Delhi Shanghai Taipei Toronto

With offices in

Argentina Austria Brazil Chile Czech Republic France Greece
Guatemala Hungary Italy Japan Poland Portugal Singapore
South Korea Switzerland Thailand Turkey Ukraine Vietnam

Oxford is a registered trade mark of Oxford University Press
in the UK and in certain other countries

Published in the United States
by Oxford University Press Inc., New York

British Library Cataloguing in Publication Data

Data available

Library of Congress Cataloguing in Publication Data

Jordan, Andrew, 1968–
The coordination of the European Union : exploring the capacities of
networked governance/Andrew Jordan and Adriaan Schout.
p. cm.
Includes bibliographical references.
1. European Union. 2. Public administration—European Union
countries. 3. European Union countries—Politics and government.
I. Schout, Andriaan, 1961– II. Title.
JN30.J58 2006
341.242′2—dc22   2006017470

Typeset by SPI Publisher Services, Pondicherry, India
Printed in Great Britain
on acid-free paper by
Biddles Ltd., King's Lynn, Norfolk

ISBN 0-19-928695-7   978-0-19-928695-9

1 3 5 7 9 10 8 6 4 2

To
Lauren, Ben, Sophie, and Lisa

Foreword

The ambitions to develop appropriate and effective collective policies in Europe continue to provide great challenges to both policymakers and analysts. Specifically within the European Union (EU), successful policy-making requires persistent endeavours to weave together into a single fabric the multiple needs of many different countries, each with its own specificities and idiosyncrasies. We can observe over the years processes of evolution and experimentation—older forms of governance and newer forms, some the product of explicit design, others the results of adaptation to circumstances. Moreover it is evident that a good understanding of what is happening requires not only careful observation of the 'macro' processes of policy development by and via the institutions of the EU, but also examination of the 'micro' processes of policy development within individual countries, not least the considerable variations among them.

Studies of EU governance mostly focus on only one of three dimensions: the EU level; the member state level; or the policy domain. Andrew Jordan and Adriaan Schout in this volume seek to address all three dimensions together. The reasoning is that: first, a focus on only one level of governance provides a very inadequate picture of what is happening; second, we need to dig deep into the variegated practices of individual countries; and, third, we need to relate processes and substance to each other. But to do all of this in a single study is indeed a daunting task. Nonetheless these authors aim precisely to put as much as possible of these three dimensions under the microscope, each bringing to the study an accumulation of expertise from their previous research.

In particular Jordan and Schout thereby seek to shed further light on several current preoccupations for analysts of European policymaking. They use 'coordination' as a running theme for exploring policy processes, with the aim of providing more precision to a term that is often used loosely. In so doing, they try to relate the burgeoning literature on EU governance to established theories of public administration and management. They also address a number of important questions about networked governance, a topic that is hotly disputed in the analytical literature. In addition they tackle the issue of how to distinguish between 'old' and 'new' modes of governance, a tantalizing distinction for all of us who work on EU policymaking.

Professor Helen Wallace
Robert Schuman Centre
European University Institute, Florence, Italy

Preface

The central puzzle addressed by this book is how should the European Union (EU) manage horizontal policy objectives like cross-border terrorism, drug crime, and environmental pollution when it is simultaneously divided into different administrative levels and competing policy sectors? For us, this puzzle first surfaced in relation to the ambitious Treaty-based commitment to integrate environmental thinking into the development and implementation of policy in all sectors—a very testing policy challenge commonly know as environmental policy integration (EPI). But in the course of writing this book, we have been struck by how many similar horizontal objectives and policy integration principles exist for other areas of the EU's work. These include, to name just a few, development cooperation with industrializing countries, better law-making, subsidiarity, deregulation, sustainability, gender equality, and social and also cohesion policy.

Evidently, 'better coordination' is something that many different parts of the EU aspire to achieve. But how can it be achieved when the EU's popular legitimacy is at an all-time low, its hierarchical steering capacity is increasingly being questioned, and (particularly after the 2004 EU enlargement) its member states are more, not less, diversified? Significantly, these problems and the governance challenges they provoke were aired in, but not resolved by, the European Commission's 2001 White Paper on governance.

In this book, we take EPI as a case study of how the EU is responding to these governance-related challenges. It is a good challenge to take as it covers a thirty-year period, many actors, and, like many other cross-cutting policy objectives, several levels of governance. Heads of state have pledged to achieve EPI on very many occasions, so at least on paper, adequate high-level political commitment is not an immediate problem. What we want to explore in this book is whether or not the EU has the administrative and institutional capacity needed to put this political commitment to EPI into effect.

EPI was formally adopted as an overarching objective of EU policy in the 1997 Amsterdam Treaty. Article 6 states that 'environmental protection requirements *must* be integrated into the definition and implementation of . . . Community policies . . . in particular with a view to promoting sustainable development' (emphasis added). Environmental policymakers at EU and national level were justifiably proud that Article 6 had elevated EPI to a guiding principle of EU policymaking. By 1998, the EU had a clear, Treaty-based commitment to achieve EPI and an innovative new 'mode' of governance—dubbed 'the Cardiff process'—to put it into practice. At the time, the Cardiff process was one of the Commission's 'big ideas' on coordinated environmental policymaking. Its appearance seemed to herald a whole new phase in environmental policymaking. Rather than regulate the sectors by imposing standards on them from the 'outside-in', the Cardiff process involved the creation of a multi-actor partnership (or network) which aimed to bind the various policy sectors together into a continuing process of target setting, reporting, and reviewing. In so doing, the various sectoral formations of the Council of Ministers were supposed to develop a wider and deeper sense of ownership for environmental problems that has traditionally been the case (Wilkinson et al. 2002: 5). This, DG Environment hoped would, in turn, encourage the sectors to find ways to 'design out' environmental damage from their policies at a much earlier stage in the EU policy process. Admittedly, EPI was and still is a fairly radical idea, that no EU member state is even close to implementing. But it works with the grain of best practice ideas disseminated by the United Nations and the OECD.

But then what happened? A senior Dutch official, Hugo Von Meijenfeldt, who had been intimately involved in negotiating Article 6, wanted to know how it should be translated into the nitty-gritty of daily policymaking in the EU. He organized a workshop in Luxembourg for the network of EU coordinators in the national environment ministries, which tried to translate the bold and lofty aspiration 'to integrate' into practical implementing steps in the member states and various EU institutions.

It soon emerged that his concerns were widely shared, at least by his opposite numbers in other national environment departments. Would, many asked, Article 6 and the Cardiff process network be sufficiently powerful to bring about the necessary cultural change in the sectors, or would it have to be supported by more detailed administrative and bureaucratic changes that govern the way in which individual EU policies are made? Both the OECD and the UN had already flagged the need to institutionalize EPI in policymaking systems, but nothing of this sort had been attempted in such a complex multilevel governance system as the EU. More importantly, would the establishment at EU level of a new mode of governance like the Cardiff process provide a sufficient governing response, or would supporting steps at national level also be required? During the workshop it soon emerged that national policymakers were not the only ones struggling to comprehend the full meaning of Article 6; Commission officials were also wondering how to ensure that the integrated policy strategies, targets, and timetables generated by the Cardiff process did not simply gather dust on shelves, but would lead to real policy change in the sectors. In all these respects, the Luxembourg workshop identified many more questions than answers.

In this book we hope to show that the way society responds to practical, 'real world' policy challenges like better horizontal and vertical coordination, necessarily raises profoundly important issues that are—or at least should be—directly relevant to the continuing debate about the precise meaning and practical implications of *governance* in the EU. The European Commission's White Paper on governance triggered a great deal of academic comment and debate about topics such as the viability of 'new' modes of governance, the organization of mechanisms to enhance stakeholder participation in EU policymaking, and, ultimately, the legitimacy of the whole European integration project. But even though the terms 'coordination', 'policy networks', and 'governance' are—at least conceptually— deeply interconnected, when we scoured the governance-related literature looking for a better theoretical and empirical understanding of the management of policy interdependence in the EU, we were surprised to find very little. Very few scholars appear to have grappled with the more administrative and bureaucratic implications of tackling growing policy interdependence in a complex, multilevel political system such as the EU.

In a sense, there is a worrying dichotomy between those who write about and study governance, and those (like Hugo Von Meijenfeldt) who need ready answers to complex, cross-cutting policy challenges like EPI. Policy documents produced by the EU display an implicit hope that simply talking and writing about 'governance' will somehow solve all the complex coordinating dilemmas by magically creating a sense of 'shared ownership'. The problem is that when everyone is responsible for delivering on a particular coordinating challenge, in practice no one is. To give just one example, the EU ministers responsible for cohesion policy recently agreed that the integration of territorial competitiveness should be taken into account when new policies are formulated in all fields. This should not be done through new legal frameworks but through 'multilevel govern-ance'—read, less prescriptive forms of coordination amongst networks of like-minded actors.[1] But precisely how will these networks emerge? How will they be structured? And how will their performance be guaranteed? As yet, the emerging literature on 'new' and more networked modes of governance has not really resolved these and many other management issues.

Invoking 'governance' (in the general sense of less hierarchical forms of steering) as a response to these and other problems, is understandable given the need for more interactive and multilevel cooperation across nearly all policy fields. However, the EU governance literature still has not fully explored what governance *actually* means in terms of implemen-table steps at the various administrative levels of the EU. This lack of precision hampers the development and testing of governance theory. In the prevailing literature, governance is strongly (and in some cases, exclu-sively) connected to the challenge of managing interorganizational net-works. Yet, there is still no agreed view on how new coordinating networks like Cardiff should be managed and/or connected to 'older' modes of governance like regulation. In fact, academics are still struggling to agree common definitions of associated terms like the 'open method of coord-ination' (OMC). More frustratingly, as it is currently conceived, the gov-ernance debate in the EU does not offer practitioners like Hugo Von Meijenfeldt the policy-relevant advice that they need to translate new coordinating objectives like Article 6 into everyday practice. Many policymakers that we spoke to during the writing of this book realized that new, multilevel coordination capacities may have to be created and managed to address increasingly interconnected policy processes. But very few have the time or, frankly, the political incentive, to identify what this may involve by way of new bureaucratic procedures, staff training, or network management.

By studying how the EU has sought to employ different modes of governance—both old and new—to address a coordination challenge (the environment), we hope to add empirical flesh to what has, for the most part, been a somewhat overtheorized debate about the empirical extent and mechanisms of governance in the EU. In so doing, we try to make new connections between the literatures on coordination, networks, and govern-ance. The creation and subsequent functioning of networks has tended to be explored in national settings, and largely from the perspective of interest intermediation (i.e. the lobbying of the EU). But how well do networks perform as governing devices in much more polycentric and multilevel settings like the EU? How do they emerge—spontaneously and in a largely 'self-organized' manner? Or do they need to be much more consciously created and subsequently managed by a central network manager? Finally, what kinds of links need to be made between coordinating networks at EU level and the coordinating capacities of the participating actors? Clearly, the two are potentially highly interrelated, but how does this play out in practice?

We have incurred a large number of debts since we started to write this book in 2001. We would first like to thank Hugo Von Meijenfeldt for sparking our interest in how networks could be used to engineer policy coordination in the EU. We would also think to thank the many officials and politicians in the EU who kindly agreed to share their experiences with us. We owe a special vote of thanks to our friend and colleague Martin Unfried (of the European Institute of Public Administration in Maastricht), who helped us in the first, critical stages of the project. He started the work on Germany and the European Parliament, ably assisted by Sarah Blau, who at the time worked for the European Parliament's Environment, Public Health, and Food Safety Committee.

Finally, we would like to acknowledge the financial support provided (especially to Andrew) by the UK Economic and Social Research Council (Award No: M535255117) and the Leverhulme Trust, which awarded him a Philip Leverhulme Prize fellowship in 2004. The National Europe Centre at the ANU in Canberra kindly offered Andrew a visiting fellowship in 2005, which allowed him to complete the final drafts of many of the chapters. Adriaan Schout would very much like to thank the European Institute of Public Administration and the Clingendael European Studies Programme in The Hague, for allowing him the research time to complete this study.

Andrew Jordan and Adriaan Schout

Canberra and Maastricht

November 2005

Note

1. For example, *Territorial state and perspectives of the European Union: towards a stronger European territorial cohesion in the light of the Lisbon and Gothenburg ambitions,* Presidency paper endorsed by the Ministers for Spatial Development and the European Commission at an Informal Ministerial Meeting on Regional Policy and Territorial Cohesion, 20–1 May 2005, Luxembourg.

Contents

Contents

List of Tables and Boxes

List of Abbreviations

APS	Annual Policy Strategy (European Commission)
BNC	*Beoordeling Nieuwe Commissievoorstellen* (Committee to Assess New Commission Proposals (Netherlands)
CIM	*Coordinatie Commissie voor International Milieuvraagstukken* (Netherlands)
CoCo	Coordination Committee for International Affairs (Netherlands)
CoCoHan	Coordination Committee at Senior Management Level (Netherlands)
COREPER	*Comité de Représentantes Permanentes* (Permanent Representatives Committee) (EU)
DEFRA	Department for Environment, Food and Rural Affairs (UK)
DG	Directorate General
DGEP	Directorate General for Environmental Policy (Netherlands)
EAP	Environmental Action Programme
ECJ	European Court of Justice
EEA	European Environment Agency
EEB	European Environmental Bureau
EEC	European Economic Community
EIA	Environmental impact assessment
EPG	Environmental Protection Group (UK)
EPI	Environmental policy integration
EPINT	Environmental Protection International (UK)
EPRG	Environmental Policy Review Group (European Commission)
EU	European Union
EU-EPI	Environmental Policy Integration at EU level
GAC	General Affairs Council (EU)
GRI	Group for International Relations (European Commission)
Hebdo	*Hebdomadaire* (meeting of the *chefs de cabinet*) (European Commission)
IA	Impact assessment (European Commission)
ICER	Interdepartmental legal team (Netherlands)
IEEP	Institute for European Environmental Policy

IMPEL	Implementation and Enforcement of Environmental Law network (EU)
IVO	International VROM meeting (Netherlands)
JCME	Joint Ministerial Committee on the EU (UK)
MEP	Member of the European Parliament
NEPI	'New' environmental policy instrument
NEPP	National Environmental Policy Plan (Netherlands)
NGO	Non-governmental organization
OECD	Organization for Economic Cooperation and Development
OMC	Open method of coordination
RIA	Regulatory impact assessment
RIVM	*Rijkinstitut van Volkegezondheid en Milieu* (National Institute of Public Health and Environmental Protection) (Netherlands)
SDC	Sustainable Development Commission (EU)
SDS	Sustainable development strategy (EU)
SDU	Sustainable Development Unit (UK)
SEA	Strategic Environmental Assessment
SG	Secretariat-General (European Commission)
SIA	Sustainability impact assessment
SPP	Strategic Planning and Programming Initiative (European Commission)
UK	United Kingdom
UKREP	United Kingdom Permanent Representation
UN	United Nations
VROM	*Ministerie voor Volkshuisvesting, Ruimtelijke Ordening en Milieubeleid* (Dutch environment ministry) (Netherlands)
WCED	World Commission on Environment and Development (UN)

Part I

Introduction

1

POLITICAL AMBITIONS AND COORDINATION CAPACITIES: THE MANAGEMENT OF HORIZONTAL AND VERTICAL INTERDEPENDENCE

The task [of governing the European Union] is not easy. The step by step integration, which has characterised the [EU's] development, has tended to slice policies into sectoral strands, with different objectives and different tools; over time the capacity to ensure the coherence [*sic*] has diminished.... The [EU] Institutions and the Member States must work together to set out an overall policy strategy. For this purpose, they should... refocus the Union's policies and adapt the way the Institutions work....

> European Union White Paper on governance,
>
> (CEC 2001: 28)

What we need is a continuous political dialogue, not within the Councils but within the Commission, where there are real problems.... [B]reaking those [Chinese walls] down and getting the Directorates-General to talk to each other in the preparation of policy... is the single most important area of improvement.

> Michael Meacher, UK Minister for the Environment,
>
> (HC 842ii Session 1998–9, col. 128)

A more coordinated European Union?

In recent years, the European Union (EU) has come under mounting pressures to adapt itself to a host of new policy challenges, some of them internal and some external. One of these is the growing importance of horizontal policy problems such as international terrorism, people trafficking, drug crime, regional competitiveness, and unsustainable development. The need to respond to these problems has been greatly exacerbated by a set of more internal challenges such as EU enlargement, economic reform, and continuing doubts about the efficacy and legitimacy of the so-called 'Community Method' of coordinating by legislating (Majone 1996; Jachtenfuchs 2001). Together, the recent combination of these external and internal challenges has forced the EU to re-evaluate its whole understanding of *governance*, or approach to societal steering. Many of the newer—or "wicked"—problems confronting the EU are especially problematic because they severely challenge the established means of governing and are, therefore, not amenable to standard (i.e. national or single sector) policy solutions (Rittel and Weber 1973). Crucially, many of the themes raised in the Commission's White Paper on governance quoted above, powerfully highlighted the need to find new ways simultaneously to *coordinate* (or govern) greater horizontal and vertical interdependencies in the EU. It is this particular aspect of the governance debate that we address in this book.

We approach the governance debate from a coordination perspective. Much has been written about EU policy coordination. In this chapter we shall demonstrate that one major stream of the existing literature relates to the management of EU affairs within individual member states (e.g. Kassim 2000; 2001). Another, much younger stream deals with coordination at EU level; that is, using different instruments to align the actions of the member states to EU policies either through 'old' regulation or through new and 'soft' instruments (Eberlein and Kerwer 2004). However, these two strands of the coordination literature have largely developed in isolation from one another. Apart from the odd cross-reference (e.g. in the White Paper quoted above), practitioners and scholars tend to ignore the need for the European Commission and the member states to work *together* throughout the policy process to tackle policy coordination challenges. In the quotation above, a national politician, Michael Meacher, implies that this is a task for the Commission to deal with. He is not alone in this view. During the writing of this book, we came across many other actors at national level who fully expected the Commission to manage growing policy interdependence in the EU. And yet, the quotation at the beginning of this chapter makes it quite clear that the Commission feels that policy interdependence is a shared challenge, which requires a shared response.

Failing to see policy coordination as a shared challenge has, we contend, major implications for the governance of the EU. As discussed in more detail below, the Commission needs the pressure from the member states to think and act in terms of horizontal interdependence (e.g. by producing more coordinated policy proposals that respect the principle of subsidiarity) across *all* phases of the EU policy. In short, the responsibility for interconnecting policies in the EU is not simply a matter of acting either at EU or at national level, but of working at both levels in a context of multilevel interdependence. The national coordination literature (Kassim et al. 2000; 2001) starts at the other end of this problem, since it focuses on what the member states (could) do to coordinate their input to decision-making in the Council of Ministers. However, it glosses over the equally important question of what member states have to do to fulfil the EU's policy coordination objectives with respect to boundary spanning challenges such as immigration, crime, and sustainable development. Similarly, if the zenith of the traditional Community Method of coordinating by legislating has, as is now being argued, been passed, the debate about new coordinating instruments should not simply focus on their deployment at either national or EU level. The capacity of actors at both levels needs to be brought into the equation. To give just one practical example, the efforts to make the European economies more competitive (the so-called 'Lisbon' process—see below) requires actions to be taken by a plethora of public and private actors at all levels of governance (High Level Group 2004).

In an attempt to address the 'mismatch' between these policy coordination challenges and its internal capacity to respond (Eberlein and Kerwer 2004: 122), the EU has accelerated its search for new coordination instruments. For example, 'czars' have been created to coordinate responses to shared problems such as global terrorism; groups of Commissioners have been created to tackle cross-cutting challenges like economic competitiveness (CEC 2005g); steps have been taken to create the unified 'diplomatic service' (the European External Action Service) and EU foreign minister provided for by the draft EU Constitution; and many new independent regulatory agencies have been formed to play a coordinating role in more technical policy areas (Everson et al. 2000; Flinders 2004: 531–2).

While noting some of these initiatives, in this book we aim to explore the role—both real and potential—played by one particular family of coordinating devices, which have come to be known as 'new' (Héritier 2001; 2003), 'newer' (Hodson and Maher 2001: 801), or 'soft' (Meyer 2004: 814) instruments or modes of governing. In particular, we address what is needed to ensure these new modes function effectively at national *and* at European levels. There is, as yet, no common definition of 'new modes of governance' let alone agreement on what their use in the EU entails (de Burca and Scott 2006). Symptomatically, they are mentioned but not defined in the 2001 governance White Paper. Normally, they are defined in relation to what they are not, that is the traditional Community Method of coordinating primarily via legislative means. This involves the Council of Ministers adopting legislative proposals drawn up by the European Commission (Scott and Trubek 2002: 4–5; ibid: 2–3). According to Héritier (2001: 2–3), new modes can be broadly defined to include voluntary agreements, different forms of self-regulation, soft law, and open methods of coordination (OMC)[1] as practised under the Lisbon process.[2] The open method is a particularly 'soft' form of coordination (Stubb, Wallace, and Peterson 2003: 152), because it involves states mimicking one another's best practices via guidelines, peer review, benchmarking, and policy-learning activities in a way that induces *voluntary* rather than obligatory policy convergence—and hence coordination (Scott and Trubek 2002: 5–6).

As is becoming increasingly clear, these new modes do not entirely replace but instead complement the 'old' Community Method of legislating (Eberlein and Kerwer: 2004; Jordan et al. 2007; Trubeck and Trubeck 2007). For us, the crucial point about new modes of governance is that they seek to build upon the EU's existing capacity to achieve its policy goals not through legislating or creating and/or altering markets, but via more '*networked*' forms of (multilevel) governance (Stubb, Wallace, and Peterson 2003: 148; Schout and Jordan 2005) (hereafter 'networked governance'). This trend towards networked governance in general and new modes in particular, is by no means unique to the EU; it is occurring in many sectors and political systems (Kooiman 2003; Goldsmith and Eggers 2004; Rhodes 1997a; 2000b; Lyall and Tait 2005; Koenig-Archibugi and Zürn 2006), in which central bodies 'have become increasingly dependent upon the cooperation and joint resource mobilization of policy actors outside their hierarchical control' (Börzel 1998: 260). This shift from hierarchical to more diffuse forms of societal steering is said to typify the transition from government to governance (Flinders 2002; 2004).

Until recently, the concept of policy networks was used mainly to understand why 'good' policies adopted centrally fall down at the implementation stage (Kickert et al. 1997a: 2). On this view, networks do all sorts of 'bad' things like frustrate attempts by central bodies to coordinate, retard policy innovation, and generally delegitimize policymaking (Kickert et al. 1997b: 170–1; Marsh and Rhodes 1992). But in actively exploring the coordinating potential of networked governance, the EU is implicitly adopting a much more positive perspective on the governance transition (see Peters 2000: 40),[3] which *suggests* that when properly harnessed (i.e. managed) networks are, in some situations, capable of providing an alternative means of fulfilling complex policy goals to hierarchy. This is because in modern policy systems (particularly polycentric ones like the EU), central bodies have a diminishing capacity to exert hierarchical authority, and should instead be viewed as a participant—albeit a special one—in interorganizational networks.

This view has been expressed by Kickert et al. (1997*b*: 171), who write:

the existence of networks cannot be denied. It is far better to face this fact and analyse how they work, looking for ways to improve them rather trying to ignore or abolish them.

There is certainly no shortage of policy networks in the EU. On the contrary, the EU is often said to be replete with them (Peterson 1997: 17). Similarly, the academic literature on EU policy networks is voluminous, but it is only relatively recently that scholars have started to analyse 'how EU policy networks can be structured and managed in order to serve the greater European good' (Peterson 2004: 133) (as opposed to the 'good' of private interests) (Metcalfe 2000). This need for new forms of policy network analysis raises fundamental questions about *inter alia* the vertical coordination between member states and EU-level actors like the Commission, as well as that spanning different policy sectors. So, for example, if greater coordination is to be pursued through networks, what are the implications for the actors involved? Are the networks likely to be self-organizing and possibly also self-managing? If not, what kind of coordinating capacities does that demand from, for example, the network, and what steering role (if any) does any central body (e.g. the Commission) need to play? And finally, what kinds of coordination obligations and requirements does all this impose on the network participants, principally the member states?

Drawing on a detailed case study of the handling of a relatively well-established horizontal policy objective (environmental protection), this book begins the task of addressing these questions. Then, we should be in a better position to judge whether the interest now being shown in new modes of governance is warranted. In Chapter 2, we define coordination capacities as mechanisms that facilitate coordination within networks of interdependent actors. They do this by: helping the participants to exchange information amongst themselves; identifying issues requiring coordinated solutions; and arbitrating when conflicts cannot be settled informally by the participants.

The remainder of this chapter proceeds as follows. In Section 2, we briefly review the debate which has emerged around the concept of governance. We show that while this debate is commonly (and sometimes exclusively—Rhodes 1997a) framed in terms of networks, it has not satisfactorily clarified how horizontal and vertical coordination can be simultaneously addressed in and by networks. In Section 3 we explain what we mean by coordination. Then we show why the coordination of a cross-sectoral, boundary-spanning challenge like environmental protection is especially difficult to achieve in a complex multilevel governance system such as the EU. In Section 4 we describe the three most widely known and intensively studied modes of coordination—that is, hierarchy, markets, and networks—in more detail, and then relate them to the steps taken by the EU to achieve greater environmental coordination at EU level. We show that the emerging pattern is one of moving away from more hierarchical approaches involving regulation, to those relying more heavily on markets and networks. In Section 5 we outline the essential characteristics of the environmental coordination challenge, and then in Section 6 we draw together the different strands of our argument and identify our research questions. In the final section we introduce the remainder of the book and highlight what we believe is particularly distinctive about our approach to understanding the coordinating ability of modes that rely upon networked governance.

Extending the coordination debate in the EU

Exploring the capacity of new modes of governance

The literature on new modes of governance in the EU is growing rapidly but the 'empirical evidence is neither conclusive nor does it permit a full evaluation of the possible scope and success of new governance' (Eberlein and Kerwer 2004: 122–3). Moravcsik (2005: 366) is correct when he observes that 'controlled empirical studies... have been extremely modest'. In particular, insufficient effort has been invested in exploring precisely what networked governance requires in terms of establishing and sustaining the relevant networks (i.e. if they do not spontaneously or otherwise successfully 'self-organize', who or what will step in to manage them and how?) and ensuring that the network as well as the participants are equipped with the necessary internal coordinating capacities.

In this study we systematically explore how well networked governance is performing in practice by taking the environment as a detailed test case. Environmentalists have long argued that when environmental policy is simply preoccupied with rectifying the environmental impact of sectoral policies, public policy as a whole will not be sufficiently coordinated and, consequently, society will fail to develop more sustainably. It would be far better, they claim, if environmental thinking was integrated into the development of sectoral policies at the start, so as to 'design out' pollution, natural habitat loss, and other forms of environmental damage.

Greater environmental coordination—or 'environmental policy integration'—EPI—is a long-standing aim of EU policy and a principle of good governance in the Organization for Economic Cooperation and Development (OECD) (OECD 2002a). EPI was included in Article 6 of the preamble to the 1997 Amsterdam Treaty. This clause states that 'environmental protection requirements must be integrated into the definition and implementation of...Community policies... in particular with a view to promoting sustainable development.' Similar clauses can be found in EU law and policy documentation which promote the integration (or mainstreaming) of many other policy concerns, ranging from gender equality and regional policy, through to development cooperation and social policy. The key thing which we want to investigate in this book is: has this new principle been supported with adequate coordination capacities to ensure its implementation?

Shortly after the formal signing of the Amsterdam Treaty, the EU established a new mode of governance known as the Cardiff process[4] to implement the new legal commitment to EPI at EU level (or 'EU-EPI'[5]). Crucially, this new mode sought to harness the coordinating power of networks to achieve EU-EPI. By binding themselves together into a shared network (the term used at the time was actually 'partnership' (CEC 1998)—see Chapter 3) collectively to report on and review the steps needed to implement EPI, the various sectoral formations of the Council of Ministers were supposed to develop a 'sense of ownership' for environmental problems that had hitherto been absent (Wilkinson et al. 2002: 5). Crucially, Directorate General (DG) Environment's role in this arrangement was not to impose standards on the sectors from the outside (as was predominantly the case under the Community Method), but instead to initiate a self-sustaining process of intersectoral and interinstitutional learning and acting. However, by the mid-2000s, deep disillusionment had set in as the process of reporting slowed to a standstill, and an effective and enduring cross-sectoral coordinating network failed to materialize, in spite of the very high-level political commitment to create one. A recent

Commission stocktake rather glumly concluded that EPI was 'still largely to be translated into further concrete results for the environment... the [Cardiff] process has failed to deliver fully on expectations' (CEC 2004b: 31).

Although the Cardiff process is not *stricto sensu* an open method of coordination (for a historical overview, see De la Porte (2002)),[6] it does, as we shall explain in Chapter 3, share many of its core features (Scott and Trubek 2002: 5; Homeyer, Klasing, and Kraemer 2004: 14).[7] Importantly, having operated since 1998, it represents a good empirical test case of the coordinating potential of networked forms of governance.

Why link multilevel governance and coordination?

By proceeding in this way, we hope to achieve a number of new things. First, we hope to add some much needed empirical flesh to what has, for the most part, been a somewhat over-theorized debate about the empirical extent and effectiveness of governance,[8] not only within, but also beyond the EU (Eberlein and Kerwer 2004: 122, 136; van Kersbergen and van Waarden 2004: 165; Kooiman 2003: 4–5; Flinders 2002: 55). In Chapter 2 we show that the appearance of the term governance has successfully (re)problematized the vexed question of societal steering. Thus, under a 'government' approach, it is commonly assumed that society is steered from the centre (normally by the state), whereas in a 'governance' model, 'society actually does more self-steering rather than depending upon guidance from government' (Peters 2000: 36). In this book we explore the extent to which a particular new mode of governance (i.e. the Cardiff process) has facilitated the necessary degree of self-steering or self-organization among the key participants (i.e. the sectors) that large parts of the governance literature seem to assume. Having done that, we should be able to offer a more rounded assessment of the coordinating potential of new (and older) modes of governance in the EU.

Second, our study aims to make new connections between networked governance in different administrative settings. For the most part, the creation and subsequent management of networks has tended to be explored in national settings,[9] where the networks and the means to manage them (i.e. through state-led steering) are better established (Kickert et al. 1997c; Klijn and Koppenjan 2000; Koppenjan and Klijn 2004). One of the aims of this book is to explore how far these insights can be applied to the more polycentric and multilevel setting of the EU, where vastly greater coordination is required across and between different levels of governance.

Third, in order to capture completely the full horizontal and vertical complexity of many coordination challenges in the EU, we look across the full cycle of policy development; that is, from the development of Commission proposals through to co-decisionmaking with the European Parliament. We also take a vertical slice through the different layers of governance in the EU to expose the day-to-day operation of policymaking in three member states, namely Germany, the Netherlands, and the UK, as they interact with EU-level processes.[10] Finally, in view of the interdependence between levels of governance and phases of decisionmaking, we also analyse the coordination capacities within the European Commission and—for the first time—the European Parliament. The Commission is potentially important because of its administrative and management skills; the European Parliament on the other hand is a potentially important source of political pressure on the other actors to work together in networks. To our knowledge, these multiple dimensions have not been systematically examined in one volume before.

Coordination: what is it and why is it so difficult?

Coordination challenges in the EU

Coordination is one of those analytical terms that is regularly used but seldom defined satisfactorily (Wildavsky 1996: 131). Therefore, in Chapter 2 we draw upon the work of Metcalfe (1994), who has helpfully separated out the most important meanings and plotted them onto a scale, ranging from loose forms of coordination which are suitable for simple tasks, to more tightly integrated systems aimed at the management of more controversial and/or encompassing tasks.

Coordination is notoriously difficult for *any* policy system to achieve—it has been aptly described as a 'philosopher's stone' (Seidman 1970) or 'Holy Grail' (Hanf 1978) of all policy systems—'ever sought, but always just beyond reach' (Rhodes 2000a: 359). There are, however, good reasons for believing that coordination in the EU will be an especially difficult nut to crack. Peters and Wright (2001: 158) note that 'managing the problems of fragmentation, sectoralization and policy interdependence is not peculiar to Brussels, but the extent and nature of these problems in Brussels is of a different order from that prevailing in the member states.' One obvious reason is that EU decisionmaking is both highly expansive and multi-modal (Peterson 1995). That is to say, it stretches from everyday 'micro-level sectoral decisions' that shape individual items of policy right up to the grand, 'high politics' decisions taken in intergovernmental confer-ences that shape the wider constitutional structure of the EU (Peters and Wright 2001: 159). In our analysis, we shall look at all points on this continuum, but especially the more mundane, 'everyday' decisions.

Another reason is that the EU has an extremely fluid and almost con-stantly expanding agenda of policy problems (Peters and Wright 2001: 158), each of which brings together many actors, sectors, and member states in a complex game of three-dimensional chess. Furthermore, if agendas are this fast moving, it may well limit the time that political leaders can devote to championing any particular coordination issue, hence the desire to institutionalize EPI in the administrative and political system of the EU (OECD 2002a; EEA 2005a). Strong political support is often pinpointed as a sine qua non of effective coordination (Peters 1998b: 52), but it is also dependent on effective coordination. A chicken and egg problem is potentially at stake here: political support influences coordin-ation, but coordination also creates political support. By identifying con-flicts between sectoral policies, effective coordination capacities can clarify the issues that politicians should look at. Coordination capacities, there-fore, help to make issues political. Rather than looking at either the 'polit-ics' or 'administration' of policy coordination, in this book we investigate the extent of their mutual interdependence.

A third reason is that successive enlargements since 1957 have brought more and more member states into the EU, some of whom have relatively weak internal coordinating capacities (Council of the European Union 1999), or who need time to readjust to the demands imposed by EU membership (Jordan and Liefferink 2004). The perceived need (as expressed in the governance White Paper) to incorporate a much wider array of stakeholders in EU-level decisionmaking only adds to the practical problem of policy coordination.

Another reason is that coordinating in a multilevel, multi-actor system such as the EU, extends the 'policy chain' almost to breaking point (Peters and Wright 2001: 157). At a very basic level, it involves negotiating within and between national ministries (intra- and interministerial respectively), as well as coordinating right across the interface with different EU institu-tions. It is widely known that the addition of a European dimension to any coordination problem adds extra potential for inconsistent policymaking (CEC 2001b: 44). Even something as apparently simple as the sequence in which decisions are taken at EU and/or national levels, can complicate the search for an adequately coordinated solution.

Fifth, the EU is arguably more deeply sectorized or 'pillarised' (Peterson 1997: 5) than most national systems (Peters and Wright 2001: 161). Thus, each sector has *inter alia* its own sectoral Council of Ministers, DG of the Commission, European Parliament Committee, and set of lobby groups. As a result, 'turf battles' between sectoral interests are 'frequent, but the "firewalls" between sectors are high and often impermeable' (Peterson 1997: 5). Moreover, each sector has its own major multi-annual strategy or set of strategies running at EU level (Agenda 2000, Better Regulation, the Environmental Action Programmes, etc.). These currently total well over sixty and synchronizing them is a major administrative headache (CEC 2001b: 44). Just to complicate things still further, the incentive for a given sector to distribute information to cognate sectors on likely spillover effects, let alone ameliorate them at an early stage in the policy cycle, can often be quite low. Thus, intersectoral conflicts tend to be bottled up, overloading the already overburdened coordinating capacities of the Council of Ministers (Schout and Jordan 2005).

Sixth, coordination is even more complex when governance (as in the EU) is multilevel. There are several aspects to this. We have already noted that while it may be possible (and perhaps even preferable) to tackle cross-cutting problems at EU level, the EU institutions cannot be expected to deliver more coordinated policies on their own. The Commission is a relatively small organization: it is structurally dependent on national administrations (Dimitrakapolous and Richardson 2001; Kassim 2003a: 161), 'which themselves suffer from implementation problems' (Peters and Wright 2001: 161). To give one practical example, even if the Commission were able to produce (as it now being asked—see Chapter 7) much more coordinated proposals that satisfy the principles of subsidiarity and better regulation, it remains heavily reliant on other actors to translate them into (and implement) EU policy.

The second aspect is that national administrative coordination systems were originally designed to coordinate national policy in domestic settings (see above), not to manage policy in supranational settings like the EU (Peters and Wright 2001: 156–61; Peters 1998a: 295–6), so they are arguably still not yet fully equipped to make up for any 'management deficit' at EU level (Metcalfe 1994: 273). EU membership brings with it new coordination challenges, which even the best organized member states have not completely addressed (Kassim 2003a; 2003b). Often a clash emerges at the national level between officials who work more on

EU-related issues (i.e. the EU coordinators in foreign affairs and sectoral ministries), and those whose work is more oriented towards national objectives. Getting administrations at all levels to 'think European' still remains a challenge, despite countless 'Europeanization' initiatives, particularly at national levels (Jordan 2002a; 2003; Schout and Bastmeijer 2003).

The coordination of specific policy challenges

These basic institutional and political features make the EU difficult to steer (i.e. govern), but even more problems come into focus if we look in more detail at what Peters and Wright (2001: 159) refer to as 'micro-level sectoral decisions' associated with a particular coordination challenge like EPI. By this, they mean the development, adoption, and implementation of individual items of policy. Although the Commission has generally taken the lead in advocating EPI at EU level (see Chapter 3) and, as the formal initiator of all new EU policies, has a special responsibility to ensure it is achieved, it suffers from coordination problems of its own (Kassim 2003a: 158–9; Jordan et al. 2007). As the sectoral DGs have their own objectives, and have to respond to demands from their own client groups and lack time, it is naive to assume that they will automatically give the environment an equal status to their own sectoral interests. This effectively means that DG Environment must monitor new policy proposals developed by the sectoral DGs to ensure they do not jeopardize EPI at EU level. This could well involve covering different levels of governance and different stages of the policy process: not easy.

In addition, every DG must ensure there is adequate support within the respective formation of the Council. Commission officials in the sector DGs will be most strongly motivated to keep an eye on the environmental consequences of their actions if they know that the Council welcomes ambitious environmental objectives. The link between the different levels of governance is thus potentially crucial. The various Commission DGs will only be sufficiently motivated if their national counterparts show they are strongly committed to EPI (i.e. vertical interdependence). At the same time, EPI requires environment officials to shift their current focus on developing new environment policies towards 'greening' policymaking in sector DGs and sector Councils. This means that national environment officials have to monitor and, where appropriate, offer their political support to, the early phases of policymaking, so that the Commission knows that EPI is being taken seriously (i.e. horizontal interdependence). However, we have already noted that their support should not be assumed to exist, given that many national officials already find it a challenge to 'think (and act) European' in their own sector, let alone in relation to cognate sectors. EU-EPI, therefore, unhelpfully combines both dimensions (i.e. vertical coordination between the EU and states—in our case, the coordination of EU affairs within each sector—and horizontal coordination across sectors (i.e. EPI)). Hence it is very much a *double*, not a single coordination challenge, requiring simultaneous vertical and horizontal coordination (Héritier 2001: 2).

Improving coordination: exploring the available tool kit

The three main modes of coordination

The near universal agreement on the desirability of 'better coordination' (Pressman and Wildavsky 1984: 133) belies a great deal of disagreement about the best way to achieve it (Thompson et al. 1995: 3; Thompson 2003). Traditional accounts of governance focus on the two most commonly known and best-understood modes of coordination, namely hierarchies and markets. More recent scholarship has added a third mode to this list, namely networks (e.g. Kaufman et al. 1985; Powell 1990; Börzel 1998: 255; Kooiman 2003; Thompson 2003; Wollman 2003).

The popular image of hierarchy 'is one of a top down command structure, where the flow of direction is "downwards" from higher to lower tiers in a pyramid type matrix' (Thompson 2003: 24). Hierarchy works best where the parts of an organization are well integrated from top to bottom (Peters 1998a: 298), and where there are clear rules and standards to ensure that subordinate bodies act in a coordinated manner (Thompson 2003: 23). Crucially, none of these conditions are fully satisfied in the EU. The underlying ontology of hierarchical tools is that social actors are generally unwilling to coordinate and have to be 'coerced' into doing so (Peters 2003). The most commonly known means of achieving this is by regulating, but:

[T]he advantages of hierarchical coordination are lost in a world that is characterised by increasingly dense, extended and rapidly changing patterns of reciprocal interdependence, and by increasingly frequent, but ephemeral, interactions across all types of pre-established boundaries, intra- and interorganisational, intra- and intersectoral, intra- and international. (Scharpf 1994: 37)

Market mechanisms, on the other hand, work rather differently. The assumption here is that the 'invisible hand' of the market will incentivize the self-interest of participants to coordinate in a more effective way than the hard and blunt 'stick' of regulation. Advocates claim that markets do not require a conscious, organizing centre (Thompson 2003: 24). However, the market is not necessarily a realistic means of coordinating activities in all policy settings. Indeed, 'the market' is not a given—politically complex steps may sometimes have to be taken to create it as well as the necessary 'buyers' and 'sellers' (Peters 1998a: 298). All these steps may well amount to an exercise in hierarchy that may lie beyond the grasp of multipolar governance systems such as the EU (Peters 2003).

Finally, there are *networks*. Definitions and interpretations abound (Börzel 1998; Thatcher 1998), but in essence, they are 'characterised by informal relationships between *essentially equal* agents or social agencies' (Heywood 2000: 19) (emphasis added) (see also Börzel 1998: 254). Through their informal interaction in networks, actors gradually identify common concerns and solutions to them. Coordination in networks is therefore built, above all, on *trust* and loyalty rather than administrative commands (hierarchy) or prices (markets) (Thompson 2003: 30). For Thompson (2003), in networks there is typically a 'kind of *equality of membership*, where *joint responsibility* holds' (emphasis in original). Scholars disagree, however, on the origins of trust. Does it arise from repeated interactions, from common values, or something else (Tenbensel 2005: 273)?

Nowadays, many scholars view governance in the EU through the prism of networks (e.g. Marks 1993: 402; Peterson 1995; Peterson and Bomberg 1999; Eising and Kohler-Koch 1999). For them, the EU *is* 'a network organization' primarily because there is no single authoritative figure (Sbragia 2000: 220). It is indubitable that the EU is replete with networks, that many important decisions are made in networks, and that networks are such potentially powerful steering devices that the Commission occasionally goes out of its way to create them (Sbragia 2000: 235). Networks would certainly appear to be consistent with the less 'top down' role that the Commission pledged to fulfil in its governance White Paper, where it operates 'at the hub of networks of European governance rather than the apex of a hierarchy' (Metcalfe 2000: 825). It may, however, require a huge leap of faith to use the empirical fact that EU policymaking is highly networked, to claim that networks (or networked governance) are—and should increasingly be—the preferred means of governing. It is to this vexed issue that we now turn.

The interaction between the three modes

Normally, these three modes are presented as though they are almost mutually exclusive 'ideal types' (Tenbensel 2005: 268). Governance researchers, however, must be alert to (and be capable of understanding) their mutual interdependence (Powell 1990; Kjær 2004: 203–4). After all, 'it's the mix [between the types] that matters' (Rhodes 1997: 53).

The 'compatibilities and tensions' (Tenbensel 2005: 268) between hierarchy and networks are particularly germane to this study. To suggest that networks are typically 'flatter' organizational forms than hierarchies (e.g. Thompson 2003: 31) actually begs many more questions than it answers. There are some who do believe that networks—as with systems of governance more generally—are 'fit' for many purposes because they are essentially self-organizing and self-steering. Rhodes (1996: 660) goes as far as to claim that governance *is* 'self-organising, inter-organizational networks'.[11] If coordination requires little or no hierarchical steering (cf. Richards and Smith 2002: 23), then it may well be appropriate to view networks as relatively 'flat' structures. Indeed, some commentators go as far as to claim that steering networks is not only difficult (Rhodes 1997a: 15), but may even lead to perverse outcomes (Kickert 1993).

It is not difficult to see why much of the policy network literature assumes that networks are self-organizing; after all, it was originally developed to describe the segmentation of policymaking into mutually discrete sectors or 'domains' (for a summary, see Smith 1993: 56–7) comprising actors with shared interests and values (Pfeffer and Salancik 1978). When these conditions pertain, it seems reasonable to assume a priori that networks will come together and 'self-organize' to promote the interests of 'their' sector (Peters 2000: 41, 46). Before proceeding, it is important to note one practical implication of adopting this stance for EU policymaking. This is that the Commission should only facilitate existing networks (e.g. by creating Internet portals) and not try to actively manage them in any sort of conscious, hierarchical sense. This was very much the gist of the EU's White Paper on governance (CEC 2001a: 18) and many other recent pronouncements from the Commission.

By contrast, others believe that it is inaccurate (and possibly even dangerous) to assume a priori that networks will 'self-organize' in response to each and every policy problem (Schout and Jordan 2005). When policy problems cut across many different sectors and/or actors with conflicting values, the potential value of networks as governing devices may need to be rigorously questioned. For Scharpf (1994: 42) the *key* question is, do

17

network structures successfully emerge 'among otherwise unrelated, and self-interested, individual or corporate actors'?[12] If the answer, is either 'no' or 'not easily', more active forms of central (i.e. hierarchical) steering may need to be explored (Klijn et al. 1995). Otherwise, policymakers can easily find themselves dealing with 'an inter-organizational version of the tragedy of the commons in which individual [i.e. sectoral] ... rationality conflicts with collective rationality' (Peters 1998a: 299). Many wicked problems arguably fall into this category, since they encompass actors from several sectors and levels of governance.

In these situations, a central coordinator or manager may have to step in and create (and where necessary structure) coordination networks by altering the rules of the game, providing sufficient inducements to participate, or even compelling some actors to participate (Kjær 2004: 45). These activities are needed to bring down coordination costs, to provide mediation in situations in which the necessary degree of trust cannot be assumed, and to help actors recognize their interdependence (Schout and Jordan 2004). This requires considerably more than steering 'self-organising' networks; it amounts to 'meta governance' (Jessop 2002; 2003),[13] 'intergovernmental management' (O'Toole 1988), or simply 'network management' (Kickert et al. 1997c). At the national level, this task is primarily performed by core executives (Weller, Bakvis, and Rhodes 1997), which can be defined as 'the set of networks which police the functional policy networks' (Rhodes 1997a: 14).[14] But in a complex, multi-actor, multilevel governance system such as the EU which lacks a dominant political coalition or 'core executive' (Sbragia 2002: 3), there is no overall ruler capable of leading, managing, or otherwise steering everyone in pursuit of common goals. The Commission is often seen as the best candidate for performing these tasks, given its policy initiating role, its access to information, and its broader responsibility to ensure that EU policy is designed and carried out effectively. However in practice, this issue is rather more problematic than it might appear given the Commission's own internal coordination problems (see above), its modest internal administrative resources, and its insecure political legitimacy. We explore some of these dilemmas more fully in Chapter 2.

Environmental coordination in the EU

At a broad level, EPI enjoys great support from the European Council, the Commission, and the Parliament. Moreover, in Chapter 3 we shall show that many member states have established their own implementing systems at national level to address EPI. In that sense, there is at least some awareness at national level that there is simultaneous horizontal and vertical interdependence. Meanwhile, over the last thirty years or so, the EU has also tried to establish a coherent EPI system. In so doing, it has experimented with all three 'modes' of governance, but as in the EU more broadly, the more hierarchical approaches have gradually dropped out of favour, while the appeal of market and, in particular, networked approaches, has grown. By far and away the most popular mechanism used in the past has been regulation. Since the dawn of EU environmental policy in the late 1960s, over 500 separate items have been adopted (Jordan 2005), with the primary aim of compelling 'non-'environmental sectors such as transport and agriculture to reduce their environmental externalities. These activities were vertically coordinated in the sense that the policies were adopted at EU level and supposed to be implemented at member state level. However, as we shall explain more fully in Chapter 3, the EU has been trying to move away from this predominantly hierarchical approach for well over a decade, because of doubts, *inter alia*, about its environmental and cost effectiveness (in essence, the member states failed to implement EU policies as fully or as fast as the European Commission wanted) (see Court of Auditors 1992: 3; Knill and Lenschow 2000).

Greater coordination via the market (i.e. levying taxes on polluters to internalize externalities) is now being actively explored by most member states (Jordan, Wurzel, and Zito 2003). The Commission believes that the use of market-based instruments offers 'one of the fastest' and most flexible routes for environmental integration (CEC 2004b: 35). However, markets do not yet constitute a viable means of facilitating EPI at EU level because of, *inter alia*, political opposition from polluters and member states fearful of allowing the EU to secure competence in this area (Jordan et al. 2003a; 2003b; EEA 2003: 283–8). In the absence of a strong EU involvement, some states have manipulated their tax systems to internalize a significant percentage of their externalities, whereas others have not (Jordan, Wurzel, and Zito 2003). The collectively optimal level of vertical or horizontal coordination has not, in short, 'self-organized', because the EU is legally prevented from playing a wider, coordinating role, particularly on (environmental) tax matters.

Therefore, almost by default, the EU has turned to network governance, principally (though by no means exclusively—see Chapter 3) the Cardiff process. In the late 1990s, Cardiff was 'one of the EU's "big ideas" on environment' (ENDS Daily No. 1679, 3 June 2004). But after a bright start, problems began to appear and the network failed to deliver. As we shall show in Chapter 3, many of the integration reports produced as part of the Cardiff process simply described the status quo and, crucially, a number of vitally important actors, notably the European Parliament, failed to join the network. There was also little explicit creation of or linkage to functionally equivalent Cardiff processes at the national level. So on paper, the network appeared to lack sufficient vertical and horizontal coordination. Not surprisingly, the European Environment Agency (EEA) (EEA 2003: 272) recently concluded that 'the process...lacked urgency and has yet to have a significant impact on sectoral policy making, let alone on improvements on the ground' (see also EEA 2005a; 2005b).

The EU now appears to have reached a crossroads in its thinking about EPI. Regulation (at least in its traditional form) no longer seems to be a viable option, and the adoption of market-based other related new instruments is proceeding too slowly to have much of an impact in the short term. External political pressure—particularly from environmental interest groups—has undoubtedly played an important part in raising the political and legal profile of EPI among policy elites in EU. However, there are clear limits to what it can achieve when EU policymaking is so expansive and the pressure groups are relatively poorly resourced. Somehow, environmentalists are still searching for ways to respond to the OECD's appeal to embed EPI more deeply in the institutions and administrations of day-to-day policymaking (OECD 2002a: ch. 2), so that it is not so easily affected by the vagaries of the political attention cycle. As yet, however, what steps need to be taken at EU and member state level to achieve this process of institutionalization have not been comprehensively explored (but see EEA 2005b). It is this practical policy need that we seek to respond to in the chapters of this book.

In the meantime, some commentators have pushed for the Cardiff 'partnership' to be formalized into an enduring EPI network involving DG Environment, the EEA, and national environment and sectoral ministries (Kraemer et al. 2001: 7; 2002: 53). The Commission's much more guarded response, on the other hand, has been to advocate measures that simply strengthen 'existing networks of [EPI] and sustainable development practitioners and speed up the exchange of information between [them]' (CEC 2004b: 36). Crucially, these two prescriptions exhibit precisely the same ambiguities about the actual or potential role of networks as those expressed in the more theoretical literature on governance noted above. That is, do coordinating networks need to be actively created and managed, or are they essentially self-organizing and self-managing? We believe that these questions are properly a matter for theoretically guided empirical investigation. In the next section, we explain how we intend to achieve this.

Putting the pieces together

The EU has decided to rely more heavily on networked governance to tackle wicked policy issues such as environmental coordination. The first question we therefore need to address is:

(1) *What coordination tasks need to be performed within the EU's multilevel system of decisionmaking to facilitate greater EPI?*

It is already apparent from the foregoing that there are several inter-related tasks that need to be discharged:

- *identify and, where possible, quantify the environmental implications of new EU policy proposals.* This is, however, a potentially gargantuan task. Although, the Commission is producing far fewer new proposals than it did a decade ago, in 2003 it still managed to generate 371 (down from over 700 in 1990) (CEC 2003a: 31). As only a fraction of these are formally 'environmental' (and hence formally under the direct control of DG Environment), the potential scale of the EU-EPI challenge is vast. We shall see that many actors in the EU are adopting environmental policy appraisal procedures as a means to tackle this problem, but crucially none are currently working effectively or efficiently enough.
- *share information.* Do all the participants understand the environmental implications of their activities and the extent to which they undermine the implementation of EPI? The Commission can invest a lot of time and effort in trying to EPI-proof legislative proposals, but it cannot possibly be expected fully to assess all their likely impacts in a vast space comprising twenty-five separate member states, each of which spans multiple levels of governance. In short, there are very many actors that potentially need to cooperate to make EU-EPI a reality.
- *set medium- to long-term priorities.* Because EU policy is too spatially and temporally expansive to assess (and thus coordinate) everything, long-term targets and priorities have to be set. There is undoubtedly a place for large-scale, EU-level processes such as Cardiff in this respect, but they do need to be adequately backed up by more specific work planning activities operating over shorter timescales within and across

21

individual sectors. In more concrete terms, this means scrutinizing Presidency and Commission agendas to single out the policies where it is particularly important to pursue EU-EPI. Monitoring will then be required to ensure that individual Commission proposals faithfully implement these priorities.

- *share workloads.* Given the scale of the task, the interdependence between actors, and scarcity of resources, it seems very unreasonable to expect any single actor to deliver EU-EPI on its own. The Commission has pledged to assess the environmental implications of each and every EU policy proposal using a new procedure known as Impact Assessment (IA), but it cannot be expected to monitor (and hence safeguard the environmental integrity of) the subsequent negotiations through to completion. The simultaneous existence of vertical and horizontal interdependence between the member states and the EU institutions is, of course, one of the primary justifications for more network-based approaches to coordination.

- *maintain a focus on achieving EPI throughout the policy process.* An effective coordinating network will need to ensure that the ambitions of Commission proposals are not diluted during subsequent stages of the policy process, when the influence of actors, namely the member states and the European Parliament, grows more powerful.

- *identify and, where possible, resolve inter- and intrasectoral conflicts proactively.* To ensure that environmental considerations are part of the deliberations at every step of the way, actors will have to work together to identify overlapping interests and solve differences that are likely to arise. If possible, this should be done at the lowest effective level (that is, administrative subsidiarity), so as not to clog up the already overburdened EU policymaking systems (Metcalfe 1994). It should also be done proactively; it is normally far too late to postpone intersectoral differences until the Council/*Comité de Représentantes Permanentes* (COREPER) (Jordan et al. 2007).

- *act efficiently.* Discharging all these tasks will probably impose huge requirements on the network as well as the participating actors. In view of this huge workload (the Dutch instructions to COREPER amount to around seventy pages each week—there are of course other EU-level bodies to service), it is essential that any coordination capacities are designed to function as efficiently as possible.

In the concluding chapter we review these tasks and assess the extent to which they have been fulfilled.

Thus far, the EU has deployed networked governance (specifically Cardiff) to implement a series of high-level and relatively long-term integration strategies, targets, and indicators. The aforementioned list of tasks suggests that more could be done to root them (and the targets they set) in day-to-day policymaking in the EU. This assertion begs another question.

(2) In view of these tasks, do EU-level networks exist that are sufficiently equipped with coordinating capacities to mediate between the relevant sectoral actors in a way that is supportive of EU-EPI?

Here, we want to investigate precisely what kinds of (if any) networks have actually arisen around the issue of EPI. By comparing them to the tasks noted above, we should be closer to determining whether the networks are sufficiently developed. This step in our investigation connects back to a major debate in the theoretical literature on governance: that is, are loosely managed, self-creating networks fit for purpose, or is there a need for stronger forms of network management?

We have already explained that effective network management must consider the capacities both at the network and at the sub-network (i.e. actor) level (see Table 1.1). At the EU level, networks must be sufficiently equipped to arrive at agreements, monitor trends, share workloads, audit capacities of the network and of the actors, and supervise implementation (see Level I in Table 1.1). Different kinds of networks can be distinguished according to their coordinating capacities. At one end of the scale are very informal gatherings that have no substantive organization (i.e. rules and procedures governing the frequency of interaction, the preparation of meetings, and the resolution of disagreements, etc.). This category fits the more extreme reading of governance as 'governing *without* government' (Rosenau and Czempiel 1992). The coordinating capacities at network level are, in a sense, therefore limited to what the participating actors bring to the table. This may seem like a utopian ideal, but Kooiman (2003: 79), who refers to it as 'self-governance', argues that it is more common than is sometimes assumed. Therefore its existence and potential long-term viability warrant further analysis via a detailed network audit such as is performed in this book, otherwise the EU may risk building new coordinating networks that serve no real purpose.

At the other end, are stronger networks that have a central manager, who performs key tasks ranging from purely *secretarial* functions to the sort of network *management* tasks described by a number of authors (e.g. Yukl 1998: 496; Kickert et al. 1997*b*: 168–70; Koppenjan and Klijn 2004). A *secretary* mainly aims at achieving greater efficiency in decisionmaking; that is, gathering and distributing information as part of the benchmarking

Table 1.1 A framework for auditing EU coordination capacities at network and actor levels

Level of network audit	Coordination capacities within the network and at actor level	Comment
I. *Capacities of the network*: types of network	**A—An informal network with no manager.** There are interested and interdependent parties who may (temporarily) organize themselves into a network to tackle common coordination challenges, but the interdependence is not really managed. As the existence of the network depends on the willingness of each actor to participate, they do not necessarily endure and their membership may fluctuate.	This is the typical governance-based view of 'networks', i.e. as essentially self-managing organizations.
	B—A formal network with a manager. The manager contributes to the stability of the network and to the handling of issues with high transaction costs. It can function in at least two ways: **(1) Weakly—as a 'secretary'** Essentially only undertakes procedural tasks. Leadership is restricted to calling meetings and sounding out views—e.g. the rotating Presidency in the EU. Somewhat stronger secretariats may also engage in facilitating peer review processes, benchmarking, and horizon scanning as in the OMC. **(2) Strongly—as a 'network manager'** A central body that undertakes strategic organizational tasks, e.g. boosting performance by 'naming and shaming', diagnosing frictions, and stimulating new actors to join. Its tasks could include addressing potentially sensitive topics such as individual and collective administrative strengths via network audits.	This is the more government/hierarchical view of governance, in that it brings into view the need for/role of a network manager.
II. *Sublevel capacities*: the coordination capacities of the actors in the network	**A—Role and resources of the main coordination bodies.** (1) Intradepartmental: e.g. the EU-coordinating units in the environment departments. (2) Interdepartmental: e.g. the roles of foreign affairs departments and the Prime Ministers' offices in national EU-policy coordination.	We focus on the role of the environment coordinators. What we are interested in are: —number of full time employees —the descriptions of their tasks. We do not study the environment coordinators in other departments.
	B—Interdepartmental coordination capacities: (1) Hierarchical (i.e. control by the apex) (2) Bureaucratic procedures (i.e. rules of procedures) (3) Skills development and training (4) Specification of output (i.e. management by objectives) (5) Horizontal coordination mechanisms (i.e. informal relations (bureaucratic politics), liaison roles, task forces, teams, weak and strong integrators) (6) Mission statements (i.e. general value statements)	Provide inputs into the coordination process (see Table 2.1). These coordination capacities facilitate coordination (the output) as measured on a coordination scale. See Table 2.1.

and peer review exercises that are constitutive of the OMC. The latter involves much more sensitive (and hence openly political) tasks such as 'naming and shaming', bringing in new actors or excluding existing ones, developing new rules of interaction, encouraging participants to look at problems from different perspectives, possibly by 'reframing' (Rein and Schön 1996) them in a more tractable form. In this way, the network manager seeks actively to *manage* coordination in the network by, for example, transforming the values of the participants (see Chapter 2). It could conceivably also extend to creating entirely new networks although the literature on network management is divided on this fundamental point (see above).

At the same time, sufficient attention also needs to be paid to the capacities of the various participants (i.e. the five actors in our sample) (Level II in Table 1.1). In theory, each must have sufficient coordination capacities to ensure that conflicts are identified and resolved. In Chapter 2 we draw on the work of Henry Mintzberg to identify and explore the role of six coordinating mechanisms that could conceivably serve these purposes. It may, of course, be that the tasks noted above are discharged even though there is no formally constituted EU-level network (that being the essence of 'self-governance'—see above), hence the need for detailed network auditing. This observation therefore leads to a supplementary question, which we begin to address in Chapters 4 and 5.

(3) Are there sufficient coordinating capacities within the participating actors to support the operation of networked governance at EU level?

Conclusions

Having now sketched out the broad context of our study and described the analytical tools that we shall be using, we are in a position to explain how the rest of this book will unfold. Chapter 2 offers a more detailed explanation of the tools that we will employ to assess the coordination capacities at network and actor level. Our assessments of the five actors are based upon the findings of extensive in-depth interviews with *inter alia* officials who are formally or informally responsible for coordinating EU environmental policy with sectoral policies at EU and at national level.

Chapter 3 charts the changing ways in which EPI has been thought about and implemented in the EU since the 1970s. The implicit assumption that has underpinned all this activity is that more effective multi-level and cross-sectoral coordination will arise through a process of incremental, non-hierarchical learning in networks, which is not guided by a template disseminated by the EU. Drawing on the work of Elinor Ostrom, we question the validity of this assumption when, as in the EU, governance is multilevel and multi-actor. Chapter 4 tackles the first part of the 'double challenge' noted above in more detail—namely how the five actors coordinate their input into EU policymaking across all policy spheres both internally (i.e. intradepartmentally) and with cognate actors (i.e. interdepartmentally).[15]

Chapter 5 then goes on to explore the steps that each actor has taken to implement EPI within its own institutional 'space'. In effect, here we begin to explore how well each actor has responded to the second part of the 'double challenge' noted above. For each actor, we begin by introducing the organizational unit that actively champions EPI (typically the national environment department), before briefly describing how it tackles the challenge of EPI within its own institutional 'space'.

Chapters 6–10 complete our empirical analysis of EPI by analysing the administrative capacities that each of the five actors has developed to coordinate the implementation of EPI across the whole of the EU (i.e. EU-EPI). In so doing, we move on from looking at the ways in which the actors operate in their immediate institutional spaces, to how well they interact in a network or networks. Each chapter is written to fit a standard analytical framework, which is outlined in Chapter 2.

Why these five actors? The Netherlands is a well-known environmental leader in the EU and has taken active steps to implement EPI in the EU and at home (EEA 2005b). Although it is not an especially consistent long-term leader of EU environmental policy, the OECD (2002b) has recently praised the UK's efforts to implement EPI at home and in the EU; its internal EU coordination system is widely known and very much admired (Kassim et al. 2000; 2001). Therefore, it seems reasonable to expect these two to be relatively advanced in their responses to EU-EPI. Germany, on the other hand, is very environmentally ambitious, but its internal coordination system is more suspect (Deubner and Huppertz 2003). Given these basic similarities and differences, it will be useful to explore whether any of these actors provides a satisfactory model for any of the other twenty-two member states to emulate. After all, benchmarking and the sharing of best practice is what many forms of networked governance in the EU are all about. Indeed, in Chapter 3, we shall show that the Commission is thinking of moving even further down this particular road to coordination. Finally, Chapter 11 summarizes our main conclusions and from these, distils a number of policy recommendations about how best to go about using networked governance to coordinate boundary spanning policy challenges.

What is especially distinctive about our approach? First, we start from the other end of what is often perceived to be 'the coordination problem' in the EU. That is to say, we analyse what the EU demands from national and EU administrations, rather than 'the national coordination of EU policy' (Peters and Wright 2001: 162). We do not, therefore, simply examine how three member states coordinate themselves in Brussels (see e.g. Kassim et al. 2000; 2001) although this is an important aspect of our study (see Chapter 4). Rather, we try to understand what is required to manage simultaneous vertical and horizontal interdependence using networked governance.

Second, the existing literature tends to look at national coordination capacities (Metcalfe 1994) *and/or* EU coordination capacities in and around the European Commission (Metcalfe 2000; Gomez and Peterson 1994; Peterson and Sjursen 1998). However, a wicked problem such as EPI which spans many actors, many administrative levels, many policy phases, and many sectors, arguably demands a much more holistic perspective. Hence, the coordination capacities of the Commission, the Parliament, and the member states have to be seen as interrelated, not (as Meacher suggests—see above) independent. But if one level of governance in the EU requires the capacities of other levels to function effectively, specifically how does this affect the design and utilization of the various coordination mechanisms, especially new and more network governance? The current literature is still relatively silent on this matter

Third, the current literature seems content to describe the presence and/or absence of different coordination mechanisms; that is, the directly visible bureaucratic rules, procedures, and committees, as if that somehow explained coordination. However, if we want to analyse—or diagnose—coordination capacities, we have to 'probe behind the official façade by considering actual practice'—that is, the everyday politics of (un)coordination in the EU (Peters and Wright 2001: 166). Therefore we seek to 'understand the endowment of resources available to would-be coordinators, as well as the mechanisms through which those resources can be deployed' (Peters 2003: 29). To demonstrate that horizontal and vertical policy coordination in EU policy are indeed intimately interconnected, we follow the EU policymaking phases as they criss-cross the traditional divisions between 'European' and 'domestic' politics.[16]

Finally, we aim to add something new to the burgeoning literature on EPI. One strand investigates the underlying principle of EPI and charts its development over time (e.g. Weale 1993; Lafferty and Hovden 2003). Another studies the implementation of EPI in specific national and sectoral contexts (see e.g. the chapters in Lenschow 2002*a*), or it charts what has been done to implement EPI at EU level (Collier 1997; Lenschow 2005). A third strand comprises the many grey literature studies produced by a mixed assortment of think tanks and consultancies. Many of these seek to assess the effectiveness of the Cardiff process (mostly by analysing the content of the Cardiff integration strategies produced since 1998) (e.g. IEEP 1992; 1995; Görlach et al. 1999; Ferguson et al. 2001; Wilkinson et al. 2002) (see Chapter 3 for further details). This study tries to build upon all this work by looking at how EPI is managed in the actual processes of everyday policymaking in the EU. In so doing it responds to policymakers' need for more insights into the multilevel challenge of institutionalizing EPI in the administration of the EU. In particular, it explores the conditions under which particular modes of coordination (in our case new and in particular networked governance) are effective (EEA 2005*a*: 7, 9).

Notes

1. Under the open method of coordination (OMC), states 'agree to voluntarily cooperate . . . and to make use of best practice from other member states, which could be customized to suit their particular national circumstances' (High Level Group 2004: 9). Its principal features include voluntary EU guidelines, reporting by member states on their performance, benchmarking, and the identification of best practice through peer review, and 'naming, shaming, and faming'. It is being used somewhat differently in areas such as social exclusion, employment, health care, and pension reform. A key element of the Lisbon process (see below), the Commission nonetheless plays an instrumental role in OMC by monitoring and comparing best practices.
2. Launched in 2000, the Lisbon process aims to promote economic, social, and environmental renewal in the EU in the period to 2010. In the words of the most high-level review undertaken of its performance to date, it requires states to make a 'comprehensive, interdependent and self-reinforcing series of [domestic] reforms' (High Level Group 2004: 8). For further details, see Chapter 3.
3. Börzel (1998: 254) explicitly refers to this as the 'governance school' of policy networks (cf. the 'interest intermediation' school) which is especially popular

amongst German and also Dutch scholars, but is now (in books like this) increasingly being applied to the EU.

4. Not to be confused with another Cardiff process (aimed at product and capital market reform), which was also launched at EU level in 1998.

5. As distinct from EPI at national levels, which is not as complex a challenge as it involves fewer administrative levels and fewer actors (e.g. member states, EU institutions).

6. That is to say, a formal element of the Lisbon process. However, over time, the Cardiff and Lisbon processes have become steadily more entangled (see Chapter 3). In this book we try to focus on what they have in common—a strong reliance on networked forms of governance.

7. Crucially, the Cardiff process is cross-sectoral, whereas OMC is normally used to coordinate the actions of several member states 'in a given policy domain' (Scott and Trubek 2002: 4). That said, there are arguably a number OMC-like activities that can be identified within the environmental sector (for details, see Homeyer, Klasing, and Kraemer 2004).

8. Critics contend that in spite of the repeated claims made about its novelty and importance, 'there is little evidence that [they]... matter... for policy outcomes' (Moravcsik 2005: 366). Both Héritier (2001: 18) and Jordan, Wurzel, and Zito (2005) demonstrate empirically that the EU continues to rely heavily on 'old' modes of governance such as regulation.

9. Notably the Netherlands.

10. A previous study only examined the capacities in the Dutch environment ministry (Schout and Metcalfe 1999). However, it quickly became clear that there is a collective action problem at stake when problems (such as EU-EPI) span many sectors, actors, and levels of governance. In these circumstances, it makes no sense to upgrade the coordination capacities of just one member state, when the EU comprises many states and EU institutions.

11. Writing from a more sociological perspective, Jessop (2003: 1) argues that governance is 'the reflexive self-organization of independent actors involved in complex relations of reciprocal interdependence.' Like Jessop, we see governance as an umbrella concept rather one tied strongly to one mode of governing (cf. the work of Rhodes).

12. Börzel (1998: 258) makes the 'often overlooked' distinction between 'homogeneous networks' in which the actors share similar interests and 'heterogeneous networks' in which they do not.

13. Jessop (2002: 6) defines this as 'the judicious mixing of market, hierarchy, and networks to achieve the best possible outcomes from the viewpoint of those engaged' (see also Jessop 2003: 108).

14. They are 'all those organizations and structures which... pull together and integrate central government policies, or act as final arbiters within the executive of conflicts between different elements of the government machine' (Dunleavy and Rhodes, quoted in Rhodes 1997a: 14).

15. To permit comparisons to be drawn between the actors, we use 'department' as a generic term to refer to sectoral ministries at member state level, different DGs in the Commission, and the secretariats of the committees in the European Parliament. In relation to some actors (e.g. the Parliament), we qualify this broad statement. Please see the relevant empirical chapter for further details.

16. This is not to say that the implementation of policy in the comitology system is unimportant—clearly it is (e.g. Schendelen 2004)—but sadly, we cannot possibly cover everything in one volume.

2

MULTILEVEL COORDINATION
CAPACITIES

Policy efforts are more likely to be successful if participants are guided
in their creation by the results of rigorous theoretical studies of the
design principles underlying successful cooperation...

(Keohane and Ostrom 1995: 22).

Introduction

'Joining up' and 'connectivity' may appear to be new terms (Pollitt 2003:
36), but the underlying issue of how best to engineer greater policy coordination is one of the classic themes in political science and public administration (Challis et al. 1988; Chisholm 1989). The growing interest shown
in them arises from the paradox that policies appear to be increasingly
interdependent, whereas allegedly the administrative capacities for managing them are lagging behind (Hanf 1978; Peters 1998a). Despite the
forcefulness of Keohane and Ostrom's statement (above), coordination
remains a heavily contested concept. Crucially, scholars remain deeply
divided on the question of whether sensitive and complex political processes
can be structured via administrative mechanisms to achieve better policy
coordination, or everything more or less depends upon the push and pull of
bureaucratic politics in day-to-day policymaking situations.

In Chapter 1 we noted that in the EU, coordination between policy
fields is inherently (and possibly even uniquely) difficult. We argued that
network-based approaches must get to grips with simultaneous horizontal
and vertical interdependence. We then argued that this requires the presence of sufficient coordination capacities in networks as well as within
the participating actors. But what precisely is meant by 'coordination in

networks', and what do we mean by 'coordination capacities' at the level of the actors? In this chapter we set out our theoretical and methodological responses to these and other questions.

The remainder of this chapter unfolds as follows. Section 2 outlines the wider context of our study by linking two major theoretical concepts (networks and governance). Section 3 sharpens the focus on networks as our explanatory device and, in particular, on the different views on managing them. Section 4 analyses what has to be done at the level of actors to facilitate greater coordination, and presents a scale covering the different meanings of coordination. Section 5 brings together these two perspectives (i.e. the network and the actor), looks at the main phases of EU policymaking, summarizes our approach, and explains how we intend to use it to guide our empirical analysis (see Table 2.1). The concluding section brings this chapter to a close.

Networks and governance

In Chapter 1 we showed that governance is a term in good currency. However, in looking at how this term has been used to describe and better understand the operation of the EU, we are presented with somewhat of a puzzle. The EU certainly qualifies as an example of 'a system of governance without government' (Rosenau and Czempiel 1992; see also Dobson and Weale 2003: 158; Hayward 2006). In recent years, the EU has, in turn, seized on the discourse of 'governance' in general and new modes of governing in particular, to allay (the apparently widespread) public fear that EU policy processes are overconcentrated in 'Brussels' (Metcalfe 2000: 817). One of the underlying problems is that the demands placed on the EU seem to be growing at the same time as its popular legitimacy is falling (see below). The term governance, meanwhile, is intimately bound up with the whole issue of coordination (Heywood 2000: 19). A study by Perri et al. (2002: 9) described cross-sectoral coordination as '*the* eternal problem...in governance' (emphasis in the original). Finally, while governance is undoubtedly a 'notoriously slippery' term (Pierre and Peters 2000: 7), it has been commonly (though by no means exclusively) interpreted to refer to the management of complex networks (Flinders 2002: 54; Rhodes 2003: 6–7). In this book, we try to ground some of these concepts and claims in a more detailed empirical analysis of the EU.

The puzzle is this: in spite of the obvious connections between the concepts of governance, networks, and coordination, scholarship has not really examined what the appearance of governance—or, more specifically, the use of networked governance to coordinate—might imply for the improvement of cross-sectoral policy coordination in the EU (but see Schout and Jordan 2004; 2005; Jordan et al. 2007). For example, the literature which has emerged around the concept of multilevel governance has mostly been concerned with vertical coordination problems (notably the implementation of EU regional policy) (Marks 1993; Hooghe 1996; Marks et al. 1996). By contrast, our analysis seeks to understand what the emergence of multilevel governance implies for the horizontal *and* the vertical handling of policy coordination in the EU, by revealing the deep interconnections between national and EU administrative systems (on this point, see Peterson 2004: 132). Similarly, the current literature on policy networks in the EU is mainly directed at understanding their role in shaping discrete sectors of policy (see below). (Börzel (1998) helpfully refers to this as the interest intermediation school of policy network analysis.) Indeed, one reason why scholars have been so eager to adopt networks as an organizing perspective is because it seems to capture 'the "polycentricity" [of the EU], or [its] tendency to generate ever more and more dissimilar centres of decision making and control' (Peterson 2004: 118). By contrast, the science of 'network management' (i.e. of using networks to deal with instances of vertical *and* horizontal interdependence), lags behind the political desire to employ network governance (Peterson 2004: 129, 133).

If we turn to the EU's own thinking on these crucial terms, the available literature is similarly thin. Metcalfe (1994: 273), for instance, has made many references to the EU's 'management deficit',[1] but in the EU White Paper on governance it did not receive the critical treatment that many scholars thought it deserved (for a review see Schout and Jordan 2005). The purpose of the White Paper was to find new ways to match the EU's internal capacity with the growing policy challenges confronting it in a more globalized world (Eberlein and Kerwer 2003: 122). The Commission was drawn to networks because they appeared to offer a more politically acceptable means to add value to national-level activities ('doing more with the same' to use a phrase coined by Santer), by working more closely with member states. But precisely how should the EU institutions and the member states achieve this? How much cooperation is needed? Who (or what) should initiate it? When should it occur? Who should be involved? And what form (or forms) should it take to be effective? These are academically *and* policy relevant questions, but the available literature on network design are in generally 'in short supply' (Pollitt and Bouckaert

2004: 36). The Commission has certainly not added any more flesh to what it originally presented in the White Paper, fuelling suspicions that it does not really wish to depart too far from the status quo. Indeed, it once admitted that governance equates to a 'quiet revolution' in the Community Method (CEC 2002*a*: 6). This is consistent with its relatively narrow interpretation of governance: that is, reducing the quantity and detail of regulation (Better Regulation) and creating more independent agencies (Scott 2002: 61).

Networks and the governance of the EU

A network has been defined as 'a more (or less) stable pattern of social relations between interdependent actors, which take shape around policy problems and/or policy programme' (Klijn and Koppenjan 2000: 155). That the EU is heavily populated with policy networks is beyond dispute, even by the very sternest critics of network analysis. However, their role— actual or potential—in governing the EU is much more contested (Rhodes, Bache, and George 1996; Thatcher 1998: 395; Jachtenfuchs and Kohler-Koch 2004). There is no generally agreed 'theory' of networks (Pollitt and Bouckaert 2004) that we can turn to; in fact, many fundamental problems (relating to both definition and explanation) (Börzel 1998) remain frustratingly unresolved.

Even though it has weaknesses (Peterson 2004), it would be thoroughly foolish to discard the policy network approach from the available tool kit of EU analysis. For a start, the EU now professes to want to employ networks to govern the EU (see Chapter 1). Networks also have a certain academic appeal since they successfully direct attention to the multitude of state and non-state actors that interact to shape daily policy in the EU (Peterson 1995; Peterson and Bomberg 1999). This is relevant particularly in a horizontally extensive policy context such as ours, in which strong hierarchical relations are lacking.

However, pointing to growing policy interdependence and the proliferation of networks is not a sufficient explanation for how policy network analysis should be used to understand the governance of the EU. Therefore, to give a clearer direction to our research questions, in Chapter 1 we started to use strategic management, network management, and coordination theories, to study networks and their potential sublevels (see Table 1.1). Crucially, these approaches visualize a network as a much more *managed* set of interactions with a formal structure, an organizational centre, and a set of actors with administrative capacities to achieve certain outcomes. By contrast, the existing literature on networks—often implicitly—assumes that they are self-organizing and, by implication, also self-managing. This is not an especially contentious assumption to make if the policy problem is predominantly sectoral in nature. Peterson and Bomberg (1999: 8), for example, go as far as to claim that the term 'policy network':

is a metaphor for a cluster of actors, each of which has an interest, or 'stake', *in a given EU policy sector* and the capacity to help determine policy success or failure.... Actors in policy networks.... have incentives to share resources, bargain and agree on how *to 'shape' policy in the interests of their sector* (emphasis added).

In such settings, actors have the incentive to recognize their interdependence, communicate with and learn from one another, and thus develop the necessary degree of trust (see Chapter 1), even if the starting point is one of different values, information, and objectives (Alter and Hage 1992). Many studies have described the role of particularly coherent international networks, which share an expert knowledge (i.e. an epistemic community) of a policy problem (Haas 1992). This is the essence of self-organization and steering. However, it also extends to the capacities of the actors in the networks, which are also assumed to emerge more or less automatically (cf. Benz and Eberlein 1999).

In Chapter 1 we noted that these assumptions about the coordinating capacity of networks and those that participate in them need to be much more critically assessed, particularly in situations when the solution of the underlying policy problem requires greater cross-sectoral coordination. Then, the role of networks changes to one of overcoming what Peters has termed an 'inter-organizational version of the tragedy of the commons' (see Chapter 1). According to the network management literature, networks are capable of solving mutual problems exhibiting high levels of interdependence, but only when they are appropriately managed or *structured*. There are, of course, many schools of thought, and each one identifies a different type of steering mechanism (e.g. Börzel (1998) discusses the rationalist institutionalist approach of the Max-Planck School). In the next section, we develop our own contingent perspective on networks.

Networks: a contingent perspective

Elinor Ostrom (Ostrom 1990; Ostrom et al. 1994) has been at the forefront of those analysing the extent to which cooperative agreements are self-steering and identifying factors that explain why institutions for managing collective actions fail. Her work goes against the findings of game theory, which emphasizes the importance of central bodies in distributing information and setting up enforcement systems. In contrast, her work assumes that by interacting, individual parties learn that institutions are needed. Their interactions help them to identify interdependencies and the need for monitoring mechanisms and independent courts. Hence, they adapt so that gradually, an effective network emerges in a culture of trust (i.e. self-organization).

Do we see this occurring in relation to EU-EPI? In Chapter 3 we show that the Commission first identified the problem of EPI in the early 1980s. In the early 1990s it realized that it needed to coordinate better its own internal policy processes, by establishing a system of environmental policy appraisal. Now it accepts that EU-EPI is a *shared* problem; DG Environment recently asked the member states to review their own EPI systems to support the Cardiff process at EU level (CEC 2004*b*: 3). Evidently, coordination systems have emerged over the last thirty years at EU and at national level, but how effective are they? This is a question which calls for a detailed network audit.

What light does Ostrom's own work shed on this apparent failure? Although writing about local communities, Ostrom does offer a set of theoretical statements that can be employed to refashion EU network theory better to understand (and address) horizontal complexity (Schout and Jordan 2005). However, before we draw lessons for the EU from very local systems of governance, we should first explore the qualifications that Ostrom (1990: 197–206) makes in relation to her work. She argues that coordination is contingent upon a number of factors, including:

- *The size of the population.* The more participants, the higher the costs of information exchange and of monitoring. Moreover, the more varied the population, the bigger the value differences are likely to be.
- *The size of the problem or the potential benefit.* The higher the interests at stake, the more people will be inclined to work towards solutions.
- *The starting situation.* Incremental approaches will be facilitated if supportive institutions already exist. The other side of the coin is that the path-dependent character of existing institutions may just as easily impede reflexive learning (North 1990).
- *The amount and type of conflict.* The actors can differ in terms of their time perspectives, interests, cultural backgrounds, etc. All of these lead to specific tensions in the negotiations (cf. Lawrence and Lorsch 1967).

- *The available information about problems and solutions.* Identification of problems and solutions and arriving at shared world-views can be complicated in more differentiated settings. This also relates to the next point.
- *The presence or absence of leadership* (or, for us, network management).
- *Past strategies.* Previous experience of working together and the feedback effect from earlier choices may reinforce trust and hence cooperation.
- *Monitoring and enforcement opportunities.* Cooperation requires trust and may need the support of trust-building institutions (i.e. network management).

Interestingly, Rhodes (2000*b*: 81) draws up a very similar list of factors which encourage networks to function effectively.

Keohane and Ostrom (1995) have reviewed the similarities between local and international settings, and discredit the widely held assumption that the former are more governable than the latter. For example, homogenous international groups—epistemic communities (Haas 1992)—may actually coordinate themselves more successfully than a differentiated local community. Be that as it may, the conditions specified by Ostrom allow us to move away from an undifferentiated 'either/or' debate on the extent of self-organization in networks. If, of course, the conditions are not fulfilled (and networks do not spontaneously emerge), the question arises whether and how they can be created and subsequently managed.

Network management I: capacities at network level

Network management

Supporters of the bureaucratic politics model of decisionmaking would claim that the more difficult the situation, the more important the competition for influence will be (i.e. the less organizational design will matter) (e.g. Palumbo 1975; Chisholm 1989). A contingent perspective tells us that the more differentiated the actors in the negotiations, the stronger the coordination capacities have to be (Lawrence and Lorsch 1967). Or, to put it another way, should we expect to find it more demanding to set up effective networks (or for networks to self-organize) when, as in the case of EU-EPI: the participants are differentiated; there are strong sources of distrust; and sectoral networks close themselves off to newcomers once they have formed? Arguably, the answer to this question is yes, in which case there is a need for network management (see Chapter 1).

Drawing on strategic management theory (Challis et al. 1988; Egeberg 1987; Hult and Walcott 1990; Mandell 1990; Metcalfe 1993) and network theory (Koppenjan and Klijn 2004), it is possible to identify two closely related forms of management that can be used to overcome these kinds of collective action problems: leading in the *design* of networks; and *diagnosing* capacity problems at actor level (see also Chapter 1). *Network design* focuses on the question of whether coordinating structures and processes are effective. It involves ensuring that:

- the overall coordination *goals* are correctly and unambiguously specified.
- the *viability* of the network is supported. This requires defining key roles (e.g. defining the tasks of the network manager or secretariat), establishing processes for gathering and processing information, and establishing satisfactory problem-solving mechanisms.
- the appropriate actors are sufficiently *stimulated* to participate in situations when the incentives to 'self-organize' are weak or possibly even absent.

It is very important to note that a network manager does not direct the network in a formal, hierarchical sense. Rather, its role is to mediate, cajole, stimulate, and arbitrate in complex situations of mutual dependency. Thus it might be responsible *inter alia* for giving the discussions on the design of networks a clear focus, and for highlighting alternative policies. It may also question ideas, help to prevent group think, and support long-term learning amongst the participants. These tasks require *diagnostic skills*, for example the ability to carry out network audits, such as the one offered in this book. Such audits imply not only that everyone looks at their own micro-positions and capacities, but also that someone (i.e. the manager) examines the functioning of the actors and of the network from a synoptic perspective. In so doing, sufficient attention has to be paid to (c.f. Table 1.1):

- *the functioning of the network as a whole.* For instance, is a network manager needed and what kinds of services should it provide? Has any thought been given to conflict management mechanisms? And are the objectives feasible in relation to the available resources?
- *the capacities of the actors.* Trust is the glue that binds networks together. Trust will be partly based on shared common interests and can be generated by more frequented interactions (see Chapter 1). However, it will also be shaped by the capacity of each actor in the network to

function in a coordinated manner (Majone 1996). Someone has to stand above the partners and indicate weaknesses and solutions to ensure that each actor lives up to its promises, otherwise the accumulated trust could easily drain away.

Our argument thus far does not deny the horizontal nature of networks, or the need to work with the forces in the network (much like a sailor seeks to harness the power of the wind) (Dunsire 1993; Schout 2000). Network management is not an alternative but a complement to self-organization. On this view, coordination remains a political process, but it is possible, through deploying management capacities, to influence this pushing and pulling. 'It is a matter of personal preference whether one regards this as politicizing management or managing politics' (Metcalfe 1993: 174).

Network management in the EU

This discussion of network management poses two immediate questions in relation to the EU: (1) who or what should manage networks? and (2) if the Commission is to be the manager, which of the management tasks identified above should it discharge? There are different views on the first of these. One holds that the EU is already heavily involved in structuring networks (Nugent 2000: 13). Sbragia (2000), for example, claims that the EU realizes full well that it 'can better achieve its objectives with networks than without them and therefore the Commission deliberately and strategically creates them' to tackle problems *inter alia* such as policy implementation (i.e. IMPEL, Schout 1999*b*) or to deepen European integration in areas where it has limited competence, such as social affairs (Cram 1997: 132–3, 175; Mosher and Trubek 2003). The other view is that the Commission does a lot of network management, but by no means enough to contribute to effective European governance (Metcalfe 1996; 2000). Metcalfe (2000), for example, believes that the Commission's failure to lead is one of the main causes of the management deficit(s) noted above.

In practice, much depends on where the analyst is looking. The Commission does work very hard to manage some policy areas (e.g. biotechnology and structural funding), where it has a clear legal mandate and support from the member states. Metcalfe, on the other hand, is referring to a range of situations, particularly the more turbulent and pluralistic ones, in which simultaneous horizontal and vertical cooperation is more difficult to generate. He has referred to the EU's weak management as a '*structural* problem that threatens the performance of the whole system'

(Metcalfe 2000: 819) (emphasis added), not something which resides in specific policy areas or actors. Dealing with this deficit, he suggests, certainly requires internal reforms within the Commission. We discuss these in more detail in Chapter 9. However, it also requires the Commission to build sufficient *external* management capacities to steer the EU 'at the level of organizational networks' (Metcalfe 2000: 825). Our ambition in this book is not to assess the size of the entire management deficit, but instead to look at one specific policy challenge that the Commission has sought to tackle using network governance. More specifically, we ask whether is there a formal EU-EPI network, and whether and to what extent the Commission has played an active role in creating and/or sustaining the necessary network capacities.

Network management II: network capacities at the actor level

Coordination: its core meaning

This section presents our model for studying the capacities at the sublevel; that is, *within* the five actors (see also Table 1.1). The actor level is, as we explained in Chapter 1, vitally important because effective management networks require the constituent organizations to invest in the capacities to cope with simultaneous vertical and horizontal interdependence (Metcalfe 2000: 829). In order to be effective, these capacities should allow the actors to work together more effectively—that is, coordinate with one another. However, this begs another question: what do we mean by 'coordination'? In Chapter 1 we explained that coordination is an essentially contested term. At a very basic level, it means to bring different parts together to form an interrelated whole. Chisholm (1989: 13) defines it as an attempt to create 'some kind of order'. Others have used more elaborate definitions such as a set of actions 'aimed at the adoption by all the members of a group . . . of mutually consistent decisions' (Simon 1976: 139). However, in more specific terms, it remains a rather ill-defined concept, having been used to refer to totally different kinds of objectives (e.g. avoiding day-to-day conflict or producing longer-term strategies?), tasks (simple or complex?), environments (tightly or loosely coupled?), and mechanisms (coercion or voluntary cooperation?) (see Wildavsky 1996). Rather than subscribing to one particular view, Metcalfe (1994) separates the various meanings and places them on a scale, which we cover in the next section.

Measuring coordination: the Metcalfe scale

The scale distinguishes between looser forms of coordination which are suitable for simple tasks, and more tightly integrated systems aimed at the management of controversial or complex tasks. Importantly, it offers a methodology for measuring coordination and diagnosing coordination capacities. The scale identifies the following meanings of coordination.

LEVEL 1: INDEPENDENT POLICYMAKING

The obvious point of departure is to look at the way in which tasks are allocated, because if this is done efficiently it may obviate the need for additional coordination. However, in the real world where policy challenges cut across formal policy sectors, breaking up coordination tasks and allocating them to particular actors is very difficult. In Chapter 3, we explain why environmental protection is a particularly 'wicked' problem and hence not amenable to a simple subdivision of coordination tasks. Therefore, Level 1 is all about identifying the relevant actors in the policy network. That is, who is involved? In the context of our study, the most important actors are the sectoral departments (transport, agriculture, energy, etc.), foreign affairs, the cabinet offices, and the environment department (especially its EU-coordinating unit(s)). In addition, we need to explore the rules and capacities which help these actors work independently on EPI. When they cannot (e.g. because of overlapping responsibilities or because actions taken by one actor have implications for other actors), we need to understand when and how their interdependence is to be managed.

LEVEL 2: COMMUNICATION (EXCHANGE OF INFORMATION)

More often than not, the idea of independent policymaking is not appropriate, and interdependencies have to be managed. Level 2, therefore, looks at the flow of information between actors regarding possible cross-sectoral spillover effects such as pollution. However, Level 2 regards information in unidirectional terms; that is, the receiver is free to do what (s)he likes with it. The ease with which information on any potential cross-sectoral spillover effect is shared depends on, among others, the culture in the organization and rules governing its operation (see the discussion of 'passive' and 'active' information' below). For the moment, it is simply important to note that at this level, EPI is restricted to one unit simply informing another (e.g. the environmental department) of the environmental repercussions of its proposed policy on a 'take it or leave it' basis.

LEVEL 3: CONSULTATION

Consultation implies an active interest in what the other party is doing and involves giving feedback. However, consultation still does not infringe on the freedom of the other actors, as feedback may be ignored. In terms of EPI, this level would involve two sectors discussing the environmental implications of one (or even both) of their respective policies.

LEVEL 4: SPEAKING WITH ONE VOICE (AVOIDING DIVERGENCES)

The previous levels underline the individual responsibilities of actors. Level 4 involves making a collective effort to represent one position. Nevertheless, it is essentially negative coordination aimed at avoiding open conflict; it is a holding position—that is, agreeing not to disagree publicly (e.g. asking for more time to study the environmental consequences of a proposal).

LEVEL 5: LOOKING FOR CONSENSUS

This involves positive coordination aimed at finding common objectives—for example, a genuine attempt is made to adjust a policy proposal to reflect environmental considerations.

LEVEL 6: CONCILIATION (MEDIATION)

Discovering common ground is seldom easy, hence the need for outside help. Foreign affairs departments sometimes take on this task and are often regarded as neutral 'go-betweens' (see Chapter 4). Crucially, once this level is reached, coordination ceases to be informal and bilateral.

LEVEL 7: ARBITRATION

Conciliation may not be sufficient. When parties continue to disagree, someone may have to step in and take a decision. Arbitration is like going to court and letting the judge decide. Arbitration works in administrative systems such as the UK's where the prime minister is *primus inter pares*. But collegial systems (e.g. the Netherlands) have to rely mainly on conciliation by the *primus inter pares*. Importantly, Level 7 introduces an element of hierarchy into what has so far been presented as a problem of horizontal coordination. The addition of a vertical dimension is important in our analysis, because many commentators see networks, coordination, and indeed governance as a whole, as being essentially horizontal (i.e. less hierarchical) in nature (see above). It also takes us back to the vexed issue of network management.

LEVEL 8: SETTING MARGINS (DEFINING ROOM FOR MANOEUVRE)

Contrary to the previous levels, defining margins *ex ante* is proactive and strategic. It involves an early agreement on the direction the policy should take. To ensure flexibility, precise objectives may not be required early on, but this presupposes early agreement between the main actors and/or sectors.

LEVEL 9: WORKING TOWARDS A SPECIFIED OBJECTIVE (IMPLEMENTING A STRATEGY)

The highest level of coordination assumes an overall objective to which the individual units are committed. It might conceivably exist if the central apex's overall objective is to achieve EPI and all the departments simply implement that commitment. In reality, we shall show that EPI is normally only one government objective alongside many others, hence the continuing importance of bureaucratic politics and the ability of lower coordination levels to facilitate these.

THE SCALE: A SUMMARY

The Metcalfe scale is a Guttman scale, which means that each level is based on the attainment of the previous levels. This means that it operates in a 'bottom-up' manner, in much the same way as one might ascend a flight of stairs. In part, this simply reflects the way that policy is normally coordinated in the EU (i.e. within and between individual departments); if everything was coordinated in Brussels or Strasbourg, the EU would quickly overload and grind to a complete halt (Metcalfe 1994: 277). However, the practical implication of this point is hugely important: 'the more basic but less glamorous aspects of the policy coordination process' are vital (Metcalfe 1994: 288). It implies that the underlying capacities—the mechanisms to exchange information, consult, and arbitrate, etc.—need to be in place *before* political energies are invested in setting strategic objectives and defining mission statements. This is a point which does not come easily to the EU. The second point to make about the scale is that it can (as we shall hopefully demonstrate) be used directly to compare coordination in different but broadly comparable institutional settings.

Coordination: underlying capacities (input)

In addition to a tool that measures output (i.e. the coordination scale), we need a way to examine the coordination capacities through which this output is achieved in the five actors. Notwithstanding the huge differences in how coordination can be defined (see Allison 1971; Allison and Zelikow 1999; Teulings 1992; Schout 1999a), we draw on the work of Mintzberg (1979; 1983; 1989) to identify six main coordination capacities, namely:[2] hierarchy; bureaucratic rules of procedure; skills; specification of output (management by objectives); horizontal coordination mechanisms; and mission statements. Following Schout (1999a), we use Mintzberg's typology because it is widely known, includes political as well as organizational interpretations of coordination, and is applicable to many different institutional settings. Moreover, it is more explicit than the standard triad of hierarchies, markets, and networks noted in Chapter 1 (e.g. Powell 1990). However, because Mintzberg's synthesis was initially written for the private sector, we need to relate it to the more open and multilevel characteristics of the EU (Schout and Metcalfe 1999).

HIERARCHICAL MECHANISMS

In Chapter 1, we noted that according to the classical hierarchical view, central management is in control of common tasks like coordination. Following this approach, in the five actors we would typically look at the placement of tasks under a common authority such as the prime minister, the President of the Commission, or the President of the European Council. The political desire to centralize is understandable—at the very least it makes it appear to constituents that things are being done (Mintzberg 1983: 136–8). However, centralization can very quickly overload the apex and/or disappear amongst a welter of other coordination goals. Moreover, in coalition governments such as the Netherlands, central control is more or less a non-starter. Nevertheless, the immediate question for our study is whether the apex of the five actors and the EU has assumed overall responsibility for EU-EPI. Crucially, if our analysis suggests that hierarchy in this classic sense cannot be relied upon, other coordination mechanisms will have to be explored.[3]

BUREAUCRATIC PROCEDURES

Bureaucratic procedures are all about rules which standardize behaviour (e.g. when and how to apply policy appraisals), who to inform and who to penalize when things go wrong, etc. 'Red tape' is almost universally reviled in liberal democracies, but bureaucratic procedures can be immensely powerful coordinating instruments (March and Simon 1958; Bendor and Hammond 1992; Olsen 2005).

An important distinction that we introduce in relation to the EU is between standard operating procedures (e.g. when and how to appraise policies) that encourage an *active* or a *passive* exchange of information. In the case of *passive information*, the departments that are not in the lead are entitled to receive the relevant information about spillover effects, but they have to hunt around to find it. As we will argue below, this is increasingly problematic in an EU in which policies are becoming increasingly intertwined. *Active information* means that the lead department is formally *obliged* to ensure that other departments are informed and their views incorporated in the coordination process. We shall show that on paper at least, the UK offers an especially good example of an actively coordinated actor. The following quotation, which is taken from the UK environment department's guide to EU negotiations, captures the essence of active information:

> The rationale for keeping others informed, from a selfish or departmental point of view, is to try to avoid the introduction of new objectives . . . towards the end of a negotiation . . . For this reason, copying papers is not necessarily enough. The *implications* of [Commission] proposals often have to be made clear [to other departments] . . . . It may take considerable time and effort to have to do the thinking for other departments, but is likely to pay dividends both in achieving your policy aims and avoiding major hassles in the endgame of the negotiations. (Humphreys 1996: 37–8) (emphasis in original)

Because it is a proactive way of coordination, problems are detected early on in the policymaking process. Thus, when inter- or intrasectoral conflicts arise, they are dealt with. Active information thus encourages *issue coordination*. By contrast, passive coordination typically goes together with *event coordination*. This is because when coordination is reactive, conflicts tend to be postponed until a specific event (e.g. the meeting of the College of Commissioners or the COREPER) requires a coordinated position regardless of whether this is the optimal point to coordinate. Consequently, it is the event, not the issue, that is coordinated.

45

SKILLS DEVELOPMENT AND TRAINING

These aim to encourage individual officials to work in a more coordinated way (e.g. training on how to perform different types of policy appraisal, consult civil society, or manage budgets). Training can raise awareness of and build commitment to a particular coordination objective. But the contribution of training can be quite limited in a world full of multiple objectives and policy appraisal procedures (Schout 1999a). Training is therefore probably best used to reinforce skills within the context of single, sectoral objectives, rather than tackle complex horizontal tasks like EU-EPI.

SPECIFICATION OF OUTPUT ('MANAGEMENT BY OBJECTIVES')

Telling each part of an organization what contribution they must make to the achievement of a common objective is a tried and tested tool of the New Public Management (e.g. Pollitt and Bouckaert 2004). In the context of this study, the most obvious EPI-related instruments that fall into this category are quantitative targets. These can be embodied in environmental regulations such as EU Directives (i.e. more hierarchical) or in eco-taxes (i.e. more market-based). However, overloading implementing bodies with targets often encourages managers to 'cherry pick' the least demanding ones. Furthermore, the use of targets to drive performance can be a tricky business in view of the well-known measurement and attribution problems (Carter et al. 1992). In any case, in relation to EPI, there is a growing appreciation at EU and national level of the need to find new ways to produce targets (i.e. encouraging common ownership rather than imposing them from the outside) (see Chapters 3 and 5).

HORIZONTAL COORDINATION MECHANISMS

In this subsection we can draw on the work of Galbraith (1973) to identify a number of other horizontal coordination mechanisms:

- *Informal relations ('bureaucratic politics')*. The classical bureaucratic politics view of organizations (Allison 1971; Allison and Zelikow 1999) emphasizes the importance of interdepartmental bargaining and conflicts in everyday policymaking. Informal relations often arise spontaneously as individual actors identify their interdependence. In a sense, this is a good example of 'self-organization' (see Chapter 1). But the sheer size of an organization like the EU, the lack of trust between the participants, and their sharply conflicting objectives, can easily thwart the free exchange of information. To overcome such flaws, informal relations need to be proceduralized (e.g. by making information sharing obligatory (see above) (Meltsner and Bellavita 1983: 37–8, or by supplementing it with additional mechanisms (see below)).

- *Liaison roles.* Liaison officers are people that have an overview of the whole coordination problem. Typically, they monitor developments in other fields to identify overlapping interests. Officials in the other fields may not appreciate (or want to see) this interdependence, but the liaison officers might. In Chapters 3 and 5 we shall show that as far as EPI is concerned, these people may be in the EU coordinating units of the five environment departments, or they may be environmental experts in the sector departments. Proactive liaison officers are sometimes termed 'watchdogs' (or spies or policemen) (Wilkinson 1998: 121); more reactive ones are known as 'gate keepers' (or facilitators, ambassadors, or technicians) (Wilkinson 1998: 121). Liaison officers facilitate information exchanges, but they are only of limited use when differences in views and values are too pronounced to reach agreement or when trust is lacking. Problem-solving may therefore sometimes require additional coordination capacities (i.e. Level 6 and above). Usually, liaison officers need some authority within their host organizations to be effective. However, senior staff normally prefer to devote their energies to achieving their organization's 'core' tasks; the politically difficult and often time-consuming task of liaising with other parts of the organization (i.e. coordination) is therefore commonly passed down to more junior officials.

- *Task forces.* Direct contacts and liaison roles involve bilateral relations between two departments. Policies involving several units may, however, require an even more horizontal approach. A task force is a temporary committee dealing with a specific coordination problem. Participation is sometimes on an equal and voluntary basis. Voluntary participation prevents participant units from feeling overshadowed, but also constitutes the primary weakness of task forces. It may be that participants do not share information readily, that they join to delay decisionmaking, or that their starting positions are too dissimilar. In these situations, stalemates can easily arise. Moreover, task forces may need to employ other coordination capacities—that is, a set of directions and priorities (i.e. some hierarchical structuring)—to get their agreed policies to work effectively.

- *Teams.* Stalemates are often moved up to a higher level (i.e. Level 6 or higher) for conciliation. Whereas task forces are topic-related and exist only for a set period of time, teams have a permanent character and exist at a level where it is possible to adopt a synoptic perspective. Importantly, they can also help commit the apex of an organization to the day-to-day management of policy interdependence. However, in order to be effective, attention must be paid to the membership of task forces. By this we mean that the right representatives have to be involved and they must be capable of making commitments on behalf of their respective organizations. If the participants lack seniority and/or cannot commit their respective organizations to take coordinated actions, teams can easily dissolve into empty 'talking shops'.

- *Weak integrators without authority.* One way to increase the effectiveness of teams is to introduce leadership (i.e. hierarchy) in the form of an integrator or 'middleman' (Challis et al. 1988). She/he is supposed to be the guardian of the whole process without dictating the outcome. The functional division and the power relations within the team remain unaltered, but the team is complemented by someone who can strengthen cooperation by providing task-oriented and group-oriented leadership; that is, calling meetings, preparing agendas, acting as a mediator, or preventing other evasive behaviour (Mulford and Rogers 1982; Whetten 1977; Fransman 1990). An integrator's influence stems from his superior access to information. Consequently, it becomes attractive for the participating organizations to cooperate to gain that information. Lawrence and Lorsch (1967) found that people in an intermediate position (i.e. those whose goals fall between the goals of the participating actors) make the best integrators.
- *Strong integrators with authority.* The more differentiated an organization, the more difficult the work of an integrating officer will be. If consensus cannot be reached in the available time, a *primus inter pares* (i.e. Level 7) may be needed to take decisions that bind everyone together. However, as noted above, it may be difficult to find a sufficiently powerful *primus* in less hierarchical (i.e. collegial) administrative systems or in multilevel governance systems like the EU.

MISSION STATEMENTS ('SPECIFICATION OF OWNERSHIP')

Finally, mission statements seek to influence the overriding culture and values in an administrative system. Cultural change can be an immensely powerful tool to modify organizational behaviour (Schein 1985). However, the problem with mission statements is that they often embody aspirations that are disconnected from the daily life of most bureaucrats, who have to juggle multiple objectives. In organizations, mission statements therefore often reflect values that are in fact *not* part of the organization's culture; that is, they often contain a strong element of wishful thinking (cf. DiMaggio and Powell 1983; Schein 1985). Hence, they often need to be buttressed with other coordinating capacities. Moreover, formulating and institutionalizing mission statements requires the strong involvement of the apex (i.e. hierarchy) to set the right example (Selznick 1957). *Specification of ownership* can also be placed in this category. Rather than specifying clear and quantifiable *targets* (see above), this involves defining who is responsible for a common task. In an EU setting, this might include practising subsidiarity, sustainability, or 'better regulation'. In practice, goals like these tend to be so widely framed that everyone (and, in practice, therefore no one) is responsible.

Is coordination ultimately an administrative or a political matter?

These six coordinating capacities form the input side of coordination (the output being the extent to which coordination is actually achieved). They cover the traditional mode of administrative coordination—that is, hierarchy—as well as some of the more political and cultural views on organizations. Interestingly, we have also shown that concepts which are more strongly linked to market and/or network forms of organization can also be fitted into this schema. As a general principle, with higher levels of differentiation between actors, more coordination mechanisms have to be available (not just more of the same). In fact, Mintzberg (1983; 1989) argues that the six have the potential to be mutually reinforcing. Starting in the next chapter, we examine how the five actors have (or have not) employed them in pursuit of greater environmental coordination (i.e. EU-EPI).

When carefully designed, these capacities can greatly facilitate the process of coordination.[4] In reality, the amount of coordination achieved will be strongly influenced by the extent of political support received from heads of state, ministers, and higher-level managers (Peters 1998b: 52). But it would be quite wrong to assume that everything can be put down to the presence or absence of political support (Wildavsky 1996), because the way in which coordination capacities are designed can strongly influence which issues eventually acquire public attention and hence become openly political. In terms of EU-EPI, the easier and the earlier that environmental officials get involved in shaping policies developed by the sectors, the more openly political the preparations for the Council will be. The use of environmental policy appraisal provides a good case in point, as it is meant to help clarify (and hence make more openly political) important cross-sectoral conflicts (see Chapter 9). Hence, to an extent, coordination capacities are a precondition for identifying intersectoral conflicts (and thus capturing the relevant minister's attention).

During the writing of this book, we came across politicians and pressure group campaigners who were adamant that politics (e.g. political pressure developed and applied by pressure groups and politicians) is what really counts. But in our view, this overlooks the extent to which politics and administration are interconnected. That is to say, coordination depends on the presence or absence of political pressure, but political pressure/ attention simultaneously depends on the availability of coordination capacities (Schout 1999a). This is presumably why bodies like the EEA and the OECD have devoted so much of their time in finding ways to institutionalize EPI in administrative and policymaking systems. In Chapter 1, we described the relationship as that involving the proverbial chicken and egg.

A framework for analysing coordination capacities

In the empirical chapters of this book we employ the coordination scale to analyse the administrative capacities for EPI at each stage of the EU decisionmaking process. The bottom half of Table 2.1 examines the capacities (input); the top half presents the extent to which coordination is achieved (output) by each actor. Drawing on documentary and interview sources, we completed one table for each actor (see the relevant empirical chapter for details). This, we hope, will give an additional insight into the extent to which coordination capacities (input) are related to the level of coordination achieved (output). By comparing them (in the spirit of benchmarking as applied via the OMC—see Chapter 1) we should be in a better position to assess the effectiveness of coordination within each actor and point to any obvious weaknesses. The remainder of this section discusses the main phases and stages of EU decisionmaking.

The main phases and stages of the EU policy process

Two main phases can be distinguished: those stages which are dominated by the Commission and those which are dominated by political negotiations in the Council and with the Parliament. This schema is, of course, a simplification of reality, because *inter alia* the stages do not necessarily

Table 2.1. Inter- and intra-departmental coordination capacities for integrating environmental factors into the work of other Councils

Coordination level	Commission phases						Council phases				
	Initiation of new proposals	Work plans	White & Green papers	Drafting of proposals	Inter-service consultation	Presentation of proposals	Presidency agenda	Working parties	COREPER	Council	Conciliation
OUTPUT											
9 Strategy											
8 Margins											
7 Arbitration											
6 Conciliation											
5 Consensus											
4 One voice											
3 Consultation											
2 Communication											
1 Independent policy making											

Coordination capacities											
INPUT											
Hierarchical											
Bureaucratic											
Specification of output											
Horizontal											
Informal relations											
Liaison roles											
Task forces											
Teams											
Weak integrator											
Strong integrator											
Mission statements											
Role of the EU coordinating units											

follow each other sequentially. Nevertheless, it offers a good starting point for discussion and comparison. Throughout, we illustrate our arguments by referring to EU-EPI.

INITIATION—HIGH-LEVEL MEETINGS AND INTEREST GROUP LOBBYING

The Commission enjoys the formal right of initiative with respect to most environmental legislation. However, as discussed in Chapter 8, only a proportion of any proposal is actually generated internally within the Commission. Ideas for new policies often come from member states, pressure groups, and even non-EU actors (Peterson 1995). Particularly relevant for this study are those that originate from member state lobbying and which are then discussed in the high-level meetings with national officials. These two steps offer important, early opportunities for contemplating EU-EPI. For example, national sectoral officials could contact their national environmental department when lobbying for new EU policies. Moreover, the meetings of senior officials (see Chapter 3) offer an excellent opportunity to ensure that environmental issues are incorporated into long-term planning. In this way, EPI issues could, in theory, be taken on board right from the start (i.e. active information). But this is easier said than done, as it might involve trespassing on another actor's administrative 'turf'.

COMMISSION WORKPLANNING

Once the need for a new policy is accepted, a proposal is included in the Commission's workplan. If necessary, a White Paper will be written to create a broad framework for the policy (see below). Requests from the Council for more transparency and better planning stimulated the last two Commission Presidents (Santer and Prodi) to plan work more systematically, focusing on priorities and any overlaps between policies (see Chapter 9 for details). A key step in the Commission's planning is the workplan, which is presented to the Parliament at the start of each year. This plan is the result of several months of planning, prioritizing, and negotiating between DGs, which starts each February.

During these preparations, each DG produces its own 'indicative list' of proposals. These lists provide a more detailed overview of planned activities than the workplan, and could be a useful tool proactively to select priorities for EU-EPI. As will be discussed in Chapter 9, the workplan is written in both a bottom-up and a top-down way (i.e. policy officials identify possible frictions in their fields, and senior management and the Commissioners indicate their political priorities). Negotiations with incoming Presidencies of the Council also affect the future workload of the Commission. The Commission's new Impact Assessment procedure aims to support these activities (see Chapters 5 and 9).

WHITE/GREEN PAPERS AND COMMUNICATIONS

To prevent fragmentation, policy initiatives taken up by the Commission are now fitted into a broader framework of Green Papers (which initiate debates on new policies) and White Papers (which set out the wider framework of new policies). Strategic Programmes and Communications from the Commission perform similar functions. Once these documents have been adopted by the full College of Commissioners, they are sent to the Council for approval.[5] They may draw upon the outcomes of public hearings or other forms of stakeholder interaction. Once adopted, they may lead to a stream of interconnected policy proposals.

These policy statements provide a very early opportunity to obtain a more synoptic overview of new policy developments in a particular sector, and can thus be used by other actors (DGs, member states, etc.) to develop or adapt their preferences. EU policy processes are opening up to the possibility of greater cross-sectoral coordination, but are national governments and the European Parliament adjusting themselves to exploit these new opportunities? We will show that national environment officials do try to influence the content of sectoral papers before they are written. However, Commission officials believe it would be difficult to produce a strategy paper with national sectoral officials looking over their shoulders. Here is a very good example of how EU-EPI strongly challenges the established working practices in EU policymaking. We will highlight many others in the empirical chapters.

DRAFTING OF PROPOSALS (EXPERT MEETINGS)

Once a strategy has been established, the drafting of a policy proposal can begin in earnest. As early as possible, officials are expected to produce Impact Assessments ('road maps') that are publicly available on the Commission's website (see Chapter 9). Many proposals are highly technical and are informed by discussions in committees of (national) experts convened by the Commission. This could be a vitally important stage for addressing EU-EPI. However, the obvious danger is that an avalanche of suggested revisions at this stage could inundate the desk officer trying to draft the proposal. Nevertheless, this is the phase in which proposals can be shaped, often very strongly.[6]

INTERSERVICE CONSULTATION WITHIN THE COMMISSION

Any proposal that is formally adopted falls under the collective responsibility of the College of Commissioners. To prepare for the formal adoption process, a draft proposal first goes through a round of interservice consultations at the level of the *cabinets* of the Commissioners. The central body in the Commission is the *hebdomadaire* (Hebdo) meeting of the *chefs de cabinets* where the agendas of the College are prepared and possible problems solved. To unburden the Hebdo, the relevant *cabinet* members dealing with specific policies will coordinate items, so as to ensure that the *chefs* focus their energies on issues of major political importance. With regards to EU-EPI, important questions include the following: do environment officials regard this phase as a relevant point to lobby for a stronger environmental dimension via the relevant *cabinet* members? Are such interventions consistently and actively coordinated in national capitals? EU-EPI implies that they should be, but does this happen in practice? We take up these and other questions in the empirical chapters.

PRESENTATION OF PROPOSALS

Once the proposal has been formally adopted by the Commission, it will be put on the list of decisions of the College and sent to the national permanent representations, the Council, and the Parliament. In the empirical chapters we analyse the extent to which national departments systematically assess the potential for EU-EPI at this stage.

THE PRESIDENCY AGENDA

Subsequent stages are planned in close cooperation with the Presidency.[7] The Presidency is in charge of putting topics on the Council's agenda, in the context of a 'rolling agenda' inherited from its predecessor. The agendas of the Presidencies are now changing towards multi-annual and annual programmes. Each of these offers new opportunities to check the content of and coordination between new policies. In the empirical chapters we examine how far the five actors use the agenda of the Presidency to prepare their activities for the coming six months in a way that supports EU-EPI.

In theory, the agenda can be an important tool to coordinate proactively as it identifies upcoming issues. However, the Presidency cannot be relied upon to be the guardian of EPI as not all states are sufficiently environ-mentally ambitious. In fact, Chapter 3 reveals that some Presidencies have enthusiastically promoted EU-EPI since the adoption of Article 6, whereas others have largely ignored it. Chairmen are often under great political pressure to produce long tally sheets listing items of legislation adopted. In any case, including environmental objectives complicates (i.e. slows down) decisionmaking in the sectoral Councils and is therefore not welcomed. Finally, many Presidency chairmen often prefer to remain neutral and avoid supporting a 'sectoral' integration priority such as EPI.

COUNCIL WORKING PARTY NEGOTIATIONS

The technical experts from the national departments and officials from the national permanent representations will negotiate under instructions from the capitals. In the empirical chapters, we will assess the extent to which national officials coordinate their negotiating lines with their environmental departments.

COREPER

A proposal goes from a working party to COREPER when it is ripe for decision in the Council, or when political mediation is required at ambas-sador level. By this stage, many dossiers are more or less settled with only a few sticking points remaining. Relying on this late phase to achieve EU-EPI is dangerous as the proposal may effectively already be a 'done deal'. But those pushing for EU-EPI must nonetheless remain vigilant during this stage because sectoral ministries can easily insert last minute changes that dilute environmentally ambitious policies. In the empirical chapters, we assess how well the five actors respond to these and other associated dilemmas.

COUNCIL MEETINGS

The focus of attention in decisionmaking, and of coordination in member states, is the adoption of the common position in the meeting of minis-ters. As above, relying on this phase to initiate discussions on EU-EPI is unlikely to be effective.

CO-DECISIONMAKING AND CONCILIATION

With the increasing importance of co-decision, the Parliament and the Council have to reach agreement, otherwise the proposal could ultimately die. If these two bodies have different views after the first reading, the topic goes into informal and formal mediations and, after second reading, a formal process known as conciliation. This stage is inherently difficult to monitor or to influence from the outside, even though it may have a significant impact upon the final content of a policy. The chairmen from Council and Parliament require considerable leeway and flexibility to arrive at agreements in what are very often tiring, all-night sessions involving large delegations of Council officials and Members of the European Parliament (MEPs). We shall reveal that the Parliament has, in the past, used this phase to 'retro-integrate' environmental factors into sectoral proposals. But is this really an effective way to pursue EU-EPI in the long term? We seek answers to this question in Chapter 10.

Conclusions

Managing the growing interdependence between different policy levels and sectors is one of the major challenges now confronting policymakers (OECD 1995: 73). According to the OECD (1995: 73), it calls for 'a clear and consistent response across government'. Inconsistency and the failure to live up to past policy promises are common criticisms levelled at the EU. Importantly, they have also fuelled a much wider sense of popular disenchantment with the EU ('output legitimacy') (Scharpf 1999). These factors (which are summarized in the 2001 governance White Paper and in numerous Better Law Making documents from 2002) coupled with the demand for less top-down interference from 'Brussels', has fuelled a search for new (i.e. less hierarchical) modes of governance that harness the coordinating potential of networks.

The academic literature has not yet fully explored the terrain which lies between the concepts of networks, governance, and coordination. As a corollary, there are a number of important issues around the concepts of governance and network management which have not yet received a satisfactory airing in the EU studies literature. In Chapter 1, we explained that the dominant view of networks emphasizes their ability to 'self-organize'. They do this as and when actors share a set of common concerns, for example how to shape the EU in their sectoral interests. In Chapter 1, we explained that in order to understand the value of networked governance, the analytical telescope urgently needs to be turned around; that is, what tasks do networks of actors have to perform to achieve a common EU-wide coordination goal such as EU-EPI?

Working from a contingent perspective, we have suggested that this task may well require the EU to rethink the way in which it interfaces with EU networks. In view of the failure to deal with horizontal objectives such as EPI, a more active and centrally managed approach to employ new modes of governance such as networks seems necessary, given that many of the existing structures and rhythms of EU policymaking—for example, the operation of the Presidency and the development of strategic workplans (see above)—appear to be in conflict with the implementation of cross-cutting coordination objectives. In order to assess the extent to which governance by networks is a viable means of delivering greater EU-EPI, in this chapter we have presented a model for active network management. This draws attention to the role of manager, which could conceivably be performed by the Commission.

In the next chapter we discuss how the EU has responded to the challenge of EU-EPI and try to link this to the way in which different coordinating instruments—including networks—have been employed. In so doing, we start to explore whether there is indeed a formal EPI network at EU level (Question 1, Chapter 1), and assess what (if any) part the Commission plays in its functioning. Secondly, the network participants have to be—by definition—more or less equal in a network situation. Therefore, to be effective, each of the partners needs to have the necessary internal coordination capacities (as set out in Table 2.1) to establish the trust needed to glue the network together. In the context of EU-EPI, this means that each must be able to set priorities and to coordinate internally (i.e. intradepartmentally) and externally with cognate sectors (i.e. inter-departmentally). The extent to which the five actors currently fulfil these demands is the chief concern of Chapters 6–10.

Notes

1. It is a moot point whether there is one systemic 'deficit' as Metcalfe implies, or whether it is time and place specific (e.g. in particular sectors/problem areas). We should be in a better position to judge this when we get to Chapter 11.
2. Although he does not specifically use the term political coordination, Mintzberg includes bureaucratic politics under horizontal informal relations (Schout 1999a; Toonen 1983).
3. This does not mean that hierarchy as such disappears. Rather, each of the mechanisms listed below requires a measure of hierarchy, but in different roles (Schout 1999a).

4. To avoid confusion, this is not to say that administrative structures determine everything—they facilitate coordination by lowering transaction costs, and help to determine the location and timing of any political conflict.
5. White Papers are sent to the European Council.
6. By exactly how much remains a moot point (see Peterson 1995: 75).
7. At the time of writing, it is likely that new team Presidency of three member states will be rather similar to the traditional rotating Presidency (see Schout 2004; 2006).

Part II
The Multilevel Context

3

ENVIRONMENTAL POLICY INTEGRATION AT EUROPEAN UNION LEVEL: A CATALOGUE OF COORDINATING CAPACITIES

Environmental integration is a key condition for progressing towards sustainable development. It requires the unfailing and continuous commitment of all policy sectors at all levels of governance in the [European] Union

(CEC 2004*b*: 38)

Introduction

EPI is almost universally acknowledged as being 'a good thing' (Lafferty and Hovden 2003). It is, for example, to be found in the 1992 Rio Declaration, Agenda 21 (the UN's multi-chapter blueprint for sustainable development), various OECD publications, and many national sustainability strategies. In Chapter 1 we explained that the EU has repeatedly pledged to implement it, but is still finding this very difficult to achieve. It is certainly not, DG Environment argues, difficult to identify examples of sectoral EU policies for transport, agriculture, or energy that are inherently incompatible with this pledge (CEC 2004*b*: 5–8). For example, in the agricultural sector, EU policies support activities that pollute rivers and degrade biodiversity, and its fisheries policies have pushed fish stocks to well below minimum biologically acceptable levels (CEC 2004*b*: 5–7). As long as these trends continue (and without a more sustained shift to integrated policymaking), the EU will struggle to achieve the long-term sustainability targets contained in the Sixth Environmental Action Programme (EAP) (EEA 2005*c*: 18) and the EU sustainable development strategy (SDS) (CEC 2005*a*).

The main purpose of this chapter is to explore what kinds of coordinating capacities the EU has deployed to address these inconsistencies, and also to assess the level of political support received at EU and member state level. Section 2 briefly explores the intellectual origins of the EPI principle and unpacks its core meaning. Section 3 charts the changing ways in which EPI has been thought about and put into effect at EU level since about 1970. This review reveals that the Cardiff process is just the latest in a long series of incremental initiatives. Crucially, there have been no systematic audits of the type offered in this book. Section 4 then reflects on these developments and attempts to put them into context. Section 5 maps the EU's response on to the typology of coordination capacities developed in Chapter 2, and pinpoints the most obvious gaps and overlaps. The concluding section summarizes the main themes of this chapter and explores the links with subsequent chapters.

Environmental policy integration

Intellectual origins

The thinking that lies behind the concept of EPI is neither sophisticated nor especially novel. In some respects, the basic idea that 'the environment' functions as a single, integrated whole whereas the human world is divided into different parts, has been one of the guiding axioms of green political thought since time immemorial (Dobson 2000). However, it began to achieve a far wider political currency with the publication, in 1987, of an influential UN report entitled *Our Common Future* (WCED 1987: 9). The Brundtland report (as it is now commonly known) popularized the concept of sustainability.[1] One passage in particular is very widely quoted by those that write about EPI:

Those responsible for managing natural resources and protecting the environment are institutionally separated from those responsible for managing the economy. The real world of interlocked economic and ecological systems will not change; the policies and institutions concerned must. (ibid.: 9)

Brundtland's preferred solution to these mismatches was deceptively simple:

[T]he major central economic and sectoral agencies of governments should . . . be made directly responsible . . . for ensuring that their policies, programmes, and budgets support development that is ecologically as well as economically sustainable. (ibid.: 314)

Since 1987, this message—essentially 'implement EPI'—has been gradually internalized in many national laws, policy documents, and political statements.

In the last decade, EPI has undoubtedly 'come of age' in EU politics. Jans (2000: 17) even goes as far as to describe it as 'one of *the* most important principles of EU [environmental] law' (emphasis added). However, we shall show that its meaning is far from obvious and its implementation remains exceedingly problematic. It has also provoked an increasing amount of academic comment, as various authors have tried to pin down its precise meaning (Haigh 2005: section 3.11-1), and what is required to implement it (Jordan and Lenschow 2000; Lenschow 2002a). However, as noted in Chapter 1, it is still far from clear what EPI implies for the future organization of administrative and policymaking systems, hence our interest in understanding the role of coordination capacities.

Coordination and EPI: their core meanings

EPI is quite clearly a popular concept, but what does it actually mean? In an early analysis, Weale and Williams (1993: 46) concluded that there was 'no canonical statement of precisely what it might involve'. Over a decade later, the EEA (2005a: 12) detected 'little agreement' on its meaning, and indeed questioned whether this had contributed to its rapid uptake. Arild Underdal (1980: 162) suggests that a policy is 'integrated' when:

the consequences for that policy are recognised as *decision premises*, aggregated into an *overall evaluation* and incorporated at *all policy levels* and into *all government agencies* involved in its execution. (emphasis added)

The problem with this definition is that it could apply equally well to any aspect of government practice, in just about any sector of public policy. What, therefore, differentiates *environmental* policy integration from, say, agricultural or transport policy integration (Lafferty and Hovden 2003: 8)? In answering this question, it is useful to distinguish between EPI as a *principle* of 'good governance . . . ' (e.g. OECD 2000c: 2), a *process* of putting that principle into practice, and the *outcomes* that would eventually emerge from doing so.

Very often, these three usages of the term (and others—a 'strategy', a 'duty', a 'concept') are used interchangeably (e.g. EEA 2005a: 7). For instance, in 2004 the European Commission explained that the principle of EPI:

recognizes that environmental policy alone cannot achieve the environmental improvements needed as part of sustainable development. The changes required to reduce environmental pressures... can only be achieved through a *process* of environmental integration in [other] sectors. (CEC 2004b: 2) (emphasis added)

Here we see references made to the *process* of considering environmental factors in sectoral decisionmaking, and a desired *outcome*, that is, environmental improvement and, eventually, sustainable development.

At first sight, the *principle* of EPI seems self-evident: it suggests that the environment should be given a higher weighting in public policy (but see Nollkaemper 2002: 24). One of the key problems is that it does not specify *how far* environment should be integrated into the development of policies in other sectors, or indeed when and by whom, to qualify as EPI. Crucially, the principle EPI does not determine how heavily environmental factors should be weighted in the decisionmaking process, only that they are integrated into the *process* of making decisions at a sufficiently early stage (EEA 2005a: 13). There is certainly no definitive legal ruling by the European Court of Justice (ECJ) which can conveniently be cited to resolve this matter (Jans 2000: 18–19).

In order to clarify the matter, it is worthwhile distinguishing between *strong* and *weak* interpretations of EPI (Hill and Jordan 1993: 5; 1995). Weak EPI occurs when the sectors simply take environmental considerations 'into account' in the process of policymaking, but leave the core of their policies essentially untouched. According to this interpretation, EPI is in principle no stronger or more important that social or economic policy integration.[2] For example, the transport sector might discuss the ways and means of reducing the environmental burden of car transport (e.g. by fitting pollution abatement equipment), without radically challenging the underlying societal demand for greater travel.

Many environmentalists on the other hand normally subscribe to a much *stronger* interpretation of EPI, which involves the development of policies in non-environmental spheres that *consistently* benefit the environment. According to this view, EPI involves much more than simply reporting the environmental repercussions of pre-existing policy precommitments, as this treats the environment as an after thought and not, to borrow Underdal's phrase, a basic 'decision premise'. Nigel Haigh of the

Institute for European Environment Policy (IEEP), who has done more to popularize the notion of EPI in the EU than anyone else, explains that EPI essentially involves :

placing environmental consideration at the *heart* of decision making in other sectoral policies. Environmental objectives become *central* to the decision making process rather than being pursued separately through purely environmental policy instruments. (Haigh 2005: section 3.1-1) (emphasis added)

Lafferty and Hovden (2003: 10) go even further, by arguing that:

as far as *some* environmental objectives are concerned, these cannot simply be 'balanced' with the objectives of other policy sectors....[T]he EPI idea clearly indicates that environmental objectives.... must—as a general rule—be seen as *principal*. (emphasis added)

The EEA seems to sit somewhere between these two positions. While noting that the application of EPI should lead to an 'overall improvement in policy and its implementation, in line with sustainable development needs' (EEA 2005a: 7) (i.e. EPI as outcome), it seems to imply that 'environment' should have some principled pre-eminence given that it has in the past 'persistently been underplayed in other policies' (ibid.: 13).

What should now be abundantly clear is that EPI is intimately related to one of the broad themes of this book, namely the coordination of the EU. In the previous chapter we noted that coordination involves searching for what Simon (1976: 139) famously referred to as 'mutually consistent decisions'. Environmentalists often claim that most EU policymaking to date has been deeply inconsistent (i.e. poorly coordinated), and that the implicit purpose of environmental policy since the late 1960s has been to remedy this situation. They identified EPI as a new intellectual rationale for moving towards greater intersectoral consistency (i.e. coordination) in order to facilitate more sustainable development in the longer term.

A process-based view of EPI

Following Schout and Metcalfe (1999), this book is less concerned with defining the principle of EPI in an abstract theoretical sense, and more with the political and, above all, the administrative *process* through which different actors interact to develop an interpretation which actually guides and, in due course, will in some way eventually shape the outcomes of

65

daily policymaking. On this view, the practical meaning of EPI emerges in the crucible of bureaucratic conflict (Allison 1971); it is an 'ongoing process, not something that is simply "achieved" ' (EEA 2005b: 9). The actual degree (or strength—see above) of the 'integration' which emerges from this process will be determined, in part, by the political power that the different sectoral actors bring to the policymaking process. But, crucially, Chapter 2 also suggests that it will be shaped in part by the extant policy coordination mechanisms (i.e. hierarchical, bureaucratic, horizontal, etc.) that have been put in place to steer it in certain directions and which mean it surfaces at certain points in the policy cycle.

For the sake of convenience, we would like (following both Underdal and our preferred bureaucratic politics approach to understanding coordination) to interpret EPI as a *process* through which 'non-'environmental sectors consider the overall environmental consequences of their policies, and take active and early steps to incorporate an understanding of them into policymaking at all relevant levels of governance. Through this process, the practical meaning of EPI will emerge (i.e. strong or weak—see above). For our purposes, what counts is the struggle not the outcome. Whether and indeed to what extent the eventual outcomes of intersectoral struggling contribute to higher levels of environmental protection 'on the ground' or even sustainable development, fall outside the remit of this book.[3]

EPI: the vertical dimension

Another hugely important dimension of EPI to which our interpretation draws our attention is the vertical one; that is, the relationship between different *levels* of governance. There is, as was noted in Chapter 1, a growing appreciation among policymakers of the need simultaneously to grapple with the vertical *and* horizontal dimensions of EPI. Other than noting the importance of the vertical dimension (e.g. Jordan and Lenschow 2000), the academic literature does not offer any clear and consistent guidance as to how this could or should be tackled.

It is significant that eminent lawyers and EU environmental policy specialists disagree about what is implied by Article 6. Jans (2000: 22), for example, argues that Article 6 has no direct legal consequences for member states, because it refers only to '*Community* policies and activities'. But later, he concedes that there may be important *indirect* consequences as member states will be bound by any legal acts that the EU adopts to implement EPI. By contrast, Kraemer et al. (2001: 44) contends that because the text of Article 6 refers to the definition and *implementation* of EU policies, which is, of course, primarily the responsibility of member states (for further details, see Jordan 2002*b*), state actors must de facto accept some responsibility for it.

This lack of legal clarity has facilitated an ongoing political dispute at the member state level over who bears the responsibility for implementing Article 6. We hinted at this in Chapter 1 and give a much fuller flavour of it in the empirical chapters. Before we do that, in the next section we explore how the various EU institutions have interacted to shape the practical interpretation of EPI at EU level since about 1970.

Environmental policy integration in the EU: a brief history

The 1970s and early 1980s: from awareness-raising to legal codification

The history of the EU's engagement with the EPI principle is a very long one (see Table 3.1). Of all the EU institutions, the European Commission stands out as having been the most consistently forceful advocate of EPI (for more details, see Chapter 8). At first, however, DG Environment struggled to sell the idea of better coordination to the rest of the Commission, let alone the EU. In the 1970s, the more environmentally ambitious member states were still preoccupied with developing an environmental *acquis communautaire*. The more sceptical ones (like the UK) saw little or no role for it in extending these powers towards the coordination of strategically important areas of national sectoral policymaking such as energy production and transport (see Chapter 8).

Undaunted, DG Environment drew fresh political support from the publication of the Brundtland report in 1987. An important first step had, however, already been taken (largely, it has to be said, at DG Environment's insistence—see Chapter 7) in 1985, when EPI was incorporated into the draft text of the 1987 Single European Act (Article 130r). As several member states began to explore ways of incorporating EPI into their own national policy systems in the early 1990s (see Chapters 6, 7, and 8), DG Environment was able to muster political support to get this formulation reworded. This was achieved with the 1993 Maastricht Treaty on European Union, which stipulated that in future 'environmental protection *must* be integrated into the definition and implementation of other Community policies') (Article 130r (2)) (emphasis added). EPI's transformation

Table 3.1 Environmental Policy Integration in the EU: key events

1972	First EAP	Passing references made to the need for greater integration.
1983	Third EAP	First detailed statement of the need for EPI.
1985	Single European Act negotiated	Adds EPI to the founding treaties.
1987	World Commission on Environment and Development	Influential UN report popularizes sustainable development and links it to EPI.
1992	UN Rio Earth Summit/ Fifth EAP	The Fifth EAP sought to promote EPI in five economic sectors: agriculture, energy, industry, tourism, and transport.
1993	Maastricht Treaty ratified	Inserted a new reference to sustainable development and strengthened the pre-existing commitment to EPI.
1996	Treaty of Amsterdam negotiated	Established sustainable development as one of the overriding objectives of the EU and made the first explicit link to Art. 6, which extended EPI to *all* sectors.
1997 (December)	European Council, Luxembourg	Work on implementing Art. 6 begins, pushed hard by the post-1995 member states.
1998 (June)	European Council, Cardiff	Start of the 'Cardiff process': invited all relevant sectoral Councils to establish EPI strategies. Called upon the Commission to subject all major new proposals to an environmental appraisal.
1998 (December)	European Council, Vienna	Transport, Agriculture, and Energy Councils produce initial strategies. Criticized for suggesting little more than 'business as usual'. New strategies requested from a second 'wave' of Councils by 2000 (Development, Internal Market, and Industry).
1999 (June)	European Council, Cologne	Considers resulting strategies. Calls upon a third 'wave' of Councils (namely, Fisheries, General Affairs, and Finance Councils) to report in 2000.
1999 (December)	European Council, Helsinki	Reviews overall progress and calls for immediate implementation.
2001 (June)	European Council, Gothenburg	Calls for further development of Cardiff strategies. Links new EU sustainable development strategy (SDS) and the Cardiff process with the new (2000–) Lisbon process. Calls on the Council Secretariat-General to find ways to improve the coordination between Councils.
2002 (September)	Earth Summit 2, Johannesburg	Provides impetus for creating the SDS as well as thinking about the external impact of EU sustainable development in the developing world. In the run-up, the Commission suggests creating an independent 'Council' for sustainable development, to appraise critically current sectoral policies.
2003 (March)	European Council, Brussels	Calls for an 'annual stocktake' of the Cardiff process and an annual review of EU environmental policy to feed into subsequent spring Councils as part of the Lisbon process.
2004 (March)	European Council, Brussels	Presidency conclusions make little reference to the environment. First Cardiff stocktake is not ready in time (published June 2004) so is not formally considered.
2005	EU Sustainable Development Strategy	Revision of the 2001 strategy. The Commission launches thematic strategies foreseen by the Sixth EAP.

Source: Own compilation

into a fully-fledged objective of European political integration was completed in 1999, when Article 6 of the Amsterdam Treaty entered into force.

The early 1990s: putting Treaty-based commitments into practice

The adoption of Article 6 was hugely important because it completed the legal codification of EPI, elevating it from being just a narrow, 'environmental' concept, into an overarching objective of European political and economic integration. Nevertheless, even after Maastricht, the EU lacked a formal mechanism to implement EPI. DG Environment had already had one go at creating are when it published the Fifth EAP in 1992. This sought to shift the focus of environmental policy from dealing with the visible manifestations of problems (waste, pollution, etc.) to targeting their underlying causes in five target sectors. It laid out some medium- and long-term targets (i.e. specification of output) for reducing key pollutants, and recommended some appropriate instruments, including new environmental policy instruments (NEPIs) (Jordan, Wurzel, and Zito 2005).

We shall show in Chapters 5 and 9 that the Commission subsequently adopted a number of internal reforms to implement EPI in its own daily activities. These included the establishment of a new integration unit and the initiation of an environmental policy appraisal system ('green star') for all new legislative proposals. However, for reasons that are more fully elaborated in Chapter 9, the outcome of these reforms was rather disappointing. Moreover, other than issue declarations in the European Council stressing the political importance of EPI, the member states did very little to ensure that their evolving national EPI systems were coordinated with EPI-related activities at EU level. Chapters 5 and 10 also reveal that the European Parliament conspicuously failed to seize the initiative, even though it continued to push for reforms (e.g. to the structural and cohesion funds) on a more ad hoc basis that were nonetheless consistent with the broad philosophy of EPI (Lenschow 1999; 2002*b*).

By the mid-1990s, it is fair to say that while DG Environment may not have created a successful system to implement EPI, it had gained a much better appreciation of the practical difficulties that such an endeavour would eventually have to overcome. In 1995, the Commission published a progress report (CEC 1995) which demonstrated just how little had been achieved across the EU. A range of other stakeholders arrived at much more critical assessments during a wide-ranging review process organized by DG Environment, dubbed 'the Global Assessment' (CEC 1999*a*; CEC 2000*d*). This showed that the integration targets set by the Fifth EAP had not enjoyed sufficient political support among the other EU institutions (i.e. they were regarded as no more than specifications of ownership) and had not been adequately connected to integration efforts at national and sub-national levels (CEC 2000*d*: 24). Consequently, they had had little bearing on sectoral policy development (CEC 1999).

The mid-1990s: the start of the Cardiff process

In the mid-1990s, the arrival of three new willing advocates of EPI (namely the post-1995 member states of Sweden, Austria, and Finland), gave the debate a decisive push forward. With their assistance, DG Environment was able to achieve agreement on Article 6. Six months after it had been negotiated, the Commission was requested by the December 1997 Luxembourg European Council to develop an implementation strategy. It duly delivered a Communication entitled 'Partnership for Integration'. Importantly, its declared purpose was to develop 'some practical steps towards implementing the integration principle in the *daily work of the Community institutions*' (emphasis added) (CEC 1998: 3). This document marked a new and much more purposeful phase in the way that EPI was thought about and enunciated in the EU. For instance, it sought to draw many new actors, most notably the Heads of State, the European Parliament, and the Council of Ministers, into a common and ongoing process of sectoral reporting, reviewing, and target setting organized around a common network centred on the Council.

The 1998 Communication marked a formal recognition—at least by the Commission—that EU-EPI was indeed a multi-actor, multilevel problem (i.e. one exhibiting complex interdependence). But how well did the other actors respond to the Commission's initiative? During the first half of 1998, the UK Presidency worked hard to turn this new enthusiasm and commitment into a set of practical coordination mechanisms supporting an EU-level integration partnership (or network). The centrepiece of what came to be known as the 'Cardiff process' (a reference to the location of the June 1998 European Council) was a process of sectoral strategy development and reporting. The first three sectors invited to participate—agriculture, transport, and energy—were obvious choices as they were deeply implicated in unsustainable development, and had been mentioned in the 1998 Communication. In the following year, six more sectoral Councils were added to the list to bring the total to nine (see Box 3.1). By 2002, these nine formations had produced sectoral integration strategies (for details, see CEC 2004*b*), although integration activities also began in a proto fourth wave (EEA 2005*a*: 30).

Box 3.1 The three 'waves' of the Cardiff process	
First wave	Agriculture, Energy, and Transport (1998–)
Second wave	Development, Industry, and Internal Market (1999–)
Third wave	Ecofin, General Affairs (or GAC), and Fisheries (1999–)
A Fourth wave?	Education, Health, Consumer Affairs, Tourism, Research, Employment, and Social Affairs

Source: Own compilation

The late 1990s: the operation of the Cardiff process

Around this time, hopes were high that the discipline of writing and sharing integration strategies within a network of interested actors would magically generate new information, intrasectoral learning, and, eventually, a new and all-pervading sense of self-responsibility for environmental issues within the sectors. However, these hopes proved to be somewhat misplaced, not least because many of the sectors drawn into the process had never really thought about environmental issues before, let alone produced comprehensive, long-term EPI strategies (Fergusson et al. 2001). With hindsight it was also obvious that a number of important network management tasks (see Chapter 2) had not been properly clarified at the start. There had certainly been no comprehensive audit of capacities at network or actor level. The process also failed fully to engage several key actors, namely the European Parliament and the member states. Rather it relied too heavily upon the different sectors of the Council producing and evaluating their own strategies. DG Environment was an obvious candidate to fulfil the role of network manager, but neither it nor the Environment Council were asked to take this job on by the European Council.[4] Other than apply gentle pressure on the laggards, DG Environment had no effective means of ensuring that the various actors (i.e. sectors) fulfilled their assignments on time. Worse still, no one was really sure if the process had an end point or how performance would eventually be assessed and lessons learnt. And finally, as no network audit had been carried out, it proved difficult to diagnose the underlying causes of non-performance.

These concerns were born out by the first independent assessments made of the initial outputs of the Cardiff process (e.g. Görlach et al. 1999; Fergusson et al. 2001). Most of the EPI strategies were roundly condemned for being vague and unambitious. The vast majority appeared to present their policies as 'given', and hence not open to any substantial change to achieve EPI (i.e. they were at best inputs to a process of coordination (Level 1) not fully coordinated outcomes). The sectors were duly asked by the European Council to go away and try again. DG Environment presented its own critical analysis to the December 1999 European Council in Helsinki (CEC 1999b). This highlighted the lack of timetables and targets. In a much more biting assessment, the European Environmental Bureau (EEB) of environmental pressure groups claimed that '[a]ll [the] councils fail[ed] to address adequately the need for major policy reform to bring Europe within its environmental space' (EEB 1999).

The Cardiff process rolled on slowly through 2000 and 2001 as each sector tried to respond to mounting criticism that the whole exercise lacked momentum and a clear focus. In the spring of 2001, the Austrian, German, and UK environment ministries organized a joint workshop to inject new life into it. Each tabled an independent report, which came to strikingly similar conclusions. The German report found 'great variation' across the nine strategies, with some offering 'little more than a description of past policies, extant legislation, and new initiatives already "in the pipeline" ' (Kraemer et al. 2001: 4). The UK's report (Fergusson et al. 2001) also identified a considerable variation in how each Council formation had thought about EPI and reported on progress. In short, there was little or no additional coordination. Part of the reason had to do with the fact that they had not been written in a comparable way (see above). Another important factor was their historical exposure to EU environmental legislation (i.e. high in relation to transport and agriculture, much lower for the rest) (Fergusson et al. 2001: 14). A subsequent report by the Commission confirmed that many of the strategies were little more than vague 'statements of intent', which lacked few if any monitoring and review procedures (CEC 2004b: 31). Either way, the 'value added' of the Cardiff process did not appear to have been that great. And crucially for us, just one of the sectors (development) gave any thought to what new coordinating capacities were needed to implement EPI either at EU or at national level (Fergusson et al. 2001: 10).

The 2000s: The Lisbon Process and the EU sustainable development strategy

By early 2001, enthusiasm for the process in some of the sectors had declined so much that claims began to circulate in the media that the whole process was about to be terminated by the Commission. To be fair, some sectors (e.g. transport) had entered into the spirit of the exercise. However, the vast majority felt the process had been imposed on them, and were deeply reluctant to commit themselves to concrete targets and timetables. By late 2002, the production of new strategies and/or updating of existing ones had all but ceased, and the entire process began to move into the shadow of the newly emerging Lisbon process on social and economic reform. Established in 2000, Lisbon aims to ensure that the EU becomes 'the most competitive and dynamic knowledge-based economy in the world, capable of sustainable economic growth with more and better jobs and greater social cohesion'. Its appearance reflected a growing concern among some of the larger member states that what the EU needed was 'old fashioned' economic growth to provide more jobs, not EPI or sustainable development. To the very great disappointment of environmentalists, the Lisbon process initially made only passing references to environmental protection.[5] In 2003, DG Environment openly admitted that 'to many actors the environment still appears as an "add on" ' to the annual synthesis reports that are submitted to the European Council each spring (CEC 2003b).[6]

The 2001 Swedish Presidency eventually succeeded in retrofitting Lisbon with an environmental dimension (Hinterberger and Zacherl 2003). But even so, only one or two of the first set of Lisbon indicators reviewed at the December 2001 Council were 'environmental'. In fact, the current list of fourteen includes only one direct environmental indicator (namely, greenhouse gas emissions) and two indirect ones (namely, energy intensity and transport volumes). Ever since the creation of the Lisbon process, environmentalists have mounted a rearguard action to prevent it from entirely eclipsing the Cardiff process (e.g. EEB 2003: 5). For example, in October 2002, the Environment Council called on the non-participating sectors (that was education, health, tourism, etc.) (see Box 3.1) to join as part of a fourth wave. But this request (since repeated by the Commission in 2004) fell on deaf ears (CEC 2004b: 5).

Partly in response to these problems, DG Environment gradually shifted its focus and energies to the EU's SDS. Published rather hurriedly by the Commission in the run-up to the 2002 Johannesburg summit, this strategy[7]was not produced in a particularly coordinated or consistent manner. Hinterberger and Zacherl (2003: 15) argue that key inconsistencies—such as the ecologically harmful subsidies paid to the energy, fisheries, and agricultural sectors—were not resolved. Also, insufficient thought was given to how the SDS would eventually dovetail with the other main strands of the EU's sustainability policy programme, namely the Sixth EAP, and the Lisbon and, of course, Cardiff processes (EEA 2005a). The SDS, which was reviewed during 2005, will eventually set new headline objectives for different unsustainable trends (CEC 2005a: 19). The Commission expects that more detailed 'operational objectives' will then be identified in the relevant sectoral policies, through a process which sounds suspiciously like a new variant of Cardiff (CEC 2005a: 21).

EPI in the EU: taking stock and looking forwards

Whither Cardiff?

In the last few years, the different parts of the Commission have tried to rationalize these different reporting and strategy processes. DG Environment contributed by preparing the first of a series of annual stocktakes of the Cardiff process (e.g. CEC 2004b) and Environmental Policy Reviews (CEC 2003b: 22, 47) to feed into the annual Spring Council assessments, complementing the annual reviews of the implementation of the SDS. However, the 2004 Spring European Council's response to this new activity was devastatingly negative. Only four paragraphs out of a total of eighty addressed environmental issues. The environment section, which was pointedly retitled 'Environmentally Sustainable Growth', did not even refer to Cardiff. In 2005, Lisbon was relaunched as the EU's Partnership for Growth and Jobs (CEC 2005b: 24), a title which clearly downplays the more environmental dimension(s) of sustainability. Significantly, even DG Environment now appears to have stopped referring to the Cardiff process. In June 2005, its Director General admitted that while 'the idea of integration is very much alive...the Cardiff process is not going anywhere' (ENDS Ltd., No. 365: 24). The 2004 Environmental Policy Review conspicuously avoided any mention of Cardiff, and instead laid stress on relatively older and better established coordination instruments that could be deployed at member state level such as new environmental policy instruments, environmental policy appraisal, and strategic environmental assessment (CEC 2004c).

General themes and patterns

There are at least three general conclusions that can be drawn from this brief review. The first is that the EU's response to EPI has gradually evolved through a number of distinct phases. During the first phase (c.1970–80), thinking about EPI developed slowly and almost exclusively in the more environmentally focused parts of the EU, such as DG Environment. The second (c.1980–7) phase was one of agenda setting and legal embedding. However, EPI remained first and foremost an *environmental* principle, located in the environmental chapter of the founding treaties. It barely impinged upon the work of the sectors or (with the exception of the Commission), the daily activities of the EU institutions. The third phase (c.1987–96) was marked by the deeper institutionalization of the principle in EU law and some pioneering attempts to translate it into daily procedures and practices (e.g. the Commission 'green star' appraisal system—see Chapter 5). However, with the exception of the Commission, parts of the European Parliament, and other environmental actors (e.g. the EEA), its political profile remained very low. In the fourth phase (1996–2004), determined attempts were made to grapple with the practical challenges posed by the consolidation of the EPI principle in the Amsterdam Treaty. Significantly, these efforts are now engaging the 'non-' environmental sectors. But as the sectors have gradually become more aware of the potential long-term implications of Article 6, they have made ever-stronger attempts to neutralize them. ENDS Daily (No. 1679, 3 June 2004) recently concluded that 'the debate [is now] ... less of integrating environment into sectoral policies, and more of reverse integrating competitiveness into EU environmental policies.' This is very much the theme of the current phase (2004–). Witness, for example, the virtual death of the Cardiff process, the rising prominence of the Lisbon and Better Regulation agendas, and DG Environment's increasingly casual search for new and less intrusive approaches to implementing EPI predominantly at member state level. In 2005, the Commission produced a Communication on the guiding principles of sustainable development which did not contain a single reference to EPI (CEC 2005*h*).

Second, although more and more sectors have become involved in EPI-related matters, the dominant axis continues to run from the Commission to the Council. The European Parliament remains only very partially engaged in the Cardiff and Lisbon processes (see Chapter 10 for further details). Therefore, the only real source of political leadership has had to come from the Presidency. The problem here is that some Presidencies have been much more proactive than others (see Table 3.2). Consequently, Cardiff proceeded in a series of fits and starts, depending on the political ambitions and energy of the incumbent.

Table 3.2 EU Presidency initiatives in relation to EPI

Year	Presidency	Political initiative
1997	Netherlands	Moderate—helped to finalize the text of the Amsterdam Treaty, although Article 6 (on EPI) was more or less already agreed when it took over (from the Irish)
1997	Luxembourg	Weak—but the Luxembourg Presidency acted on a Swedish initiative and sought to find practical ways to implement Article 6
1998	UK	Strong—formally initiated the Cardiff process of sectoral reporting
1998	Austria	Strong—initiated studies on EPI, arranged workshops, and debated coordination capacities in the Council. Requested Commission to report on integration indicators and the impact assessment of policies
1999	Germany	Moderate—other than organizing a workshop on EPI in Bonn and pushing for the addition of a third wave of strategies, did little to take Cardiff forward
1999	Finland	Weak—did little to develop the Cardiff strategies, although Finland has supported EPI in the transport strategy
2000	Portugal	Very weak—paid no attention to EPI or Cardiff; initiated the Lisbon process
2000	France	Weak—did little to take Cardiff forward
2001	Sweden	Strong—helped to breathe new life into the Cardiff process; pushed for environmental dimensions to be added to the Lisbon process. Asked for integration strategies to be further developed. Called on the Council to find ways of improving intercouncil coordination. Pushed for all new Commission proposals to be subjected to an sustainability assessment
2001	Belgium	Moderate—but did commission an independent audit of environmental governance and EPI mechanisms
2002	Spanish	Weak—Cardiff almost completely ignored at the Barcelona summit. An Austrian government initiative to create a new high-level environment working group in the Council was not successful
2002	Denmark	Moderate—pushed for the greening of the Lisbon strategy; no committed support for agricultural reform
2003	Greece	Weak—although agreement was reached on the need for an annual stocktake of the Cardiff process
2003	Italy	Weak—strongly supported the Lisbon agenda
2004	Ireland	Weak—no new initiatives on sustainability; no systematic evaluation of Cardiff
2004	Netherlands	Moderate—main emphasis was on eco-efficiency; supported the 'greening' of the Lisbon process

Source: Own compilation

Our third and final observation is that the EU's response has been relatively incremental, with no obvious breakpoints or phase changes. There has also been no systematic review of the causes, consequences, and possible responses to disintegrated policymaking (i.e. something akin to a network audit), other than various ad hoc reports produced by DG

Environment and, eventually, the EEA (2005a; 2005b). A casual inspection of the content of the Cardiff strategies indicates that the EU lacks even a common, practical understanding of EPI; rather, every sector has its own preferred interpretation ranging from business as usual to something more in line with DG Environment's aspirations. The manner in which these competing interpretations are reconciled (i.e. coordinated) in the heat of daily EU policymaking will, we suggest, ultimately determine the practical meaning of EPI in the EU; that is, strong or weak. The outcomes of coordination will, of course, never be entirely determined by pulling and hauling; they will also depend on the presence and/or absence of administrative coordination mechanisms—rules, procedures, systems for exchanging information, and coordinating committees. These help to define who is involved in addressing cross-sectoral conflicts (i.e. just the sectors, or environment as well?), when this takes place (i.e. early or late in the policy cycle?), and who bears the cost (see the discussion of 'active' and 'passive' information in Chapter 2). They will also have a strong influence on which intersectoral conflicts are seen to be important and, by implication, which are opened up for active political debate. Given their importance, the next section begins the task (which is continued throughout the remainder of the book) of assessing precisely what sort of coordination capacities the EU has in place to pursue EU-EPI.

Mechanisms of environmental coordination in the EU

We have already explained that effective network management should consider the availability of capacities at the network and at the sub-network (i.e. actor) levels (see Table 1.1). To what extent has the EU sought to address the need for adequate capacities at these two levels?

Coordination capacities at network level

In Chapter 1 we asked whether there is such a thing as an 'EU-EPI network'. The brief historical review offered above suggests that there is no formal 'EPI network' in the EU, but there are at least three networks that are potentially relevant to the challenge of EU-EPI.[8] The first could be termed the *Cardiff process network*, which was established in 1998. It brings together the sectoral formations of the Council and is serviced by the Council Secretariat. The Council Secretariat has been described as a 'vital cog' in Council decisionmaking (Beach 2004: 415), but providing day-to-day administrative support to the Council and/or the Presidency normally consumes most of its relatively meagre resources (Hayes-Renshaw 2002: 52). Because of this and the Secretariat's relatively limited understanding of the technicalities of environmental protection/EPI, the Cardiff integration strategies emerged via a number of different routes involving different combinations of actors. In other words, the network was rather fluid and lacked strong central management. Some of the strategies were co-produced by parallel Commission DGs, some by the national departments of the state holding the Presidency, and some with the assistance of the Council Secretariat (EEA 2005a: 34). The General Affairs Council was eventually given a coordinating role, but this only ever 'consisted of . . . the development of a road map setting out the relevant policy issues where the environment is relevant' (EEA 2005b: 29).

The second is the *network of national environmental coordinators*. This comprises middle-ranking bureaucrats from the member state environment departments (see the relevant parts of Chapters 6, 7, and 8 for details). These are the main point of contact between member state environment departments and the Environment Council. Their primary responsibility is to ensure that Ministers arrive in Brussels with an internally coordinated position. The network meets formally around the time of each Environment Council meeting, but it will often meet informally before and after to work on common topics and develop future agendas.[9] It also tries to find compromises between different state positions on individual policy proposals. This involves defending positions, leading discussions, and collecting support for particular dossiers. Strictly speaking, this is a coordination network, but, like its functional equivalents in other sectors, it is primarily focused on shadowing the work of its council formation—that is, the Environment Council. In other words, it primarily addresses *vertical* rather than horizontal interdependence.

Finally, there is the *Environment Policy Review Group* (EPRG), which was specifically created in 1993 as part of the Fifth EAP to improve the flow of information between the Commission DGs and national environment departments. In theory, it could provide a potentially powerful bridge between different levels of governance in the EU. However, one major actor—the European Parliament—is not represented. And although it discusses environmental issues at a very early stage (i.e. before proposals are made), it does not play a strategic role in relation to wider Commission or Council agendas. Importantly, it has never considered the question of EPI in much detail, either in the broad, strategic sense of, say, the Cardiff process, or in relation to daily policy and politics. We return to the role of the EPRG in the concluding chapter.

Coordinating capacities at the sublevel

In Chapter 2, we drew on the work of Mintzberg to identify six coordination capacities at actor level. Although we are not yet in a position to judge their fitness for purpose at EU level, some broad patterns of use are nonetheless apparent and worthy of comment.

HIERARCHICAL MECHANISMS

Thus far, the EU has not utilized many hierarchical mechanisms in pursuit of EPI. There is, for example, no 'high representative', 'super commissioner', or 'czar' charged with pursuing EPI across the EU, in the same way that other coordination problems such as terrorism, competitiveness, and foreign policy are championed. Part of the problem is that EPI is not (yet) regarded as being politically important enough to warrant such a high-profile response. It is hard to think of a single Commission President or national prime minister in the last ten years who has vigorously and consistently championed EPI. The European Council has, admittedly, assumed some leadership, for example, by publicly endorsing Article 6, and initiating the Cardiff and Lisbon processes, even though implementation depends on other actors.

As enthusiasm for the Cardiff process waned in some sectors, environmentalists called for new coordinating capacities to be created at the apex of the main EU institutions to compensate for these deficiencies. These have included a named 'Article 6 Committee' to coordinate and inform the Council, and a new 'Environmental Policy Committee', to work with the existing economic, employment, and social protection committees (Kraemer et al. 2002: 5; 2001: 45–6). Other recent proposals include a new 'Horizontal Affairs Council' sitting within or alongside the General Affairs Council, whose tasks would include undertaking detailed reviews, disseminating guidance, and championing Article 6. New coordinating committees may be of some help, but the danger is that they could easily spend most of their time offering more and more polished summaries of the sustainability implications of sectoral policies, without really tackling their underlying causes. The need for a direct link into daily policymaking at member state level will be particularly important. It is telling that DG Environment has never (at least publicly) endorsed these and other types of hierarchical mechanism (e.g. see the 2004 Cardiff stocktake). On the contrary, it believes that 'the institutional and top-down approach of [the Cardiff] process, [now] needs to be complemented by more practical steps at both Community and national levels' (CEC 2004b: 34).

BUREAUCRATIC PROCEDURES

In Chapter 2 we defined bureaucratic procedures as rules and guidelines that seek to standardize the daily work of officials. Aside from creating and recently revising an (environmental) policy appraisal procedure—IA— (CEC 2002b; 2005c), it is not obvious from our analysis thus far, that the Commission (or indeed any other EU institution) has placed much reliance on this particular coordination mechanism. Moreover, even if policy appraisal in the Commission was perfect (the early indications are that it is not—see Chapters 5 and 9) (Wilkinson et al. 2004b: 5),[10] it is unlikely ever to be a panacea when EU-EPI is a multi-actor and multi-level problem. Therefore, in Chapter 5 we look in much more detail at the other four actors, to see whether they have installed effective policy-appraisal procedures to share information on possible spillover effects. Then, in Chapters 7–10 we analyse the flow of information (i.e. is it primarily passive or active?) at the level of daily policymaking within the five actors.

SKILLS DEVELOPMENT AND TRAINING

From our analysis thus far, the Commission is the only EU institution to train its staff in the use of environmental policy appraisal techniques. It does not, therefore, appear that this particular coordinating mechanism plays much of a role in the EU at present, although we will only be really sure when we have reviewed the five actors (i.e. Chapters 7–10).

SPECIFICATION OF OUTPUT ('MANAGEMENT BY OBJECTIVES')

The EU has, it appears, relied rather more heavily on this particular coordination mechanism. In the previous chapter, we differentiated between different subtypes, namely management by *targets* and management by *tasks*. The many hundreds of directives and regulations that the Environment Council has adopted since the late 1960s (Jordan 2005; Haigh 2005) contain myriad quantitative *targets*. These place the Commission in the hierarchical role of 'guardian' of the treaties (i.e. it has a formal right to take cases of non-implementation to the ECJ). Crucially, these targets have generally involved imposing environmental requirements on the sectors from the outside, and then in a largely reactive manner. Not surprisingly, the pace and extent of implementation has tended to be extremely patchy (Jordan 2002b), hence the political appeal of different modes of governance such as markets (i.e. environmental taxes) and networks (such as Cardiff). One of the main rationales for introducing NEPIs is to achieve a greater level of sector 'self-responsibility'. However, for political, economic, and legal reasons, most of the innovation with NEPIs is continuing at national levels (Jordan, Wurzel, and Zito 2003; Jordan et al. 2003a). The 2004 Cardiff stocktake therefore sensibly concluded that the EU's EPI strategy can never rely entirely on the adoption of NEPIs (CEC 2004b: 35).

The other remaining example of targets is that associated with the so-called 'new approach' to standard-setting in the EU, which was heavily trailed in the Commission's White Paper on governance (CEC 2001a: 21). Under the new approach (it actually dates back to a Resolution issued in 1985) (Official Journal, C136 4 June 1985), Directives only set the most essential requirements; more detailed technical standards are then negotiated between industry, pressure groups, and the European standards body, CEN. In a Communication issued in 2004 (CEC 2004d), the Commission claimed that this has great potential to facilitate EPI, particularly in fast-moving sectors such as electronics, packaging, and light manufacturing.[11] However, the 'new approach' is still embryonic in the environmental sector, but its contribution to EPI may well grow in the future.

As regards the specification of *tasks*, the Cardiff process could be seen as an example of *specification of output (management by objectives)* since it involves each sector developing its own integration strategy with targets and timetables. However, they are best thought of as mission statements (see below) as they are essentially self-determined and are non-binding.[12] Time will tell whether the quantified sectoral targets that DG Environment intends to include in the thematic strategies of the Sixth EAP will have any more hierarchical force. DG Environment hopes they will provide a 'test bed for [more] innovative approaches' to EPI, because, unlike the Fifth EAP, they will be developed in full consultation with all relevant stakeholders (CEC 2004b: 35). The problem is that as yet, they are a relatively untested instrument.

HORIZONTAL COORDINATION MECHANISMS

We have not delved sufficiently deeply into the internal affairs of individual actors to reach a definitive judgment on the relative importance of liaison roles, task forces, teams, and integrators, etc. After all, the existing literature suggests that their presence/absence is no guarantor of success; analysts need to look at how and in what form they operate in practice. For example, the Article 6 committee (mentioned above) has the potential to operate in a hierarchical fashion, but only if it is given strong decision making power and a robust monitoring capability. On the hand, if it lacks these attributes, it will be more like a coordinating *team*. The empirical chapters may also reveal the full extent to which these different subtypes coexist. Again, taking the proposed Article 6 committee as an example, we need to know if it is supported by an effective secretariat (i.e. a *strong integrator*). Or is it simply a small team of overworked Commission officials from DG Environment? The theoretical literature on coordination suggests that these seemingly subtle differences can be enormously important.

At this stage in the analysis, it is also worth noting the existence of a number of EU bodies that were specifically created to improve environmental coordination. Two of these emerged from the Fifth EAP: a consultative forum (to exchange information between different stakeholders) and the EPRG (see above). *The Consultative Forum* on environment and sustainable development produced several reports on integration-related practices such as sustainable agriculture, as well as the institutional implications of EPI (e.g. Consultative Forum 1999). But on balance, the mission and the membership of the Forum were set so broadly to render it little more than a very weak *task force*. The Forum was eventually wound up in 2002 to make way for new consultative arrangements foreseen in the EU's SDS.

Finally, it also worth mentioning the *Strauss–Kahn group of independent experts*, which was created by the Commission in 2002 with the aim of providing high-level advice on sustainable development directly to the then President, Romano Prodi. It published its first report in 2004 (Strauss–Kahn 2004). Although it has a direct link into the President and is serviced by the Secretariat General's Strategic Planning and Programming unit (see Chapter 9), to all intents and purposes it remains a roundtable, and hence is not really a mechanism for coordinating daily policymaking.

MISSION STATEMENTS ('SPECIFICATION OF OWNERSHIP')

The continuing support (e.g. expressed in repeated European Council conclusions) given to EPI/Article 6 is a type of mission statement—that is, a way to change the working culture of the EU towards sustainability. However, the main problem with mission statements is that they often present aspirations that are disconnected from the daily life of administrators. While ostensibly legal (i.e. hierarchical) in nature, the treaty-based commitments to EPI (i.e. Article 6) and sustainability (which has since been carried over into the draft European Constitution—see Coffey (2003) for details),[13] could also be thought of as mission statements. Similarly, the SDS has a strong political relevance but is also not legally binding (Hinterberger and Zacherl 2003: 14).

Conclusions

To summarize, EPI is a high-profile, long-term, and hugely ambitious goal, to which the EU has regularly committed itself. It is increasingly recognized that it has both a horizontal and a vertical dimension. However, aside from the Commission and, more recently, the Council, it is still not conceptualized (or tackled) as a *shared* challenge in the EU. Even from a very cursory inspection of the capacities at network and actor level, there appear to be a number of gaps. At EU level, the most obvious example of networked governance is that supporting the Cardiff process. However, the Commission has recently confirmed that it had produced 'mixed results' and that many of the commitments made 'are still largely to be translated into further concrete results' (CEC 2004b: 31). This failure can be partly attributed to the basic composition of the network (several key EU actors, specifically the Parliament, are not formally represented), the sharp value differences between the participating actors (namely the sectors), and the absence of a strong central manager. In the remainder of this book we will seek to identify and explore these and other contributory factors.

Although we have not delved deeply into the internal affairs of the five actors, it is already evident that the EU as a whole is heavily reliant on a small number of fairly weak coordination capacities to tackle EPI, namely *mission statements, specification of outputs* (i.e. management by targets and tasks), and some simple *bureaucratic procedures* (e.g. to produce environmental policy appraisals). Other than the Commission's own internal reforms, the EU has made very little effort to put in place adequate *bureaucratic procedures* (rules) and *horizontal coordination mechanisms* more deeply to institutionalize EPI. These could have an important role in facilitating the achievement of high-level policy objectives set by the Cardiff and Lisbon processes. Moreover, it appears as if the EU is relying more and more heavily on *mission statements* and *management by very weak tasks*. After ten years of actively debating the need for greater coordination, there is arguably a *'piling up* of strategies...that are insufficiently harmonized with one another' (Hinterberger and Zacherl 2003: 32). For instance, the EU now has not one, but two long-term environmental strategies (the SDS and the Sixth EAP), and two integration processes— Lisbon and Cardiff. There are also other important strategic activities with a strong sustainability dimension which should be mentioned, such as the reforms to the Common Agricultural Policy and the Structural Funds.

Recently, it has been argued that these activities should be 'brought together in an overarching EU environmental strategy or road map' (Wilkinson et al. 2002: 17). The idea of a supercoordinated 'strategy of strategies' may appeal to distracted politicians and overworked officials. But unless it is adequately supported by coordination capacities (i.e. mechanisms to exchange information, consult, and arbitrate) at lower levels, our theory suggests that it will always 'be superficial and vulnerable to the disruption of unresolved conflicts and the emergence of unforeseen problems' at lower levels (Metcalfe 2000: 832). This, at least, has been the experience of the Cardiff process. One way to avoid this possibility (and in so doing compensate for any weaknesses at network level) is to strengthen the vertical links between the EU and the member states. Currently, the EU appears determined to ignore this basic design principle by trying to leap straight to Level 9 (i.e. strategy) on the coordination scale without building coordination capacities from the bottom-up (i.e. from Level 1 upwards).

The EU does not, of course, necessarily have to start at the bottom and move upwards as though ascending a flight of steps. Level 9 objectives could conceivably be used to put pressure on national and EU administrative systems to push sectoral policy conflicts up through the lower levels so they can be adequately coordinated at successively higher levels, including the EU. But at the current time, the EU is not thinking or acting in this way. For instance, the existing Cardiff integration strategies pay very little attention to vertical relationships, including the capacities for coordination at EU and national levels (see above). That said, a consensus is beginning to emerge around the idea that the Cardiff process must be more deeply rooted in (and connected to) national policymaking (Kraemer et al. 2002: 70; Lenschow 2002c: 223–5). The Commission concedes this point (CEC 2003b: 23; 2004b: 34–6) in relation to the SDS, too, but it is not clear how it can be achieved when the twenty-five member states and the three main EU institutions appear to have such very different and poorly integrated administrative systems. We should be in a much better position to offer clearer diagnoses and policy prescriptions in this regard once we have analysed the five actors in more detail. It is to that task that we now turn.

Notes

1. Which it broadly defines as social and economic development that meets the needs of the present generation without compromising the ability of future generations to meet their own needs.

2. In theory, Brundtland's interpretation of sustainable development suggests that economic and social factors may, in some contexts, be pre-eminent.

3. This would require *inter alia* a highly sophisticated understanding of the way in which environmental, economic, and social policies are implemented and, in turn, (do not) translate into the policy outcomes (sustainability?) desired. For good summaries of why this might be difficult to deliver, see Parsons (1995: 600–13) and Weale (1992).

4. DG Environment does, however, have a role in overseeing the annual stock-takes of the Cardiff process (see text for details) and the thematic strategies under the Sixth EAP.

5. If sustainable development had been as important as the environment sector would have liked, the process would have encompassed society, economy, *and* the environment, but environment was not initially included.

6. In an attempt to complement the economic and employment reports prepared by the sectors (Haigh 2005: section 2.1–7), in 2003, DG Environment started to produce and submit annual Environmental Policy Reviews to each Spring Council (e.g. CEC 2003*b*).

7. The word 'strategy' is a bit of a misnomer because the SDS is in fact a rather 'confusing' 'collection of papers' produced by the Council of Ministers, the European Council, and the Presidency (Wilkinson et al. 2004*a*: 20).

8. There are, of course, others, but either they are bilateral (e.g. the joint expert group on transport and environment) or they only address one aspect of EU-EPI (e.g. the green diplomacy network, the network of environmental inspectors (IMPEL), and the new network of environmental lawyers) (for further details, see EEA 2005*a*: 34–5; ENDS Daily No. 1957, 7 October 2005).

9. There are, of course, constant and generally informal bilateral interactions between individual members.

10. Even the Commission admits that there is room for improvement (CEC 2005*a*: 20; CEC 2005*c*).

11. There were 13,500 CEN-type standards in 2003, and around 1,200 new ones are added each year (CEC 2004*d*: 7).
12. The same could be said of the sectoral targets embodied in the Fifth EAP.
13. If ratified, the Constitution will retain the principle of EPI but move it towards the back of the Treaty (EEA 2005*a*: 29).

4
THE COORDINATION OF EUROPEAN UNION POLICY: ACTOR PERSPECTIVES

[T]he effectiveness of the Council decision-making process does not depend upon new initiatives to be taken at Union level, but upon a critical review to be undertaken by the Member States themselves of the methods used by them in preparing the Council's proceedings.

(Council of the European Union 1999: 29)

Introduction

This chapter introduces the basic administrative mechanisms for coordinating EU policy in the five actors. For each actor, we describe the most important administrative parts, and explain the processes through which they seek to coordinate their input to EU policymaking both internally (i.e. intradepartmentally) and with cognate actors (i.e. interdepartmentally). To permit comparison, we begin by analysing the main coordination instruments and roles within each actor. Then we describe the mechanisms through which each coordinates the various phases of EU policymaking described in Chapter 2. Finally, we comment on how each is currently attempting to upgrade its coordination system.

Germany

The main actors and system characteristics

Germany belongs to a group of member states with a decentralized system for managing European affairs (Kassim 2003*a*; 2003*b*). Apart from the highly sensitive files, there is little political steering from the Chancellery or the two coordinating departments (since 1998, foreign affairs and finance). Formally, the head of government sets the strategic guidelines of the federal government, but in practice, this is only applied to the most contested issues (Derlien 2000). The strong role of the finance department is a legacy of the historical focus of EU political integration (i.e. on economic and trade matters) (Derlien 2000: 59; Maurer and Wessels 2001: 124). Deubner and Huppertz (2003) note the following reasons for why the overall level of coordination tends to be poor:

- the general principle that departments are independent (the *Ressortprinzip*), which encourages bureaucratic politics (see Chapter 6);
- the passive manner of coordination, which asks a lot from dependent departments;
- the highly 'event' nature of coordination, focusing on COREPER meetings;
- the predominance of coalition politics;
- the physical distance between officials working in Berlin and Bonn, as well as the various regional authorities (e.g. the Länder).

Maurer and Wessels (2001: 102) conclude that the reputation of the German system is one of 'horizontal and vertical fragmentation, old fashioned and cumbersome procedures, institutional pluralism and negative coordination.' A more recent review of expert opinions suggested that the Germans have a 'poor reputation', with no central agency that has the power to formulate a 'coherent European strategy' (Maurer 2003: 119). Not everyone believes the system is quite this bad—Derlien (2000) considers it to be comparable to the UK. Be that as it may, even very poor coordination has its advantages. For example, some commentators note that coordination in Germany is quite flexible in the sense that nothing is really finalized until the end of a negotiation (Maurer 2003).

The tendency among German departments has been to articulate their interests directly in Brussels. The search for a common position ('speaking with one voice'—Level 4) is either delayed or never really sought. This breeds mistrust, which in turn forces cognate departments to send 'minders' (*liaison roles—watchdogs*) to shadow the lead department in Brussels. Very few involved see the coordinating departments (i.e. foreign affairs and finance) or the Chancellery as honest brokers, so conflicts of view are put off until they have to be solved. The German Chancellery does not involve itself in the daily process of EU policymaking. Only in extreme cases does it step in to alter a sector department's position (Deubner and

Huppertz 2003). A good example of this was the very late intervention made by the Chancellery in the case of the end-of-life vehicles Directive, which was led by the environment department in 1999 (Wurzel 2004*b*). In this case, the national position changed completely at the very last possible moment when the Chancellor (the ultimate *integrator*) made a personal intervention.

The coordination process

The German system is highly, but also weakly, event based. The major interdepartmental coordination committee for European affairs (see Table 4.1) is the COREPER instruction meeting on Tuesday. By implication, this means that only COREPER is systematically coordinated.[1] The COREPER instruction meeting is a *team* that gathers European Affairs units and it is chaired jointly by finance and foreign affairs (i.e. two *integrators*). The department for foreign affairs is generally responsible for the dossiers negotiated in COREPER II, the General Council, the Justice and Home Affairs Council, the Development Council, and the Culture Council. The Environment Council and other councils of COREPER I are coordinated by the department of finance. This arrangement leads to the following problems. First, the finance department coordinates the more technical dossiers but its neutrality is questioned by many in the German system. Second, the system is highly reactive—the coordination meeting to bring problems out into the open is very close to the endgame in the Council.

As a general backup, there is a layered system of *teams*. The heads of the European units—the European officers (*Europabeauftragte*)—meet every Tuesday under the chairmanship of foreign affairs (or finance), mainly to prepare COREPER. However, this committee is weak. In fact, the absence

Table 4.1 EU coordination committees in Germany

Teams	Organization and tasks
Tuesday meeting	Weekly meeting, chaired by departments of finance and foreign affairs. Discusses COREPER instruction and (if time allows) solves problems
Head of Division meeting	Meets twice a month to discuss problems
European Secretaries of State meeting	Meets every 4–6 weeks

Source: Own compilation

of sectoral departments and the lack of sufficient support from higher level *teams*,[2] creates a vicious circle of ineffectual problem-solving and non-attendance. Consequently, the cabinet becomes the main forum for solving problems, but its role is restricted by the workload that has normally accumulated when this relatively late stage in the policy process is reached. The lack of early discussion on positions commonly leads to the postponement of conflicts up until the last stage before the COREPER preparation meeting. This generates a great deal of mistrust between departments, symbolized by the huge German delegations that regularly attend EU negotiations in Brussels. Consequently, coordination as a whole in Germany is reactive, conflict ridden, and—especially for those departments that are not in the lead—highly time-consuming.

In an attempt to remedy some of these defects, in 2000 the department of foreign affairs lobbied for a number of changes, which have affected departmental as well as interdepartmental relations. This was accompanied by a new coordination handbook. The main innovation is that departments have invested in monitoring units (i.e. *liaison roles—watchdogs*) better to track developments in other fields and to fight for influence. Bigger departments (such as finance) have watchdogs shadowing many different policies; this allows them to intervene at crucial stages of the policy process. By contrast, the environment department has not done nearly as much to watch cognate sectors (see Chapter 6). The more general problem with monitoring units is that they tend to lose out to line units in the battle for departmental resources.

Also at the start of the new millennium, the Head of the Chancellery recommended a set of further changes including:

- binding participation in the (often poorly attended) weekly COREPER instruction meeting (on Tuesdays);
- encouraging the European officers (*Europabauftragte*) in all departments to meet more regularly to discuss upcoming dossiers/problems;
- urging the coordinators from the departments of finance and foreign affairs to work together to ensure proactive action (i.e. establish an early warning system);
- push the German permanent representation in Brussels to produce an early warning report (three times p.a.) and issue ad hoc early warnings.

Crucially, in making these changes the Germans are (like the Dutch, see Chapter 7) trying to improve their coordination system by creating additional procedures and teams, without addressing the underlying problem: passive information. The new system has undoubtedly given a fresh opportunity to the environment department to be better informed about developments in other sectors. However, our interviews suggest that the reforms have already begun to lose momentum. Moreover, they were intended to improve communication in the Council phases, not to coordinate better the early Commission phases where the sector departments retain control. Consequently, the environment department's ability to influence dossiers at an early stage remains largely dependent on the goodwill of the sector departments. Chapter 6 discusses these failings in more detail and examines the scope for making more long-lasting improvements.

The Netherlands

The main actors and system characteristics

In some respects, the Dutch coordination system resembles that of Germany. The departments are, for example, autonomous as regards EU policy coordination. In addition, information is often exchanged passively and, as a result, coordination is focused on predefined events (event coordination). Departments are, in general, responsible for policies in their fields as they move through the policy phases. The sectors coordinate EU policies between themselves. However, environment is one of a few notable exceptions as formally the department of foreign affairs (see below) coordinates it. The key differences with the German system are the (increasing) number of interdepartmental committees for different steps in the EU policy cycle and, probably because of this, a friendlier and more informal style of cooperation.

The department of foreign affairs is a key actor in the Dutch system. It is concerned with procedural coordination as its primary task is to guide Commission proposals through the various stages and coordinating committees. One factor limiting its power is its size. Approximately fifty officials work on EU-related tasks. They are not only responsible for coordinating the different Council formations, but also deal with strategic issues such as intergovernmental conferences and EU enlargements. A second major problem is that the department's staff are often tied up coordinating routine meetings (event coordination). Consequently, they are often disparaged for providing little more than a 'postbox' service. Thirdly, the department of foreign affairs does not receive particularly strong backing from the cabinet office. The permanent representation is primarily involved in aligning positions during the

Council negotiations (although when technical dossiers are on the table, the negotiators tend to be seconded from the departments (Bos 1995; Schout 1999*a*)).

The national parliament only tends to get involved at a relatively late stage. Sector departments normally discuss the agenda with the relevant parliamentarians in the week before the Council of Ministers meets. Finally, as all ministers are in theory equal, the prime minister is only the *primus inter pares*. Disagreements can, therefore, linger on because of the difficulty in taking decisions. Apart from European Councils, in which the prime minister is involved, the cabinet office hardly plays a role.

The prevalence of passive information in the Dutch system allows lead departments in particular to play strategic games, whereas cognate departments—environment in the case of EU-EPI—have constantly to monitor developments, show interest, and check whether their suggestions have been accepted. If not, the lead may think that they have no real interest and will stop dispatching information. Dutch officials strongly favour informal coordination as it allows a quick and efficient exchange of views, especially on horizontal problems. However, it means that negotiators often have no formal instructions or reports from previous meetings (VWS 2003). However, the workload, the lack of transparency especially in the early and the later (e.g. comitology) phases, and the passive nature of coordination, render the whole system relatively inefficient.

The coordination process

Being a small and relatively open country, the Netherlands has traditionally been in favour of deeper European integration. The Dutch tend not to be critical towards new Commission initiatives; in any case, the workload (see above) and the tight deadlines prevent very detailed inspection of every new proposal. This attitude is changing now, due in large part to the country's transition from being a net beneficiary of the EU budget to being a relatively major contributor (Schendelen 2004). Moreover, enlargement has contributed to a greater societal debate about EU membership, which has *inter alia* fuelled a debate about the national coordination system (*Gemengde Commissie* 2005).

The most relevant interdepartmental coordination committees in the Netherlands are the Committee to Assess New Commission Proposals (BNC), the COREPER-instruction meeting, and the Coordinating Committee (CoCo) (see Table 4.2). In addition, there are several legal interdepartmental teams (ICERs). The BNC is located at the start of the Council phases

Table 4.2 EU coordination committees in the Netherlands

Teams	Organization & tasks
Committee to Assess New Commission Proposals (BNC)	Weekly meeting at junior level
COREPER instruction meeting	Weekly meeting at—de facto—junior level
Coordinating Committee (CoCo)	Weekly meeting gathering junior and senior coordinators. Chaired by the Junior Minister for EU Affairs
Several legal interdepartmental teams (ICERs)	Teams focusing on legal questions and implementation issues
Additional teams	Teams relating to state aid, trade policy, and environment policy. These meet usually at junior level
CoCoHan	Team at senior management level to allow strategic decisions on major EU policy issues

Source: Own compilation

when the College of Commissioners has approved a proposal. It is a 'light' committee and mainly functions to announce the new proposal, to distribute responsibilities (i.e. who is in the lead and which departments want to be kept informed), to formulate a first impression (in the form of a *fiche*—or policy appraisal), and to inform Parliament (Schout 2004). It was created to speed up legal implementation, to have more insight in financial implications, and to foster a more proactive approach (*Ministerie van Financiën* 1989). Interestingly, 'proactive' was only seen in relation to the Council and *not* the Commission phases.

The CoCo is the senior management body chaired by the State Secretary for EU affairs. Its main purpose is to conclude the negotiating instructions for ministers in the upcoming Councils. It assembles every Tuesday to discuss instructions before the permanent representatives gather (on Wednesdays). This leaves little room to discuss cross-cutting issues like EU-EPI (see Chapter 7). A long-standing problem with this committee is that it spends too much time on problems that should be resolved at lower levels (*Ministrie van Algemene Zaken* 1993). Moreover, CoCo's arbitration role is limited because it is a collegial body, which operates as a conciliation body (i.e. Level 6 on the coordination scale). Arbitration (i.e. taking decisions—Level 7) can be impossible when ministers persist in pursuing their sectoral interests. To increase further the strategic capacities of EU coordination, another high-level committee was created in the 1990s (CoCoHan—the coordinating committee at senior official level). The CoCoHan meets irregularly to discuss major policy issues and items on the agenda of the European Council. Instead of being a decisionmaking body, it mainly serves to advise senior management on EU policy matters such as legal competence or subsidiarity.

Finally, the ICERs are responsible for discussing the legal and implementation implications of a new proposal. They have produced new handbooks on a range of topics including negotiation and policy implementation. However, the Netherlands has still not dramatically improved its mediocre position in terms of implementing EU laws (Verschuuren 2004).

When asked, sector officials from most departments are generally very pleased with the way in which EU policy is coordinated, and list several positive aspects including flexible and informal ways of working. However, the weaknesses of the national system are also very well known (*Ministerie van Financiën* 1989; Soetendorp 1991; van Schendelen 1995; Bos et al. 1995; Schout and Nomden 2000; ROB 2004). The root of the problem is the passive nature of coordination, which largely persists. Hence, influencing the lead department remains highly labour intensive. Interdepartmental relations remain competitive and there is, as yet, no generally supported commitment to active information. The fact that the Dutch system is decentralized also makes the system relatively informal (cf. Wright 1996). This makes it more efficient, but there is relatively little scope for resolving issues at higher levels. Therefore, coordination problems tend to be delayed until they have to be resolved (event coordination), which in turn militates against early and full coordination of cross-cutting topics such as EU-EPI.

Several attempts have been made to improve the national coordination system (*Tweede Kamer der Staten-Generaal* 2002: 632; Haersolte and Oosterkamp 2003; Schout 2004). One of the key questions is whether a round of further incremental changes will suffice, or whether more radical changes are now required. As more and more horizontal concerns (ranging from the quality of legislation, through to equal opportunities and third-world development), are added to the agenda, demands for new coordination mechanisms and specialized teams grow. This has resulted in new committees (such as the BNC, CoCoHan, and ICERs) and new procedures (e.g. policy appraisal). However, the point is close to being reached where too many people are involved in too many coordination committees (ROB 2004). Currently, there are approximately seventy officials in the EU-coordinating units in the sectoral departments and in the department of foreign affairs working more or less full-time on running the system (Schout 2004).

The United Kingdom

The main actors and system characteristics

On paper, the UK possesses a very actively coordinated system of national government. While Germany and the Netherlands struggle to present a united front in international negotiations, the UK boasts a 'tight' set of internal mechanisms, which ensure that departments 'sing from the same hymn sheet' (see Table 4.3). Overseen by the Cabinet Office, these mechanisms have been described as the envy of other member states (Metcalfe 1994; Spence 1995). At the periphery, we find the various government departments, which take the lead on sectoral policy issues. They are expected to 'think and act European' for themselves, with some light steering from the centre as and when necessary (Jordan 2002a; 2003).

Six elements form the 'core' of the UK's coordination system. First of all, the basis of coordination is that negotiators receive a solid set of procedural instructions. These bureaucratic rules of procedure are—contrary to the other two states—of a general nature and stress active coordination. Second, the Cabinet Office holds the ring as the various departments compete with one another for resources. It was originally created to function as the 'the coordinating brain' of the entire system (Hennessey 1989: 56). Its main roles are to ensure that the UK has a consistent negotiating position on new topics and to spot conflicts as soon as they arise. As such, it is a good example of a *strong integrating role*. In spite of its small size, the European Secretariat in the Cabinet Office discharges an impressive number of responsibilities (Kassim 2000; 2001; Spence 1993). These include:

- overseeing and managing interdepartmental coordination: normally it only steps in when there are irresolvable conflicts between departments, or where there is a real danger of them occurring;

Table 4.3 EU coordination committees in the UK

Teams	Organization and tasks
Grant–Darroch meeting	Chaired by the Cabinet Office, this meeting—irrespective of the policy phase—discusses strategic issues and resolves interdepartmental problems
European Policy group & Joint Ministerial Committee meetings	Teams at departments to resolve problems at a political level and to take decisions on major new policies on the EU agenda

Source: Own compilation

- acting as storehouse of EU information (Spence 1993: 53): its guidance notes are known as 'the Bible of European business' in Whitehall (Humphreys 1996: 31);
- ensuring that EU policy issues are consistent with existing government policy: departments are expected to report differences to the European secretariat as they arise (active information) (Humphreys 1996: 32). All correspondence with the Commission and any major policy documents must be cleared in advance with it;
- coordinating major cross-cutting policy issues: these include issues such as enlargement and IGCs, as well as 'horizontal' matters such as subsidiarity and deregulation, but *not* EU-EPI;
- overseeing the system of national parliamentary scrutiny: normally, all departments are required to produce an explanatory memorandum for Parliament upon receipt of a Commission proposal.

Third, the UK permanent representation (UKREP) operates like a 'mini-Whitehall' in Brussels. UKREP is made up of a tightly knit group of around forty to fifty officials drawn from across Whitehall, who are managed by a central diplomatic corps. Normally there are two attachés handling environmental matters, but they also coordinate with other policy areas. UKREP differs from other national permanent representations in three important respects (Kassim 2000: 40–1):

- It is relatively proactive. For example, it keeps a watching brief on the Commission.
- It is in constant communication with Whitehall. Partly due to UKREP, departments should find it hard to 'go it alone' in Brussels as all positions will have been circulated in advance.
- It has an active input to the development of the national negotiating position in any given policy sector.

Fourth, many of the most well-known UK committees (for details, see Kassim 2000; 2001) have been abolished. In their place, the Grant–Darroch meeting between the Permanent Representative and the head of the European Secretariat (currently Grant and Darroch, respectively), is the only issue-based coordination committee. It meets every Friday and discusses problems that need attention. Unlike its opposite numbers in Germany and the Netherlands, it is highly issue based—that is, any topic at any stage can be discussed. A second feature that makes this committee stand out from those in the other actors is that it strongly accords with the subsidiarity principle. Even though it meets on a weekly basis, not all the departments have to be present at the same time. In fact, the agenda indicates who should attend and for how long; hence, there is a constantly changing cast of participants in its meetings.

Fifth, in addition to developing the UK's European policy and supporting the prime minister at European Council meetings, the foreign affairs department will often act as the first point of contact when there are disagreements between departments. When they cannot reach agreement, the Cabinet Office will step in. This is rare as the departments normally prefer to settle differences at lower levels.

Finally, there are two teams at ministerial level which seek to settle problems and to indicate preferred directions and priorities early on in an EU negotiation. The European Policy group meets at the level of full cabinet; and the Joint Ministerial Committee on the EU (JMCE) includes other ministers as well as representatives from Scotland and Wales. Interestingly, these committees (or *teams* in Mintzberg's terms) are permanent, but their membership is not fixed (it depends on the agenda). However, certain key departments (e.g. the department of finance) are normally present.

The coordination process

A number of important but mainly informal operating principles guide the UK's coordination process. First, there is collective responsibility; that is, departments should not depart from the position brokered in Whitehall. It has always been common practice for the cabinet in the UK to 'speak with one voice' (Level 4). In EU negotiations, the European Secretariat is the guardian of this principle.

Second, active steps are taken to achieve subsidiarity in policymaking (Schout and Metcalfe 1999): that is, all business (including EU policy) is expected to be handled at the lowest possible level to avoid bureaucratic overload. When significant differences in view exist, it is up to the departments concerned to solve them (i.e. starting at Level 1 on the coordination scale and moving up).

Third, information is typically regarded as a *shared* resource (i.e. active information). The environment department's internal handbook on negotiating in the EU even suggests that 'it is best to err on the side of wide copying: recipients can always ask not to receive papers' (Humphreys 1996: 37–8). The lead department should always point out what its proposal implies for those not in the lead.

One of the great strengths of the UK system is its ability to plan pro-actively. The actors at the core of the system play an important part, as does the extensive catalogue of Cabinet Office guidance notes (*bureaucratic procedures*) and active information. The existing literature on the UK underplays the importance of the Presidency agendas (Schout and Metcalfe 1999). Twice-yearly agendas for each department are discussed in two ways. First, the Grant–Darroch committee writes summary statements to the Environmental Policy group. During this process, future frictions and priorities are identified. Second, each department organizes a session on 'its' agenda—together with people from embassies and UKREP. Above all others, this final feature should (at least in theory) make the UK system inherently 'fit' for the challenge of EU-EPI.

In terms of the overall trend, it is important to re-emphasize that the total number of coordination capacities in the UK has declined in recent years, not increased. Meanwhile, the core principles (i.e. active coordination, issue-related coordinating committees, and proactive monitoring by the Cabinet Office and foreign affairs department) have been emphasised even more strongly by abolishing some very well-established committees.

The European Commission

The main actors and system characteristics

The Commission has a reputation of being notoriously bad at coordination (e.g. Spence 1994; 2000; Dinan 1999; Metcalfe 1996; 2000). The more important question is whether this reputation is still accurate. The administrative reforms (the 'Kinnock reforms') initiated by the Santer and Prodi Presidencies, following several well-known crises (Wise Men Report (I) 1999; Wise Men Report (II) 1999), stemmed from a general perception that things had to change—and quickly—to avoid irreparable damage to the organization's already battered reputation (Nugent 2002: 156–60).

The Commission's coordination capacities include its staff. Depending on whether and how one counts secondees and temporary experts of various kinds, the total workforce numbers between 20,000 and 30,000 (Stevens and Stevens 2001; Nugent 2000; 2001). To prevent centralization of the 'Brussels' administration, the number of Commission officials and the relevant budget lines in the EU budget have been kept stable. In view of the many functions it has to carry out, the Commission is still relatively small compared to most national administrations. The Commission is a collegial body and it has always struggled to overcome the fragmentation that arises from trying to meet so many demands—not least those from the nominating member states (Peterson 2002). The President chairs the College of Commissioners, but the Commissioners tend to take strong personal positions. Many are often ex-ministers and have strong personalities. Commissioners use their *cabinets* (or private offices) as a strong, strategic, administrative 'arm' (Nugent 2001: 126; 2002). *Cabinets* are important in the coordination of policies from the very inception of a proposal, right through their formal adoption (see below). It is also worth noting that the Commission is a physically fragmented organization, which is spread across numerous buildings in Brussels and Luxembourg. However, the administrative core of the organization comprises two dozen DGs (Nugent 2002: 144–7). The DGs are 'very roughly comparable' to government departments, 'although in terms of size they are mere shadows' of them (Cini 1996: 102).

Finally, the structure of the Commission (it is modelled on a hierarchical French-style bureaucracy) and the cultural make-up of the DGs, have complicated horizontal relations (Abélè, Bellier, and McDonald 1993; Cini 1996) (see Table 4.4). The flow of information has traditionally been top-down and passive, and coordination has tended to be event related. The major coordinating events are the Hebdo, the group for interinstitutional relations (Group for International Relations (GRI)—which prepares for COREPER and conciliation)—and the meeting of the College of Commissioners. The Hebdo (see Chapter 9) is the meeting of *chefs de cabinet* chaired by the President's *cabinet chef*. This body prepares the meeting of the Commissioners on Wednesday and is preceded by meetings of the 'special *chefs*'. Information is exchanged informally beforehand, but final problem-solving is often delayed until this event.

Table 4.4 Coordination committees in the Commission

Teams	Organization and tasks
Special *chefs*	Regular meeting of technical *cabinet* members
GRI (group for interinstitutional relations)	Preparation of COREPER and Conciliation meetings (weekly)
Hebdo	Weekly meeting of the *cabinet chefs* preparing the weekly meeting of Commissioners
College of Commissioners	Weekly meeting of the Commissioners to discuss technical and strategic issues and to resolve differences

Source: Own compilation

The central player in the coordination process is the Secretariat General (SG), which serves under the Commission President. Importantly, its main task is to guarantee coherence, internal transparency, and a continuing focus on political priorities. In spite of its central position, the SG has traditionally suffered from resource constraints[3] and a lack of high-level political support. Consequently, it has tended to shy away from its formal responsibility to coordinate the Commission through processes such as policy appraisal. Chapter 3 noted that the expertise and the political muscle needed to back up DG Environment's 'green star' policy appraisal system was never deployed. Moreover, the SG was not in a position to stop environmentally damaging proposals from going through to the College even when DG Environment was unhappy with the quality of the appraisals produced (see Chapter 5). But the situation has changed in the last three years, especially with the advent of the new impact assessment (IA) process (see Chapter 9).

Finally, there are the *cabinets*. These have various functions such as monitoring political choices within the Commissioner's own DGs and guarding the (national) interests of the Commissioner (Spence 1994). Each *cabinet* member (approximately six per DG) is tasked with following developments in specific policy fields. In this way, they play important roles in internal coordination by detecting new issues early on and, if necessary, initiating dialogues. At the end of the decisionmaking process, they participate in the 'special *chef*' meetings (see above) and support the preparations of Hebdo and the College of Commissioners.

The coordination process

Policy-planning has never been one of the Commission's strengths. However, there is now a rolling process that leads to regular updates and culminates in the writing of job assignments. In an attempt to improve coordination, the Santer Commission started the Strategic Planning and Programming (SPP) initiative in an effort to match ambitions to resources and to respond to continuing complaints about internal fragmentation. The SPP (which is a *bureaucratic procedure*) aims at increasing efficiency, consistency, and strengthening inter-DG consultation (CEC 2000*a*; 2002*b*). The early rounds (starting in early 2001) did not overcome the strong sectoral positions taken by DGs. Moreover, as the Lisbon agenda shows (see Chapter 3), coherence and focus remain key challenges—and not just due to the internal competition for resources (see also CEC 2004*a*: 4).

The first step in the coordination process is the development of an indicative list of proposals by each DG. This list includes any future work related to adapting existing legislation, reviews, White Papers, etc., and is the basis for the Commission's early reflection on next year's programme (an Annual Policy Strategy—APS), published every February. During the rest of the year, this is discussed at various levels in the Parliament and the Council, so that the Commission's work programme can be finalized at the end of each year. In the meantime, as part of the newly revised IA system, officials have to write and update a short road map indicating the objectives of a proposal, the main policy options, any potentially affected DGs, and the need for outside consultation (Adelle et al. 2006). Close to 200 road maps are currently available on the Commission's website. For major proposals, an 'extended impact assessment' must also be produced (see Chapter 5).

IAs are, of course, not the first attempt to improve the internal coordination of the Commission. Williamson, who was Secretary General from 1987–97, drew upon his time in the British Cabinet Office, to try and upgrade the organization's internal coordination systems. After the fall of the college in 1999, the pace of these reforms was accelerated, focusing in particular on financial management and career development, but also work planning. A recurring theme of these changes is the desire to create a culture of early consultation, through work planning and codes of conduct that support early coordination (e.g. the SPP). Responsibility for horizontal coordination is decentralized to the 'lead department' which is implored to act in 'a real culture of cooperation' (CEC 2004a: 9). Steps are also being taken to ensure that agreed proposals are delivered on time and in a suitably transparent manner (see also CEC 2001a; 2002b).

These many and varied reform steps have heavily bureaucratized the Commission (in the positive sense—see Chapter 2) (cf. Olsen 2005). But how successful have they been? In a recent review, Cini (2005: 4) concludes that that the jury is still out on whether they have succeeded. By studying a horizontal coordination challenge (EU-EPI), we will also look at how the Commission interacts with other actors (Schout and Jordan 2005). New institutional (path dependency) theory (e.g. Scott 1995) suggests that the Commission will remained poorly coordinated. But as will be discussed in Chapter 9, we arrive at a slightly different conclusion.

The European Parliament

The Parliament is arguably the most difficult actor of the five in our sample to coordinate in view of the wide variety of sources of differentiation. The main actors that need to be coordinated are, of course, not civil servants but politicians, namely the 732 MEPs. Their primary duty is to represent their electorates and champion their grievances. Unlike civil servants, they are not necessarily trained in the ways and means of smoothing over conflicting priorities. Moreover, there are major differences between those representing green and less-environmentally oriented countries, big and small states, left and liberal parties, and the older and the more recent member states. Finally, the Parliament is fragmented into a set of functional committees, each of which supervises a discrete policy area.

There are, as we shall explain below, two main routes to coordinating the work of the Parliament: via political grouping, and via administrative mechanisms. As it is composed of MEPs, the task of coordinating the Parliament will always be more overtly political than in the three member states discussed above. However, the Parliament is not entirely political. It has an administrative secretariat (see below) that supports the work of the committees and the conciliation process. It comprises around 4000 officials (2005),[4] about 400 of whom are administrators performing the same sort of roles as civil servants in the three member states.

The main actors and system characteristics

The MEPs represent the core of the Parliament. The vast majority belong to one of the seven main political groups (see Box 4.1). Members who do not belong to any are known as 'non-attached members'. A political group must include MEPs from more than one member state and have a minimum number of members to be officially recognized. These groups draw on more than 160 national parties (Jacobs and Best 2004) and possess privileges in the internal proceedings of the European Parliament (Faas 2002: 9). For example, they control the committee assignments, which are distributed proportionally to the size of the party groups in the plenary, and also the distribution of key positions (e.g. chairs and vice-chairs) in key bodies (e.g. in the bureau and the committees). The political position of an MEP is not entirely dependent on the line taken by his or her political group. Nevertheless, there is considerable party discipline (Hix et al. 1999). Each political group has a chairperson, a bureau, and a secretariat to manage its workload and provide continuity. The groups are of central importance for coordination as they influence the appointment of *rapporteurs*—that is, the MEP that shepherds a specific policy proposal through the parliamentary system (see below).

Box 4.1 Political grouping in the European Parliament (as of 2005)	
PPE–DE	Group of the European People's Party and European Democrats (268)
PSE	Group of the Party of European Socialists (198)
ALDE	Group of the Alliance of Liberals and Democrats for Europe (88)
Greens/ALE	Group of the Greens/European Free Alliance (42)
GUE/NGL	Confederal Group of the European United Left/Nordic Green Left (41)
IND/Dem	Independence/Democracy group (36)
UEN	Union for Europe of the Nations Group (27)

Source: Taken from the Parliament's website (www.europarl.eu.int/facts/1_3_3_en.htm (17 October 2005))

An MEP may have multiple and potentially conflicting roles. He or she is, for example, normally: a member of a committee and a substitute to another one; a member of a political group; a citizen of a particular country or a member of a national political party; and an affiliate of a particular lobby group. All these complicate the quest for (and study of) greater coordination in the Parliament. A 'whipping' system (as exists at national level) is not a viable coordinating device because MEPs are not representatives of a European 'government' as such. Moreover, their reappointment depends on national parties and not on the political group at EU level. However, MEPs recognize dependence on the wider group, which ensures some basic level of party discipline (Corbett et al. 2005).

In the past, there have been unofficial 'grand coalitions' comprising (until 1999) the Socialists (PSE), the European People's Party and the European Democrats (PPE–DE), as well as deals between the two biggest parties (i.e. the Christian Democrats and the Liberals). This has consequences for voting on the second reading of proposals subject to co-decisionmaking, where a qualified majority is required. Achieving a qualified majority could involve splitting the PPE–DE, which is the strongest group.

The other main actors are the twenty or so standing committees, which have been described as the 'legislative backbone' of the Parliament (Neuhold 2001) (see Table 4.5). Everything in the Parliament falls under the competence of one or more of these committees. In practice, the Parliament's Secretariat distributes new legislative proposals to the responsible committee(s). This reinforces the fragmentation of EU policymaking in the Parliament. There is a close relation between the committees and their counterparts in the Council and the Commission DGs. However, they are not perfectly matched. For example, a food safety issue with a

Table 4.5 Standing committees of the European Parliament (as of 2004–5)

	Members	Substitutes
Foreign Affairs, human rights, common security, and defence policy	77	76
Development and cooperation	34	34
Budgets	47	38
Budgetary control	34	31
Economic and monetary affairs	49	45
Employment and social affairs	49	42
Environment, public health, and food safety	63	60
Industry, research, and energy	51	51
Internal market and consumer protection	41	38
Transport and tourism	51	49
Regional development	51	49
Agriculture and rural development	41	40
Fisheries	34	20
Culture and education	35	35
Legal affairs	26	25
Civil liberties, justice, and home affairs	52	49
Constitutional affairs	28	27
Women's rights and gender equality	36	24
Committee on petitions	25	9

Source: European Parliament website: www.europarl.eu.int/activities/expert/committees.d (July 2005)

strong agricultural component (e.g. related to animal feeding stuffs), could be handled by the agriculture committee, or the committee that covers environment and consumer affairs.

The Environment Committee (strictly speaking, the Committee on Environment, Public Health, and Food Safety) is a strong committee with a broad range of responsibilities, but it is not a 'sustainability' committee which takes a holistic perspective across all policy fields (Burns 2005) (see Chapter 5). There have been proposals—for example, by the Liberal group—to move some of the Environment Committee's responsibilities over health and consumer affairs to other committees. These were partly motivated by the desire to weaken its ability to support strong environmental policies.

The committee chairs are key players in the coordination process, in view of their position in the conference of presidents and their mediating roles vis-à-vis other committees. Another key player is the *rapporteur* (see above), who leads the discussions on a dossier in a given committee and brings together the views of its members with his or her own. These are summarized in a written report. When this has been adopted by the committee, it becomes the main basis for discussion, amendment, and (eventually) adoption by the plenary. The *rapporteur* is usually in close informal contact with the Commission, the General Secretariat of the Council, and the Presidency of the Council, and is thus a vital cog in the EU policy machine. The growing power of the Parliament, the pressure for more efficient policy management between it and the other EU institutions, and the more informal negotiation style brought about by co-decisionmaking, have all dramatically increased the importance of the *rapporteur's* work. As has been noted often, a good *rapporteur* can have a huge influence on the final shape of a policy (e.g. (UK) Cabinet Office 2003: 53).

Another important coordinator is the President, who oversees all the activities of Parliament and its constituent bodies. He or she presides over its plenary sittings, monitors procedures, and chairs the meetings of the bureau and conference of presidents (President and Political Group chairs). He also represents Parliament in all external relations and in negotiations with the Commission and Council (e.g. he or she attends European Councils). The Conference of Presidents (see Table 4.6) is the main political planning and mediation body that supervises the distribution of dossiers over committees and mediates if the Conference of Committee Chairs cannot solve disputes between them. This body establishes the size and terms of reference of parliamentary committees and delegations and draws up the timetable and agenda for plenary sessions.

Meanwhile, the bureau is the administrative arm of the Parliament, and is composed of the President and the fourteen Vice-Presidents (see Corbett et al. 2005). It is responsible for the Parliament's budget and all

Table 4.6 Coordinating committees in the European Parliament

Teams	Organization and tasks
Conference of Presidents	Organizes the practical aspects of the Parliament's work and decides on all questions relating to legislative planning (i.e. the timetable and agenda for plenary sittings, the composition of the committees and delegations, and their remits and legislative programmes)
Bureau	Guides the Parliament's internal functioning (including its budget estimates and administrative and financial organization)
Conference of Committee Chairs	Monthly meetings to discuss upcoming plenary meetings and to mediate between committees

Source: Own compilation

organizational and staff matters. The Vice-Presidents have specific responsibilities such as conciliation or relations with national parliaments. These bodies do not play a direct role with respect to EU-EPI, in the sense that there are no common positions formulated on policies or strategies. However, they indirectly influence EU-EPI when there are fights between committees over the distribution of dossiers.

In addition to the politicians, there is the secretariat, which serves the committees, assists in the writing of reports, and is a vital component of the day-to-day running of the Parliament. Its tasks include preparing documents, taking notes, and ironing out intercommittee relations. It also keeps a close eye on developments in the Commission and Council. Like the Secretariat of the Council, it is also the 'memory' of the organization, amidst an ever-changing cast of MEPs and *rapporteurs*. Its central position in the negotiations gives its advice considerable weight.

Finally, MEPs also coordinate outside these formal structures. Informal contacts are vital to bring amendments into other committees. As an MEP may be a full member of one committee, and a substitute member in another, double membership can facilitate horizontal coordination. They often also belong one of the so-called 'intergroups', which are made up of MEPs with common interests. These range from single issues like animal welfare through to broader themes (e.g. disarmament) (Dinan 1999: 277). It is difficult to know the total number of these more or less informal gatherings, but they probably do not exceed sixty (Corbett et al. 2005). Crucially, there is no intergroup related to EU-EPI. One senior Parliamentary official suggested to us that EU-EPI would benefit greatly from having something comparable to the 'Kangaroo group', which has the horizontal objective of contributing to the four freedoms.

The coordination process

ADMINISTRATIVE COORDINATION

Because the Parliament is essentially a political animal, administrative coordination has to be distinguished from the political coordination that occurs in and between the political groups. The administrative coordination facilitates the allocation of work between committees, the appointment of key actors (e.g. the *rapporteurs*, shadow *rapporteurs*, and draftsmen), and the way in which the work of the committees is integrated. This part of the coordination process is closely related to individual proposals going through the decisionmaking phases. There is generally little scope for identifying priorities or workplanning proactively due to the Parliament's inherent control function. The political coordination is primarily based on activities of individual MEPs and remains to a large extent within the political group.

The most visible mechanism to engineer cross-sectoral policy integration is for one committee to write an opinion on a dossier supervised by another committee. Opinions only concern a number of key issues. They aim at changing a number of paragraphs in a Commission proposal and do not involve continuous discussions on the proposals throughout the entire policy process.

The influence this gives to cognate committees varies. First, the Parliament's rules of procedure mostly focus on the (much more high profile) task of distributing proposals between the committees. There are very few formal rules to stimulate cooperation between committees. The exchange of information between committees is therefore predominantly passive.[5] There is no obligation to consult. Hence, the Environment Committee must know which reports in related committees might have an environmental impact, before it can do anything to influence them. Second, workloads and imbalances in the expertise within and between committees impede thorough scrutiny. Third, the relations between committees range from the outright hostile to the more cooperative and this, evidently, has a profound impact on coordination. The difficulties may stem from different values (e.g. agriculture versus environment) and may be intensified (or ameliorated) by the political affiliations of the respective chairpeople, *rapporteurs*, and draftsmen.

Finally, in view of the limited impact of opinions, MEPs are sometimes not interested in spending a great deal of time writing them. Opinions from one committee may be completely ignored by another. Opinions are increasingly less recognized as a valuable tool for managing cross-cutting issues (Corbett et al. 2005), or addressing the fragmentation of the Parliament.

Nevertheless, opinions are widely used. The Secretariat allocates dossiers based on an agreed list of responsibilities (see Annex VI of the Rules of Procedure) and advises on any overlaps where a cross-committee opinion would be welcome. However, due to the heavy burden borne by all committees, there is only so much time that can be devoted to writing them. Although it is responsible for an inherently horizontal policy issue, the Environment Committee is not the most active committee when it comes to influencing other committees. Between 1999 and 2004, it had 308 own reports and produced 119 opinions. By contrast, the Committee for Industry, Technology Policy, Trade, and Energy (with

Table 4.7 Opinions produced by the Environment and Industry Committees (1999–2004)

Committee	Reports	Opinions
Environment Committee (ENVI) (53 MEPs during 5th Term)	308 Reports	Total Adopted: 119
		Industry, External Trade, Research, and Energy: 20 Regional Policy, Transport, and Tourism: 23 Agriculture and Rural Development: 13 Budgets: 9 Economic and Monetary Affairs: 8 Legal Affairs and the Internal Market: 16 Budgetary Control: 6 Employment and Social Affairs: 3 Fisheries: 6 Culture, Youth, Education, Media, and Sport: 3 Women's Rights and Equal Opportunities: 0 Citizens' Freedom and Rights, Justice, and Home Affairs: 5 Constitutional Affairs: 4 Petitions: 1 Development and Cooperation: 2
Industry and Transport Committee (ITRE) (68 MEPs during 5th Term)	193 Reports	Total Adopted: 210 (212)*
		Environment, Public Health, and Consumer Policy: 41* Regional Policy, Transport, and Tourism: 29 Agriculture and Rural Development: 7 Budgets: 12 Economic and Monetary Affairs: 16 Legal Affairs and the Internal Market: 17 Budgetary Control: 4 Employment and Social Affairs: 9* Fisheries: 4 Culture, Youth, Education, Media, and Sport: 7 Women's Rights and Equal Opportunities: 3 Citizens' Freedom and Rights, Justice, and Home Affairs: 7 Constitutional Affairs: 4 Petitions: 0 Development and Cooperation: 13 Foreign Affairs, Human Rights, Common Security, and Defence Policy: 36 Conciliation: 1

*Items of legislation where two committees were responsible (shared positions).

around fifty members) had 193 and 210 opinions (see Table 4.7). The overall figures are telling in one other specific respect: the Industry Committee had forty-one opinions dedicated to environment, while the Environment Committee had just twenty opinions directed at the industry committee. Our interviews confirmed that the Environment Committee tends to look at the Environment Council and less to what happens in other areas—or at least that it has limited ambitions to use opinions to influence other negotiations. Intense disputes between Committees over the lead do, however, arise. In certain cases, mechanisms for reinforced cooperation between committees are established, obliging the lead committee and the opinion-giving committee to coordinate their work to the maximum extent. However, the effectiveness of this arrangement varies (Chapter 10).

Once a committee has been selected it nominates someone to draft an opinion. This is essentially a political bargaining process similar to the allocation of a *rapporteur*. However, the posts of *rapporteur* and draftsman are not equally important. An opinion essentially consists of a list of amendments to the proposal referred to the committees if it is a legislative text, and of suggestions for the resolution[6] submitted by the Committee responsible in the case of a non-legislative text. The work of a draftsman is often made difficult due to time pressures and a general lack of information in a system which basically relies on passive information. There is a widespread dissatisfaction with the treatment of opinions by the lead committee—and with this, the extent to which horizontal coordination between committees is possible. Several attempts have been made to treat them with more care, building, where possible, on more formal and organized contacts between *rapporteurs* and draftsmen.

POLITICAL COORDINATION

The administrative coordination system is subdivided into sectoral committees (resembling a typical divisionalized organization). However, there is an overlay on top of the committee structure in the form of political groups. These groups provide linkages between MEPs (potentially resembling a matrix structure). As noted above, MEPs from one group can inform their colleagues in other committees of their views. Moreover, MEPs are connected through various national channels and groupings. This opens up the question of the extent to which administrative coordination is really very important compared to these political linkages. As will be discussed in much more detail in Chapter 10, political coordination is highly inefficient and does not lead to an ongoing exchange of views as occurs in the national administrations discussed above.

Reform

The discussion of the previous actors showed that there are reform processes going on in each of them. The reason for this, as will be discussed in Chapter 10, is that internal coordination problems have been spotted by the Parliament—notably by its Secretariat—but there has been little thought into how to respond. The consequences that this may have on the political incentives to further a horizontal policy objective like EU-EPI will be discussed in Chapter 10.

Conclusions

In Chapter 1, we suggested that EU-EPI challenges the five actors in two interrelated ways: the coordination of EU affairs; and the integration of environment into the work of others sectors. This chapter has described how effectively the five actors tackle the first element of this double challenge—namely, the coordination of their input into EU policymaking across all policy spheres. This represents the general organizational foundations for addressing a complicated, cross-sectoral challenge such as EU-EPI.

In this chapter we have shown that the five coordination systems have certain key characteristics. In terms of the most obvious similarities, the three states and the two EU institutions all give a high level of responsibility for coordination to the lead department/committee. All five rely extensively on informal relations to exchange information and settle disputes. In this respect, all are decentralized.

However, there are also significant differences in the status quo and the direction in which they are heading. First, the UK is more centralized than the other four; it has a strong but small coordinating 'core'. Second, it has a system that is highly focused on looking ahead whereas the other four are reactive. Moreover, the UK has specific mechanisms to achieve this; Germany and the Netherlands currently do not. Our analysis suggests that this is not simply a function of the UK's system of single-party government; it is also closely connected to the make-up of their respective administrative systems (i.e. the roles of the Cabinet Office and UKREP, combined with the strong Grant–Darroch meeting). Also the way in which agendas—particularly Presidency agendas—are used contributes greatly to proactive coordination. The ability to behave proactively is, therefore, to an extent determined by the administrative structure of interdepartmental relations.[7]

Third, there are essentially two distinct types of coordinating systems. One type (e.g. the UK) is based on active information and coordinates when issues become a problem. Having been heavily criticized for its poor internal coordination in the past, the Commission may now be moving in this direction. The other type (e.g. the other four actors) is characterized by passive information and highly event-related coordination. This distinction is closely connected to a set of other characteristics (e.g. passive systems suffer from workload problems because the coordination efforts fall on the shoulders of the 'non-lead' departments).

Fourth, apart from the Parliament, it is striking how much effort all the actors have put into reforming their systems. These changes aim to make the respective systems more proactive and reliable. However, the addition of new procedures and teams in the Netherlands and Germany has simply led to more time and resources being tied up in trying to improve internal coordination. By formalizing their coordination systems and making them 'heavier', Germany and the Netherlands may actually have made their coordination problem worse ('perverse incremental changes'— Schout 2004). Hence, there is seemingly continuous demand for more reforms and even more coordination mechanisms. Thus, what we can observe is a set of divergent reactions: while the UK is actually simplifying its coordination mechanisms, the other actors are expanding theirs to cope with increasing policy interdependence.

To conclude, in spite of recent reforms, at least four of the actors are still struggling to respond to the first element of the double challenge— namely the coordination of their input into EU policymaking across all policy sectors. This does not bode well as the five seek to respond to the (even more complex) 'double' challenge of EU-EPI (see Chapter 1). The next chapter explores what steps each of the five actors has taken to respond to the second part of the 'double challenge'—namely EPI—in its own institutional space. Then, the empirical chapters (6–10) analyse how the five have responded to both elements of the 'double challenge' of coordinating the Europeanization of national policymaking and EPI.

Notes

1. Compare with the Dutch system which has 'event meetings' for new Commission proposals, and COREPER and Council meetings, as well as for implementation issues.
2. Namely, the monthly meetings of the division heads and the state secretaries. However, the long intervals between meetings prevents timely feedback.

3. It has approximately 500 officials, around half of which are policy officials (own calculations; see also Nugent 2000: 153).

4. In 2002, the Parliament reported that there were 3,591 officials, 103 temporary staff, 565 political group staff, and 1,500 individual assistants (European Parliament 2002b). Enlargement added more than 1,000 officials to this list (European Parliament 2005).

5. For example, rule 46 stipulates that 'should the Committee . . . wish to hear the view of another Committee', then it may ask the President to give the other committee the status of 'opinion giving Committee' (see also Chapter 10).

6. The opinion amends proposals for legislative acts referred to the Committees. The resolution submitted by Committees concerns non-legislative texts. It may or may not be taken seriously by the bodies to which it is addressed (i.e. the Council, Commission, and European Council). Importantly, the Cardiff and Lisbon processes do not involve legislative procedures (such as co-decision), so the Parliament has to rely on resolutions.

7. Evidently, this does not mean that politics are unimportant. The Major government in the UK (1990–7) struggled to coordinate EU affairs (Wallace 1996; 1997).

5

ENVIRONMENTAL POLICY INTEGRATION IN THE EUROPEAN UNION: ACTOR PERSPECTIVES

[A]ction at national level is needed to deliver on the commitments [to EPI] made at the Union level, as in many areas [EU] competence is limited.

(CEC 2004*b*: 2)

Introduction

The previous two chapters first looked at how the EU as a whole has sought to implement EPI at EU level, and then examined how the five actors coordinate their respective input to EU policy processes (i.e. the first part of the 'double challenge' referred to in Chapter 1). In this chapter we will explore the steps that each actor has taken within its own jurisdiction to implement EPI, acknowledging (as the Commission does in the quotation above) that EU-EPI involves coordinating across many levels and actors. This chapter therefore explains how the five actors have responded to the second part of the 'double challenge'—namely implementing EPI in their own institutional space. For each actor, we begin by introducing the main unit of the organization that actively champions EPI, before briefly describing how its thinking about EPI has evolved over time. We then identify which coordination mechanisms exist within each actor to facilitate EPI. The final section identifies the main similarities and differences between the five.

Germany

The national environment department

Established in 1986, the Federal Department of Environment, Nature Conservation, and Nuclear Safety has approximately 850 employees. It is an independent organization with relatively extensive competences covering water, soil, and air, though some of these are shared with the regional Länder. The department is itself an amalgam of various 'environmental' functions which it inherited from the departments of agriculture, home affairs, and health. Its compartmentalized structure has not, however, prevented it from developing many highly ambitious 'end of the pipe' environmental policies (Wurzel 2004*a*). Germany has an extensive and highly profitable industry producing 'end-of-pipe' technologies (OECD 1993: 207), so it was hardly surprising that Germany should interpret EPI primarily in this way (Jordan and Lenschow 2000). But there is a growing recognition that EPI demands more than just cleaner technologies driven by strong environmental regulation. This was very much the gist of the 1993 OECD performance review of German environmental policy, which praised continuing attempts to decouple growth from pollution flows but criticized the failure to integrate environment into sectoral decisionmaking (OECD 1993: 205–15). This theme was again raised by the OECD in its 2001 review, which praised Germany's progress in combating climate change and pursuing ecological tax reform (OECD 2001: 2), but highlighted continuing contradictions in current policy, for example in relation to coal subsidies (see also German Council of Environmental Advisors 2004: 13).

Müller (2002) argues that there are two main structural bottlenecks impeding the adoption of a more integrated approach in Germany: those lying between different policy sectors; and those separating national and regional authorities. At various times both these have stifled attempts to pursue greater coordination. For example, in the early 1970s, the federal government tried to foster EPI by creating a national system of environmental impact assessment, but it was soon blocked by the sectoral departments. Environmental impact assessment was not actually introduced until 1990, when Germany came under external pressure from the EU to implement a 1985 Directive (Müller 2002: 59). The story with respect to many types of new environmental policy instruments is very much the same (Wurzel et al. 2003). Here, the environment department tried to push the idea of eco-taxes throughout the 1980s and 1990s, but was persistently blocked by the sectoral departments. Ecological tax reform only really got going after the election of Germany's first red–green coalition in 1998 (Wurzel et al. 2003: 133). Germany does not even have an integrated set of environmental statutes. An integrated statute book was supposed to enter into force in 2000, but work has now halted until the respective competences of the federal state and the Länder have been clarified (BMU 2004).

National EPI initiatives: A brief history

The government defined environmental protection as a cross-sectoral challenge as long ago as 1976. However, this soon ran aground on the rocks of intersectoral fighting (Jänicke et al. 2002) (see Table 5.1). It is notable that many of the instruments which were first discussed in this period (e.g. environmental planning, green cabinets, environmental policy appraisal, and strategic environmental assessment) are only now being actively discussed and implemented in Germany (c.f. the Netherlands and the UK). No ruling party in Germany has ever attempted (even at a

Table 5.1 German environmental policy and EPI: key events

Date	Landmark	Remarks
1971	Publication of the first environmental pro-gramme	EPI identified as a guiding principle
1971	Work begins on a national environmental impact assessment system	Eventually abandoned in the teeth of opposition from sectoral departments
1976	First levy (i.e. a tax) on waste water adopted	Germany emerges as a European leader in the use of NEPIs
1986	Creation of the German environment department	
1990	EIA finally implemented in Germany	Primarily due to EU pressure; implementation remains deficient
1990	Adoption of ambitious, cross-sectoral climate change reduction target	Helps to drive cross-sectoral integration
1998	Election of a Red–green coalition	Adopts several ambitious long-term targets; ecological tax reform initiated
1999	Red–green coalition initiates ecological tax reform programme	Steps taken to develop a national environmental policy appraisal system
2002	Publication of a national sustainability strategy	New advisory Cabinet Committee on the environment created
2004	Publication of an interim report on the 2002 strategy	

Source: Material assembled in Wurzel et al. (2003) and Wurzel (2004a).

rhetorical level) to change fundamentally the agriculture, transport, or industry sectors in order to implement EPI. According to the German Council of Environmental Advisors (German Council of Environmental Advisors 2000; 2002), EPI-like targets and strategies have traditionally been formulated by the environment department, but have never generated sufficient support in the German cabinet to make a difference. The one exception is probably climate change policy. Here, the setting of international greenhouse gas reduction targets in 1990 triggered a ten-year process of cross-sectoral policy planning. However, the implementation of the resulting policies has lacked the support of the sectors, and Germany's attempts to fulfil its international targets would almost certainly be failing had it not been for the post-1989 'windfall' effect of unification.

The prospects for implementing EPI grew significantly in 1998 with the election of a red–green government. This formulated some concrete political projects to green the agriculture and energy sectors. The energy sector project links the closure of nuclear plants with a national target for renewable energies (i.e. to double the current share by 2010) and co-generation. Meanwhile, the 2000–1 BSE crisis triggered a public debate on the need for a fundamental reorientation of the agricultural sector. The department in question (agriculture and food) was (much like its counterpart in the UK) reorganized and renamed (in this case to 'Consumer Protection, Food, and Agriculture'). The new minister explicitly stated that the government wanted to achieve ecological modernization in the agriculture sector as a matter of urgency. One of the most prominent decisions was to aim to ensure that 20 per cent of German farming was organic within ten years, as well as to raise the environmental standards of conventional farming. The German Council of Environmental Advisors (2002: 48) confirmed that important first steps have been taken, but German environmental non-governmental organizations (NGOs) continue to complain about the slow pace of change (BMU 2004).

Concerning transport policy, there was some 'green' wording in the coalition treaties of 1998 and 2002 as well in the German sustainable development strategy (see below). But there is not—as is the case in the agriculture field—a strong political desire at high levels to engineer a fundamental change. EPI-related policy objectives have begun to appear, but the government still does not talk in terms of a drastic process of reform (*wende*).

In summary, there is growing evidence of structural change in the agriculture and energy sectors, but this has more to do with external drivers (international regulation in the case of energy; trade–economic pressures in relation to farming) than domestic ones. Crucially, in spite of repeated political commitments to achieve EPI, the German public discourse overwhelmingly supports technological solutions to pollution control, 'forced' by strong regulatory standards (Wurzel et al. 2003). In its official submission to the 1992 Rio Summit, the German government even argued that this approach was 'to a large extent identical with the aims and demands of... Agenda 21 [the international UN sustainable development action plan]' (quoted in Beuermann and Burdick 1997: 91). However, there is a growing appreciation that the two are not the same, and that sustainable development implies a much more radical and thoroughgoing overhaul of German sectoral policymaking (e.g. Beuermann 2000: 110–11; OECD 2001).

The National EPI System

A NATIONAL SUSTAINABILITY STRATEGY

Soon after assuming power, the red–green coalition agreed to develop a national sustainable development strategy, embodying clear objectives (SPD-Bündnis 90/Die Grünen 1998). The strategy, which was officially published in 2002 and is currently being reviewed, contains a number of potentially significant institutional innovations. Significantly, the preparation of the strategy, which the OECD (2001: 28) criticized for being 'very slow', was also very weakly coordinated with EPI-related activities at the Länder (e.g. Agenda 21 processes) and EU levels (the Cardiff process, etc.). Importantly, in 2003 the German Chancellor made no reference to sustainability objectives during the debate on social and financial reform ('Agenda 2010') (German Council of Environmental Advisors 2004: 1).

NEW COORDINATING BODIES AND COMMITTEES

The red–green government (1998–2005) did not significantly alter the basic structure of the environment department to improve EPI. But it did create some new coordinating bodies to produce the sustainable strategy. In 2000, a committee of secretary of states was established for this purpose (*Staatssekretärausschuss für nachhaltige Entwicklung*). This body, which is chaired by the Chancellery, is now recognized as Germany's standing green cabinet (OECD 2001: 28). It is supported by a new advisory council for sustainable development, which is composed of seventeen independent experts. So far, it has produced two reports (in 2002 and 2004). Importantly, all these changes focus on national level developments; thus far, there has been no direct link to EU-EPI, and (unlike the UK and the Netherlands) no national level Cardiff-like process.

AN ENVIRONMENTAL POLICY APPRAISAL SYSTEM?

The red–green coalition also amended the Common Ministerial Rules of Procedure (*Gemeinsame Geschäftsordnung*) of the federal government, which describes the bureaucratic procedures for law-making. There is one article (§44) that can be read as requiring a kind of 'impact assessment'. It obliges sector departments to describe the consequences of their policy proposals on the finances of the federal, regional, and municipal levels.[1] There is, however, no requirement to undertake an environmental appraisal, or even to pay special attention to environmental matters in regulatory impact assessment. Only later in §45 does the order mention that all relevant departments must be involved 'early' (*frühzeitig*) in the process. With respect to EPI, it obliges the lead department to inform the environment department of any significant environmental impact. In practice, this means nothing more than normal interdepartmental information-sharing (i.e. Level 1 or 2 on the coordination scale), which in Germany is in any case quite passive (see Chapter 4). The German government, therefore, cannot be said to have a formal environmental policy appraisal system. In fact, traditionally there has not been a national system of strategic environmental assessment within Germany, although one is now being created for certain plans (e.g. transport plans) to meet the requirements of an EU Directive on strategic environmental assessment.

Conclusions

Germany's very strong regulatory past casts a long shadow over its more recent attempts to grapple with the more horizontally complex task of implementing EPI and developing more sustainably. The federal government has acknowledged that there is an urgent need for administrative improvements to facilitate EU coordination and EPI, a view supported by the German Council of Environmental Advisors (2004: 1). The OECD (2001: 28) maintains that 'at all levels of government, Germany still faces significant problems that hamper better integration.' There is, for instance, still no effective system of environmental policy appraisal in Germany, and, consequently, no formal system for assessing EU proposals. As the German EU coordination system is quite passive, this places the onus very much on the environment department to find out what the sector departments are doing. To make matters worse, the environment department shows no real appetite for remedying this gap. In fact, many officials regard 'procedural' measures such as EPI as an attempt to weaken the 'successful' German regulatory approach to environmental policy-making (Jordan 2003; Wurzel 2004a). In 2001, the environment department responded to these deficiencies by creating new working groups (e.g. in the transport sector) to improve the administrative coordination of EU-EPI. In this sense, Germany is finally beginning to respond to both elements of the 'double challenge'.

The Netherlands

The national environment department

Environmental protection was first institutionalized in Dutch policy in 1971 when a Directorate-General for Environmental Protection (DGEP) was created in the new department of public health and environmental protection (Liefferink 1997: 213). From its inception, the DGEP worked closely with the agency that later developed into the National Institute of Public Health and Environmental Protection (RIVM). In 1982, the government created a new department (of Housing, Physical Planning, and Environment – in Dutch 'VROM'), which grew significantly in political importance after 1988 (Jansen, Osland, and Hanf 1998: 288), when the regular publication of long-term environmental plans (*milieubalans*) commenced (Liefferink 1999).

The national environment department has traditionally been a strong advocate of EPI (Jordan and Lenschow 2000). Each directorate is responsible for EU policies in its own areas and most have appointed officials to track EU policies (see Chapter 4). These officials deal with the negotiations in working parties and monitor relevant developments in other Councils. However, the extent to which they have the time and the seniority to do this varies between directorates. These differences can partly be explained by, among others, personal interests and the workload associated with national policy development. The national environment department, in summary, is still not a particularly Europeanized department, with much of the onus falling on its EU coordinating unit. By contrast, some sectoral departments, such as economic affairs, agriculture, and transport, have appointed one or more officials who monitor the work of the Environment Council on a more or less full-time basis. The commitment (and hence capacity) to monitor other Councils is less developed in the national environment department.

National EPI initiatives: a brief history

The Netherlands is a member of the 'green troika' of member states that significantly shaped the direction of EU environmental policy in the 1980s and 1990s (Liefferink and van der Zouwen 2004) (cf. Bressers and Plettenburg 1997: 109). The strong international/EU orientation of Dutch environmental policy arises from the belief that for a small country it is tactically more effective to work with Europe than to pursue national ambitions unilaterally (see Table 5.2). More recently, the Dutch have tried to move beyond seeing 'environment' as a stand-alone problem and recognize the wider sustainability dimensions. This shift has led to a conscious policy effort to address EPI through long-term planning processes, coordinated across national, EU, and international levels (Jordan and Lenschow 2000).

The national EPI system

The long-standing desire to implement EPI (or what the Dutch refer to as 'external integration') (Muijen 2000: 155) is reflected in the national environmental policy plans (NEPPs). Each plan is produced collectively by the departments most concerned in collaboration with wider civil society. Rather than regulate, the Dutch environmental policy style (Zito et al. 2003) is to rely on covenants (or voluntary agreements—see Chapter 3) to implement the contents of NEPPs. The latest environmental policy plan (NEPP 4) presents the 'innovation of systems towards sustainability' (*systeeminnovatie naar duurzamheid*) as its main theme.

Against this background, new ways are being explored to codify environmental policy principles in sector policies, involving extensive dialogue within government as well as between government and civil society (Backes and Ozinga 2002). A core element is 'an agenda of transition' which aims to manage sustainable development patterns in the field of energy/emissions, biodiversity, and agriculture. The latest plan includes concrete, long-term targets and indicators for these sectors. However, intermediate targets are often missing. Environmental NGOs claim that these are absolutely vital as they force the pace of change in the short to medium term (*Stichting Natuur en Milieu* 2001). The national

Table 5.2 Dutch environmental policy and EPI: key events

Date	Landmark	Remarks
1971	Creation of the department for Public Health and the Environment, with a Directorate General for Environmental Protection	Publication of a 'Priority Memorandum on the Environment' (*Urgentienota Milieuhygiëne*) is followed by a surge in new environmental laws
1980	National EIA system created	
1982	Environmental policy placed in a stronger department for Housing, Spatial Planning, and the Environment (VROM)	
1983	Inclusion of the Environment in the National state constitution (*Grondwet*) (Article 21)	
1984	First steps towards environmental planning taken by VROM (1985–9)	Encompasses an integrated, target group approach
1987	Strategic environmental assessment system is formally established	Targets waste, water, energy, and some land use plans
1988	First national 'state of the environment' plan published by RIVM	
1989–90	First national plan (NEPP), reformulating Dutch environmental policy	Introduces a new steering approach with quality targets
1993–4	Second NEPP	Incorporation of the General Provisions Act into the new Environmental Management Act
1995	Introduction of national environmental appraisal system ('e-test') for legislative proposals and policy plans	
1997–8	Third NEPP	
2001	Fourth NEPP	
2003	Creation of a new scoping procedure under the e-test system known as 'Quick Scan'	

Source: Adapted from Liefferink (1995); Liefferink and van der Zouwen (2004)

environment department's reluctance to agree to intermediate sectoral targets underlines the widespread belief that EPI should be achieved by decentralizing responsibilities (to economic sectors and departments), and improving the flow of information about the environmental implications of government actions (i.e. through independent reviews and environmental policy appraisals).

By contrast with Germany, the Netherlands is a front runner in the field of environmental impact assessment, and has also innovated in the use of strategic environmental assessment at national level (see OECD 2003 for details). Since the late 1980s, the Dutch government has also subjected all national legislative proposals to an environmental policy appraisal (or 'e-test'). At first the e-test system was very informal and its environmental effectiveness was unclear (Verheem 2004). In 1994, the government developed a more formal environmental policy appraisal system as one part of a wider Market Operation, Deregulation, and Legislative Quality Plan (Marsden 1999). The Dutch 'e-test', which is a form of strategic environmental assessment (SEA) (Sheate et al. 2001), is one element of a battery of different testing schemes, including the Business Impact Assessment and the Practicability and Enforcement Assessment (Nooteboom 2002; VROM 2003). Its purpose is to provide civil servants, the government, and members of parliament with better environmental information. In order to support departmental officials, new coordinating capacities (i.e. a Joint Support Centre for Draft Legislation and training facilities) were established (Verheem and Tonk 2000). Importantly, the e-testing regime covers all national legislation, as well as national measures that implement EU requirements (Ruiten 2002). After a critical external review in 1999, the e-test regime was reformulated and renamed 'Environmental Assessment of Legislation' (see VROM 2003; Verheem 2004).

Conclusions

Even though many new policy and administrative measures have been put in place, the implementation of EPI in the Netherlands remains problematic. First of all, the ownership of environmental objectives is not equally supported by all the policy sectors (VROM 2001: 13). Backes and Ozinga (2002: 3) argue that the national environment department needs to put more pressure on other departments to produce more e-tests and to use the resulting information to inform their decisions. Currently, only around 5 per cent of policy proposals are actually e-tested (Verheem 2004). Drawing upon the findings of a consultancy analysis commissioned by the environment department in 1999, Ruiten (2002: 1) claims that '[n]o rules or regulations have changed significantly due to the results of an e-test.' This is because lead departments often regard them as just one of a number of administrative hurdles that have to be cleared before legislation can finally be adopted (Ruiten 2002). Very often parliamentarians and environmental pressure groups (who may be involved in the drafting process; they may even produce information for the e-test) are not formally involved. Many may not even be aware that an e-test has been, or may be, produced (Ruiten 2002). Finally, the whole process is informal and, in contrast to most other aspects of Dutch life, relatively opaque. It is not externally reviewed or verified (e.g. by the Support Unit); the national environment department simply checks whether a test has been produced.

Secondly, because of these and other failings, the OECD (2003: 29) concluded that the Dutch government's ambitious aim of achieving sustainability by 2010 appears 'increasingly difficult to achieve, particularly for the agriculture and transport sectors' (see also Hanf and de Gronden 1998: 177–9). This pattern is confirmed by the national 'state of the environment' reports, which suggest that too many important environmental trends are running in the wrong direction (e.g. RIVM 2003).

The United Kingdom

The national environment department

The UK created the world's first national environment department in 1970. Although it was named the department of the environment, for the first twenty years it mostly focused on local finance, urban quality, and at various times, transport issues (Jordan 2002*a*). Judging by the number of administrative reorganizations and name changes that have occurred since 1970, very few politicians have really known what to do with it. For instance in 1997, it was amalgamated with the transport department, then, following the BSE crisis in 2001, it was pulled away and fused with agriculture to form the Department for Environment, Food, and Rural Affairs (DEFRA).

Throughout much of the department's life, the most 'environmental' part—that is the Environmental Protection Group (EPG)—has been a neglected backwater (Jordan 2002*a*). For our purposes, EPG's most important subcomponents are the European/international division—EPINT (Environmental Protection International)—and the Sustainable Development Unit (SDU), which is the guardian of the national EPI system (see below). Currently, the European coordination unit in the department is staffed by a couple of full-time officials. This may appear small, but it reflects the UK's active, subsidiarity-based coordination system. It does not, for example, lead in the development of the environment department's negotiating position in the EU; that is the responsibility of the various line units and divisions. Rather, its main task is to ensure that information moves around the system (active coordination), although in the past it has intervened to change the negotiating position of another division (DoE 1993: 13).

National EPI initiatives: a brief history

EPI is a long-standing, but as yet still unfulfilled, aspiration of UK policy-makers (see Table 5.3). In the 1970s, the UK tried to integrate by fusing all the environment-related parts of Whitehall into a single department (see above). It also sought to impose environmental standards on other sectors by regulating. It generally resisted any EU involvement in EPI. The environment department maintained that 'controlling pollution will continue to be a major concern [of the EU] and the [UK does] not want to see . . .

Table 5.3 UK environmental policy and EPI: key events

Date	Landmark	Remarks
1969	First environmental White Paper	Advocates a regulatory approach; no mention of EPI
1970	Creation of the Department of the Environment, the world's first environment department	Given the task of developing a cross-government approach to environmental protection
1976	The Department of the Environment loses its transport functions	A separate Department of Transport is created
1973	The UK joins the then EEC	The UK envisages a very minimal role for the EEC in determining national environmental affairs
1985	After a long fight, the UK finally agrees to adopt the EU's EIA Directive	Had fiercely resisted formalizing EIA
1990	Publication of second environment White Paper	First coherent statement on EPI. Growth in the size of the environmental protection group in the environment department. Several new mechanisms are created to implement EPI
1990	The environmental protection group finally creates a European coordinating unit	Previously, EU work was treated as a (relatively unimportant) subset of international environmental affairs
1992	First of a series of annual White Paper updates published	
1997	A new Labour government; pledges to 'green government'	Existing EPI mechanisms strengthened, and a new Parliamentary audit committee is created
1998	Treasury signs rolling public service agreements (PSAs) with all sectoral departments	Some agreements include clear environmental targets, but the vast majority do not
1999	Publication of a new sustainability strategy	Promises sectoral strategies and targets, but few ever appear
2001	Adoption of the EU Directive on SEA	UK successfully limited its focus to plans (and not policies)
2004	A new integrated appraisal system is created	Brigades together several 'sectoral' appraisal systems
2005	Publication of a revised sustainability strategy	Contains few new EPI initiatives or mechanisms

Source: Based on Jordan (2002a) and Russel and Jordan (2004) [those] commitments neglected in order to extend [environmental policy] into other areas' of EU policymaking (ENDS Ltd. No. 69: 14).

In the 1980s, domestic attitudes to the environment and Europe changed (Jordan 2003), and the UK emerged as one of the first member states to examine ways of pursuing EPI at the national level (Jordan 2002*a*; 2002*c*). A major White Paper was produced in 1990 containing several new coordinating capacities: a green cabinet committee; a network of 'green' ministers in every department; a system of annual reporting; and the publication of guidance on how to undertake environmental policy appraisals. But as has been widely reported (Hill and Jordan 1993; 1995), these innovations failed to produce sufficiently integrated outcomes. The cabinet committee and the green ministers hardly ever met, and the guidance on environmental policy appraisal was politely ignored by the sectoral department (Russel 2004).

The national EPI system

A Labour government entered office in 1997 promising to breathe fresh life into the national EPI system (Jordan 2000). In 1999, it launched a new sustainable development strategy (DETR 1999), backed up by an annual reporting system. However, it was widely criticized for being insufficiently innovative, and short on specific objectives and targets (Sustainable Development Commission 2004).

Targets (*management by objectives*) are, however, increasingly included in the annually updated Public Service Agreements that all departments have had to sign up since 1998 (H.M. Treasury 1998). The 2002 Public Spending Review (H.M. Treasury 2002) White Paper includes over 130 of these 'outcome-focused commitments'. Departments are expected to report on their progress in their annual departmental reports. The results are then fed into the next budgetary cycle. However, they are very few in number (i.e. around seven per department), of which only a handful are environmentally related (some departments have none). Although each Public Service Agreement normally contains a statement of who is responsible for the delivery of the targets (James 2004), they are framed in such general terms that they are effectively little more than *mission statements*.

Labour also created a Parliamentary committee to audit EPI and a special cross-departmental SDU (located in the national environment department) to champion EPI and sustainability across Whitehall. Labour also increased the status and external profile of the network of green ministers (see below); produced a new sustainable strategy (in 1999—subsequently reissued in 2005) on sustainable development; and relaunched the national environmental policy appraisal system (Russel 2004).

THE GREEN CABINET COMMITTEE (ENV)

This cabinet committee (on paper, *a strong integrator*) is supposed to be the principal decisionmaking body for national environmental policies. But because the UK has a very subsidiarity-based decisionmaking system (Chapter 4), ENV tends not to meet very much. The Parliamentary audit committee has instructed it to take a more 'more interventionist' position (HC 426-I Session 1998–9: para. 2). One of the underlying causes is that not enough environmental issues are pushed up the Whitehall decision-making system for ENV to deal with. In large part, this arises from the failure of sector departments to produce sufficient numbers of environmental policy appraisals to advertise the fact that they are developing policies that are not supportive of EPI (see below).

THE GREEN MINISTERS

Labour has tried to give the green ministers (*liason roles*) a larger and more visible role. They meet more regularly (*teams*), and produce annual reports. Each green minister is supported by one or two officials who are supposed to champion EPI in their respective departments (*gatekeeper*). But the environment department insists that its ministers should not be 'green policemen' (*watchdogs*) (HC 517-I Second Report Session 1997–8: para. 25). But without this added element of hierarchy, sector departments do not instinctively support EPI. This highlights the importance of the ownership dogma identified in Chapter 1.

ENVIRONMENTAL POLICY APPRAISAL

According to guidance published by the national environment department, an environmental appraisal should have been carried out '[w]henever a policy or programme—*including any under negotiation in the EU*—is likely to have a significant effect on the environment' (DEFRA 1998: para. 5.1) (emphasis added). However, detailed research reveals that only sixty-one appraisals were actually undertaken in the period 1997–2002, of which forty-seven (78 per cent) were produced by the environment department (Russel and Jordan 2004; 2005). Very few of the sixty-one met all of the environment department's best practice criteria; most were deficient in almost every respect. The fundamental problem was that there was no formal requirement of sectoral departments to produce or publish environmental policy appraisals. By contrast, over 500 appraisals were produced in the same period under the Cabinet Office's system of regulatory impact assessment, which assesses the potential impacts of new proposals on business, charities, and the voluntary sector.

In the late 1990s, the environment, health, and transport departments began to experiment with more integrated forms of appraisal, which sought to bring environmental, social, and economic impacts together in one metric. However, Integrated Policy Appraisal was not, as these two departments hoped, rolled out across the rest of Whitehall. Instead (and as part of a wider attempt to make policymaking more efficient and interconnected) (Russel 2004), in April 2004 the government 'collapsed all eleven of the government's [sectoral] appraisal systems [including environment policy appraisal] into a single, more integrated form of appraisal' (Jordan et al. 2003) In effect, the new regime, which will be overseen by the Cabinet Office, simply extends the existing system of regulatory impact assessment to encompass more sectoral concerns (ENDS Ltd., No. 358: 48; Jordan et al. 2003: 123; HC 1259 Session 2004–5: 4). Although this could increase the number of appraisals performed, environmentalists are deeply concerned that the high environmental ambitions of the environmental policy appraisal system (see Chapter 8) will be sacrificed (Russel and Jordan 2004; 2005). The parliamentary audit committee suggested that it 'will [not] do anything to help address the failure by departments ... to improve their performance on environmental policy appraisal of policy measures' (HC 261, Seventh Report, Session 2004–5: para. 10).

Conclusions

Why has EPI not penetrated the heart of mainstream decisionmaking in an administrative system with a very well-developed culture of active information sharing? There are two primary reasons. First, most Whitehall departments are, at heart, not very green (Jordan 2002a: 24). So while information on shared concerns such as EU affairs and economic policy is actively disseminated, for domestic policy concerns with a much lower political profile (e.g. EPI), the level of coordination achieved appears to be considerably lower. The Cabinet Office has not been vested with the power to force departments to adopt EPI, and the environment department is politically too weak to force other departments to amend their policies. Second, the environment department in the UK is not nearly as environmentally minded as some of its counterparts in continental Europe. Consequently, the environmental protection group has often had its work cut out to implement EPI within the Department of Environment, let alone the rest of Whitehall. So, while the national EPI system looks strong on paper, many of its core elements underperform (OECD 2002*b*: 26–7, 28).

THE EUROPEAN COMMISSION

Many parts of the EU expect Commission officials to act as the legal and political guardian of EPI, because they often lack the time or the incentive to do this for themselves. The Commission—in practice, DG Environment—has actively sought to develop this guardianship role, for example through the EAPs and various Treaty amendments (see Chapter 3). However, the Commission has discovered to its cost that if it takes up the challenge of EU-EPI, other actors tend not to feel so compelled to pay attention to it.

The Commission's environment 'department': DG Environment

DG Environment was established in 1981 (see Table 5.4) and is endowed with several coordinating capacities. The most relevant are: its mission; its organizational and political resources; various incentives for its officials to work on EPI; and the unit for sustainable environment. To carry out its mission, DG Environment has two deputy DGs and five directorates. Including support staff, about 400 officials work in DG Environment. Due to its size (it is one of the smaller DGs), only a few people actively monitor developments in the sectoral DGs. Most of the staff in DG Environment devote their energies to formulating new environment policies to target these sectors. 'Policing' the work of other DGs is avoided, as is clear from, for example, the loose and open-ended targets listed in the Fifth and Sixth EAPs (see Chapter 3).

The Commission's EPI initiatives: a brief history

The European Commission has been trying to green itself and the rest of the EU for almost twenty years (see Table 5.4 and Chapter 9). The debate on what EU-EPI should seek to achieve and through what means has,

Table 5.4 The European Commission and EU-EPI: key events

Date	Landmark	Remarks
1967	Passage of the first EU environmental law	On dangerous chemicals (EEC/67/548)
1972	Stockholm environment summit	Shortly afterwards, member states decide to accelerate EEC environmental policy
1973	Creation of the Environment and Consumer Protection Service (ECPS) in DG Industry	A small unit with a handful of staff; it is the precursor of DG Environment
1981	Creation of DG Environment	
1983	Adoption of the First EAP	Makes the first explicit reference to EPI
1987	Single European Act introduces a Treaty commitment to EPI	The new commitment is perceived to be a sectoral (i.e. environmental) matter
1987	Adoption of the Fourth EAP	Whole subsection devoted to EPI; announces new environmental appraisal procedures in the Commission ('green star')
1993	Commission adopts an internal Communication on steps needed to put EPI into practice; creates an Integration Unit in DG Environment	Initiates the green star procedure; also linked to a network of integration 'correspondents' and an annual reporting process
1997	Luxembourg European Council	The Commission begins work on designing a new mode of governance to pursue EU-EPI
1998	Commission publishes 'A Partnership for Integration'	An explicit attempt to build a cross-sector network to implement EPI at EU level
1998	Cardiff European Council	Beginning of the Cardiff process; Commission invited to report on progress
2001	European Council in Gothenburg	The EU adopts a sustainable development strategy (SDS) produced by the Commission; Heads of State call for the Cardiff process to be revitalized
2002	Commission adopts the Sixth EAP	EPI is one of the strategic priorities
2003	Start of the new EU impact assessment regime	Commission publishes its first Environmental Policy Review; identifies EPI as one of three main priorities
2004	Commission publishes the first Cardiff 'stocktake'	First of an annual series; identifies new ways to strengthen EU-EPI and develop links to national EPI systems
2005	Commission develops a series of thematic strategies under the Sixth EAP	This work runs in parallel with an updating of the EU SDS

Source: Based on Lenschow (2002a) and Wilkinson (1995; 1997)

however, proceeded jerkily. On the one hand, awareness of the environment has undoubtedly increased across the Commission. Awareness has been raised in the other sectors through macro-level initiatives such as the Cardiff process and the SDS (see Chapter 3). On the other hand, doubts continue to exist regarding the Commission's commitment to supporting DG Environment's aspirations. These have, if anything, been compounded by the recent emergence (and growing importance) of the Lisbon and Better Regulation agendas. In a frank assessment, the Commission admitted that 'environmental integration commitments [in the EU] are still largely to be translated into further concrete results for the environment' (CEC 2004*b*: 4), but then said conspicuously little about how it intended to rectify this problem.

The Commission's EPI system

The Fifth EAP incorporated several EPI-related initiatives within the Commission, namely: an integration unit in DG ENV; integration correspondents; the 'green star' system of environmental policy appraisal; a subgroup of green Commissioners (which was quickly abolished); and an annual evaluation of the environmental performance of individual DGs.[2] As is now well known from external and internal examinations (e.g. Wilkinson 1995; 1997), none of these were particularly successful.

THE SUSTAINABLE DEVELOPMENT UNIT

Because this unit (see Chapter 9 for details) has tended to lack high-level political support even within DG Environment, it has struggled to be an effective champion of EPI and environmental policy appraisal. Crucially, it lacks staff and, according to our interviewees, would probably have been better off as horizontal unit in the Secretariat General under the President. It has, however, played important roles in other areas (e.g. coordinating the Cardiff process). But even here its impact has been patchy to say the least (see Chapter 3).

IMPACT ASSESSMENT

Under the 'green star' system, important new proposals were supposed to be marked with a star in the workplan indicating that the lead DG would produce an assessment specifying how environment considerations were to be taken on board during the formulation of the proposal. Writing five years after its initiation, Wilkinson (1997) found no evidence that any environmental appraisals had ever been produced. The enthusiasm in lead DGs for assessments was lacking, and the available methodologies were simply not available to those charged with producing them.

In the early 2000s, the Commission moved on to implement a new and more formal system known as impact assessment (IA) (see Chapter 3) which has later developed into a much more transparent system of publicly accessible 'roadmaps'.[3] Despite some critical early reports on its performance (Wilkinson et al. 2004*b*), the system certainly does have a higher profile outside DG Environment than 'green star'. The Commission's website claims that there is a culture of greater transparency and open evaluation (CEC 2004e: 4). But whether the greater uptake of appraisal leads to more EPI at the level of individual sectoral policy proposals, is (as UK is also finding) still far from clear. In 2004, IA was 'refocused to give greater attention to factors that are widely considered to be important to productivity and hence to the competitiveness of the EU' (CEC 2004e: 5).

THE ENVIRONMENTAL CORRESPONDENTS

The network of environmental correspondents (*liason roles*) in each DG was created to support and encourage the writing of environmental policy appraisals, but their influence has been mixed. In some DGs, they acted more as gatekeepers than watchdogs. On the whole, though, they remained peripheral to the process, lacked authority, and were easily distracted by their sectoral affiliations and concerns (see Chapter 9).

GREATER CONSULTATION AND BETTER BUDGETING

In addition to these instruments, the Commission has recently underlined the need for early consultation and exchange of information between DGs to ensure consistent and sustainable policies (Chapter 4). Moreover, under the influence of the European Parliament and NGOs, EU financial support for regional and agricultural projects is now increasingly tied to adequate compliance with the habitat, nitrates, and birds directives (this conditionality is known as 'cross-compliance'). These successes have been achieved largely because of external political pressure (Lenschow 1999; 2002b; Haigh 2005; see also Chapter 10).

Conclusions

Having briefly reviewed the EPI mechanisms in the Commission, it is evident that the dominant approach has been to rely on persuading the sectoral DGs to accept ownership instead of issuing more and more top-down obligations. The IAs and the greater openness are part of a new system that seeks to heighten awareness of other values and to prevent cross-cutting issues from becoming a problem later on. But sharing ownership for sustainable development also neatly exempts DG Environment from having to invest time and resources in leading the rest of the Commission. However, the question remains as to whether this approach is an obstacle to, or a precondition for, the fulfilment of EPI. It also remains to be seen whether the underlying problem is one of a weak coordination capacities or limited political leadership from the apex of the Commission.

The European Parliament

According to Hey (2002: 133), the Parliament is a '*potentially* progressive force in EPI' (emphasis added). It most certainly played a key part in bringing about the greening of the EU's structural and cohesion funds (see Table 5.5), but has never quite realized its potential to be a force for greater EPI. In fact, for much of the last thirty years, it has remained at the

Table 5.5 The European Parliament and EU-EPI: key events

Date	Landmark	Remarks
1973	Creation of the first Environment Committee	
1985	Negotiation of the Single European Act	Parliament granted the power to cooperate in environmental decisionmaking
1987	Adoption of the Fourth EAP	Parliament supports the inclusion of a sub-section on EPI
1992	Adoption of the Fifth EAP	EPI section strongly endorsed by the Parliament's environment committee
1993	Adoption of a Regulation on Structural Funds	Parliament successfully campaigns for all regional programmes to be subject to an EIA
1996	Decision on Trans-European Networks (TENS)	Parliament successfully campaigns for all transport projects to be subject to a strategic environmental assessment (under the co-decision procedure)
1998	Review of the Fifth EAP	Parliament uses the conciliation procedure to stress the need for much greater EPI
1998	Commission publishes 'A Partnership for Integration'	Parliament requested to revise its internal procedures accordingly; no formal response received (as of 2005)
2001	European Parliament publishes a resolution on 'Preparing for the Gothenburg European Council'	Informal proposal by an MEP to set up a Parliamentary 'Committee for Sustainable Development' has little impact
2003	Resolution on the preparation for the 2003 Spring European Council	Parliamentary committees fail to agree a common way to input to the spring summit (under the Lisbon process)
2004	First annual Cardiff stocktake published	Makes no mention of the Parliament's potential role
2005	Relaunch of the Lisbon process	Still no formal role for the Parliament

Source: Based on Lenschow (2002a) and Wilkinson (1995; 1997)

margins of the policy debate about EPI in the EU. After the Cardiff European Council in 1998, the Commission expected the Parliament to join the partnership for integration (Chapter 3), but it still has not. To this day, the Parliament remains partially disengaged from the Cardiff, as well as the Lisbon and SDS, processes (see Chapter 10). Furthermore, it has never initiated an internal review of the practical steps it could take to increase its own contribution to realizing more EU-EPI.

The Parliament's environmental champion: the environment committee

The European Parliament decided to set up an Environment Committee in 1973. It was the twelfth specialist parliamentary committee to be created since the Parliament first met in 1952. Its original membership of thirty-six was subsequently increased to sixty to cope with successive enlargements of the EU. At first, it was primarily an advisory body, but the introduction initially of the cooperation and then, more recently, of co-decisionmaking, has boosted its influence considerably (Burns 2005).

In theory, the committee is in a good position to champion EU-EPI as it has relatively broad horizontal remit, which goes well beyond the traditional confines of 'environmental policy' to encompass public health and consumer policy. In practice, its role is limited in at least four different respects. First, the Parliament's influence differs considerably across its remit; that is, it has limited powers of consultation in the agricultural and fisheries areas. In these areas, it has to resort to less direct devices such as producing reports and holding conferences to influence the Commission and the Council. Second, the environment committee is already heavily occupied with its own sectoral work (see Chapter 10). Crucially, the advent of co-decisionmaking has effectively concentrated workloads on a limited number of permanent committees, namely those dealing with the environment, regional and transport affairs, and industrial policy. For example, these three committees alone handled almost 60 per cent of all the new legislation between 2001 and 2002 (European Parliament 2002a: 6). Third, as the Cardiff, Lisbon, and SDS processes are not following the traditional (i.e. Community Method) route of regulation, the Parliament is robbed of what is effectively its most powerful weapon—co-decisionmaking. Finally, as discussed in this and the previous chapter, more practical administrative and political matters hamper its ability to function horizontally.

The Parliament's EPI initiatives: a brief history

So far, the Parliament has made several contributions to the debate about sustainable development in the EU (e.g. the Hulthén report for the Gothenburg Council in May 2001) (European Parliament 2001*b*), but it has done very little directly to shape the Cardiff process or to restructure itself to facilitate EU-EPI. The most visible way in which the environment committee has made its views known has been through the issuing of resolutions,[4] that are then subjected to a formal vote in the plenary.

There are some general indications that influencing the work of other sectors could be rather difficult. First, there are sectors (such as agriculture) that are hugely relevant to EPI which are not subject to co-decisionmaking. Consequently, the Parliament's influence is weakened.[5] Second, there is the assumption that the present committee structure of the Parliament leads to a very fragmented policy style where intercommittee coordination is rather limited. In Chapter 4, we saw how the internal capacities to achieve greater internal coordination across all issues are weak to non-existent. Interestingly, the Parliament is still to embark upon the internal evaluation of its rules and procedures that it has repeatedly promised to complete. In 1998, the Commission requested the 'Parliament [to] review its current organizational arrangements to ensure that in its decision making it takes account of the need to integrate environment into other policies' (CEC 1998: 7). In contrast to the Council and the Commission (which both took active steps to institutionalize EPI in working procedures), we still await a concerted response from the Parliament.

This is not to say that the Parliament has done nothing whatsoever to promote EU-EPI. There were at least two prominent examples during the 1990s when it actively supported greater EPI. The first was connected to the integration of environmental aspects into the 1993 and 1999 regulations specifying the operation of the Structural Funds (Lenschow 1999). Here, the Parliament supported the idea that the regional development programmes should undergo an environmental impact assessment. In each successive regulatory reform during the last fifteen years, the role of environment and sustainable development was strengthened, and always with the active support of the Parliament.

The second was the introduction of a new requirement to subject Trans-European Network projects to a strategic environmental assessment. In 1996, the European Parliament used its co-decisionmaking power to help a network of environmentally minded actors green the EU's transport policy

(Hey 1998: 256). Interestingly, Hey argues that the same coalition made a lot less progress in areas such as taxation, agriculture, and fisheries, where the Parliament enjoys much less formal power.

The Parliament's EPI system

There is no formal EPI system in the Parliament as such. For example, the environment committee does not formally appraise Commission proposals, or routinely subject its own legislative amendments to an appraisal, although on occasions it does ask the EEA for technical advice. The Committee's secretariat has no internal capacity to monitor other policy sectors (i.e. a *liason role*). The monthly meetings of the heads of division provide one opportunity to flag any horizontal issues to the relevant committees. The officials in the secretariat also have informal contacts with several Commission DGs such as environment, enterprise, transport, and energy. Other sources of information also serve as an informal early warning system. Thus individual members of the Environment Committee are very often tipped off by NGOs about the potential impacts of a particular dossier which may still be in the Commission phase.

EU-EPI can also be facilitated if and when a particular committee member influences the work of another committee via their colleagues of the same political group or nationality. A case in point was the coordination between the energy and environment committees on a proposal to promote electricity from renewable energy (adopted by the Council in September 2001). Here, cross-sector and multilevel coordination was facilitated because the German *rapporteur* (Mechthild Rothe) enjoyed good contacts with members of the environment committee, several national environment departments, and MEPs. At the time, Ms Rothe was a member of a network which supported renewable energies (Eurosolar). Crucially, it was these informal relationships that most strongly facilitated coordination, not the more institutionalized *bureaucratic procedure* of offering committee opinions (see Chapter 4). This example nicely illustrates the potential for vertical alliances to be built between member states, national parliaments, and the European Parliament. However, currently, these are almost entirely dependent upon the personalities involved. When and where these informal contacts are absent, the system's potential for achieving greater coordination is surprisingly weak.

Conclusions

The Parliament has adopted several resolutions in which it urges the Council to do more to implement EU-EPI. It has also repeated its plea for a new interinstitutional arrangement to resolve questions relating to EU-EPI and sustainable development. However, it has not yet revised its own organizational structures to facilitate EU-EPI. When it comes to daily policymaking, the Parliament's capacity to push for EU-EPI largely depends upon its traditional, regulatory-based powers (e.g. co-decisionmaking). But these are, in turn, vested in sectoral committees, as opposed to some central coordinating body. Overall, the working style of the Parliament is very fragmented and intercommittee coordination is poor. As information is transferred in a very passive manner (see Chapter 4), the day-to-day pursuit of EU-EPI is heavily reliant on a particular committee or MEP taking a close interest in the work of another. This form of coordination is, of course, very unreliable in a world of multiple objectives and rapidly changing political agendas.

Conclusions

Looking across the five actors, there are obvious similarities in the way they have responded to the challenge of EPI (Table 5.6). First, in terms of timing, a broadly synchronous pattern of change is apparent. In the 1970s, all five created new environmental administrations to develop higher environmental standards in their respective institutional contexts. The most common coordination mechanism employed was hierarchical—that is, the production of environmental legislation. However, at least two (the UK and the Netherlands) sought to integrate policymaking by fusing environmental departments with sectoral functions such as housing and local finance, to create 'integrated' environmental departments. Germany later attempted the same thing. However, 'building big' failed to tame the sectors. This was because the integrated departments were all set up as typical divisionalized organizations with a decentralized responsibility for managing different sectors of environment policy. Horizontal coordination is, as we explained in Chapter 2, notoriously difficult to achieve in such settings. Meanwhile, sectoral policies continued to fall under the control of sectoral departments and the degree of horizontal environmental integration remained low.

In the 1980s, appreciation grew of the need to integrate environment much more consistently into the work of the sectoral departments. At this

Table 5.6 EPI initiatives taken by the five actors: a comparison

	Germany	Netherlands	UK	European Commission	European Parliament
Is there a cross-sectoral organization?	No, the environment department is primarily environmental	No, but the environment department does cover urban issues and housing	Yes, the environment department has covered (at various times) transport and agriculture	No, the environment department is primarily environmental	No, but the environment committee does cover public health and consumer policy
When was an environment department created?	1986	1982	1970	1981	1972
Are there long-term sustainability targets?	Yes, some set for energy, agriculture, and taxation	Yes, in the NEPPs	Not yet—but they were promised in 1999	Yes—in the EAPs/SDS	No
Is there an explicit EPI system?	Yes, from 1998	Yes, from 1989	Yes, from 1990	Yes, from 1993	No
Is there a formal appraisal system covering policies?	No	Yes (1995–), but poorly implemented	Yes (1990–), but poorly implemented	Yes (1993–), but poorly implemented. Relaunched in 2002	No
Summary	Attempting to integrate, but the 'regulatory' approach dominates	Strong advocate of EPI through long-term societal planning	Highly sophisticated national EPI system, but of questionable effectiveness	Novel EPI system, but lacks the support of sectoral DGs in the Commission	Intermittent but effective champion of EPI; its power is strongest in the later stages of the EU policy process

Source: Based on text and Jacob and Volkery (2004)

time, the three states and the Commission began to develop integration strategies, which (in the case of the Netherlands and (to a lesser extent) the Commission) embodied more specific long-term targets (*specification of output*). Over time, these have gradually evolved into overarching sustainable development strategies. Finally, in the 1990s, all the actors (with the sole exception of the Parliament) attempted to strengthen the operation of their EPI systems by creating new coordination capacities, such as green cabinets (*teams*) and environmental policy appraisal regimes (*bureaucratic procedures*). So far, these have not produced the coordinated outcomes that many environmentalists hoped for. Of the actors that have most stringently applied environmental policy appraisal (i.e. the Commission, the Netherlands, and the UK), it has not proven to be the panacea that many expected, hence the growing interest in ever more integrated forms of appraisal (e.g. in the UK and the Commission).

The second striking similarity is that although four of the actors have developed quite complex EPI systems on paper and some have set long-term EPI targets, the new administrative resources that have been invested to support and sustain these activities is actually quite limited. For example, a great deal is expected of policy appraisal in the UK, the Commission, and the Netherlands, but only the latter has actually created new administrative capacities (i.e. a help desk) to support it. Significantly, very few sector officials have the training, the administrative support, or the political incentives to use appraisal to pursue EPI.

There are, however, also significant differences in the way the five actors have responded. Just as there is no secular convergence towards a common approach to coordinating EU policy (see Chapter 4), the five actors do not appear to be converging upon a common system of EPI. On the contrary, each actor appears to be following a strikingly different pathway that reflects its own cultural and political make-up. For example, the UK's EPI system has been grafted onto its strong and internally well-coordinated system of central government. In general, it amounts to a relatively bottom-up approach to achieving EPI which seeks to move step-wise up the coordination scale (i.e. from Level 1 to 9). The UK system is also relatively closed; that is, there are relatively few opportunities for civil society to become involved. By contrast, the Dutch approach follows the consensual national policy style of bringing different stakeholders together to agree long-term plans (NEPPs) incorporating specific targets. New coordinating capacities have been created (the environmental appraisal and the help desk, etc.), to ensure that daily policymaking supports the achievement of these targets. Germany on the other hand is, like the EU, struggling to move away from a highly regulatory past (Wurzel et al. 2003) and develop new integration strategies and targets. But like the EU (see Chapter 3), it is pursuing this in a very top-down manner (i.e. jumping straight to Levels 8 or 9 on the coordination scale), with few new administrative coordination capacities to build coordination from the bottom (i.e. moving upwards from Level 1 on the scale). Although we will analyse these differences in much more detail in the next five chapters, it is already apparent that each actor relies on a different combination of the six coordination capacities identified in Chapter 2. These differences are summarized in Table 5.7.

Table 5.7 EPI coordination capacities in the five actors

	Germany	Netherlands	UK	European Commission	European Parliament
Hierarchical	Yes: a green cabinet committee	No	Yes: a green cabinet committee	No	No
Bureaucratic	No	Yes, environmental policy appraisal	Yes, environmental policy appraisal	Yes, environmental policy appraisal	No
Skills/training	No	Yes, on environmental policy appraisal	Yes, on environmental policy appraisal	Yes, on environmental policy appraisal	No
Specification of output	Yes	Yes	No	No	No
a. Targets	Yes	Yes	No	Yes	No
b. Tasks	Yes (to implement sectoral strategies)	Yes	Yes (to produce sectoral strategies)	No	No
Horizontal coordination mechanisms	Yes	No	Yes	No	No
a. Informal relations	Yes	Yes	Yes	Yes	Yes
b. Liaison roles	Yes	No	Yes	Yes	No
c. Task forces	No	No	No	No	No
d. Teams	No	No	Yes	No	No
e. Weak integrating role	No	No	Yes	Yes	No
f. Strong integrating role	No	No	Yes	No	No
Mission statements	No	No	Yes	No	No

Source: Based on text and Jacob and Volkery (2004)

In conclusion, in the last ten years in particular, all five actors have, to varying extents, made a serious effort to coordinate better their own internal activities in pursuit of EPI. As many EPI-related activities fall within the formal competence of the member states (Chapter 1), it is important to ensure they are sufficiently well organized to work with other states and the EU on cross-cutting issues. However, in spite of all these efforts, the EPI systems in all five actors suffer from a number of serious weaknesses. More worryingly, these five were deliberately selected as pioneering states (Chapter 1), but at least one of them (the Parliament) has still not taken steps to reorganize internally. In spite of the European Commission's plea for a multilevel approach (see the epigram at the start of this chapter), what is already striking about all five is that European coordination and EPI (the first and second parts of the 'double challenge') are treated as separate rather than interconnected challenges. In the three states, the EU-coordinating units are the natural focal point for organizing cross-sectoral coordination, but in practice they tend to focus on coordinating *environmental* work destined for the Environment Council, not EPI. Meanwhile, national EPI systems tend to be focused on national policies, rather than sectoral policies created by the EU. Furthermore, the EU-coordinating units in the environment departments are already far too overloaded with environmental policy work, to start interfering in the work of the sectors, either nationally or in the EU. In the next five chapters we analyse more fully each actor's individual contribution to the development and functioning of an EU-EPI coordinating network, starting with Germany.

Notes

1. §43 also states that the responsible department should explain how far the proposed legal act corresponds with EU law, hence the name Law Impact Assessment (GFA) (see also Jacob and Volkery 2006).
2. The details were presented in an *internal* Commission Communication entitled 'Integration by the Commission of the Environment into other Policies' (CEC 1993: 5).
3. It was originally intended to be a system of sustainability impact appraisal (SIA) (see the Conclusions of the 2001 Gothenburg summit), but the 'S' was dropped during inter-DG discussions.
4. A resolution is a policy statement, which may or may not be taken seriously by the bodies to which it is addressed (i.e. the Council, Commission, or European Council).

5. According to Maurer (2002: 61), after the environment committee, the other committees which have significant co-decision powers are: economy (17 per cent), legal affairs (15 per cent), transport (9.5 per cent), research (7.2 per cent), and education and culture (6.6 per cent).

Part III

Member States

6

GERMANY: A REACTIVE AND PASSIVE COORDINATOR?

We often go to Environment Council working groups with an entire football team. Other departments seem to have enough capacities to monitor our work in Brussels. We cannot . . . do that to other Councils, so we lose out.

(An official from the German environment department)

Introduction

Germany presents a rather curious case study of how different actors in the EU are adjusting to the multi-actor, multilevel challenge of EU-EPI. On the one hand it is often described as a paragon of environmental virtue—an environmental 'pioneer' or 'front runner' in the development of EU environmental policies (Pehle 1997a; Pehle and Jansen 1998; Wurzel 2004a). On the other hand, often it is described as one of the least coordinated member states (Metcalfe 1994), which relies heavily on what we term *bureaucratic politics*. The German system is often criticized for not only being highly fragmented (Siwert-Probst 1998), but also conducive to a form of 'institutional cannibalism' in which different line departments fight hard with one another for influence (quoted in Maurer 2003: 119). That said, the dominance of one type of coordination capacity—*bureaucratic politics*—does offer ample opportunities for cross-sectoral coordination when other departments have the lead. Some have even argued that bureaucratic politics is the *only* way to coordinate in complex and dynamic situations (e.g. Palumbo 1975; Chisholm 1989). Derlien (2000) and Maurer (2003), for example, appear to take a similarly positive view, praising the flexibility and openness of Germany's coordination mechanisms. Having noted these apparently conflicting views, what does a detailed empirical analysis of Germany's management of complex, horizontal policy objectives such as EU-EPI reveal about its overall capacity for coordination? In short is the German system fit for purpose?

The links between national and EU-EPI

Advocating EPI in the EU

Germany has not done as much as the UK and the Netherlands to advocate EPI at EU level (see Chapters 4 and 5). Until recently, Germany had neither an environment plan nor much experience with environmental planning. Nevertheless, in 1997 Germany played an important part in strengthening Article 6 of the Amsterdam Treaty. At the time, the departments of environment and economic affairs reached an early agreement on a positive German position (Unfried 2004). According to officials from the environment sector, Germany regarded Article 6 as a major chance to improve the position of environmental interests while maintaining a level playing field (Unfried 2000; 2004).

After the change of government in 1998, more support for the integration principle was expected from the German government. In December 1998, the then environment minister, Jürgen Trittin, announced that EPI would be one of the priorities of the upcoming German Presidency. In concrete terms, the German Presidency in 1999 duly organized a workshop in Bonn to discuss the administrative aspects of EPI. A study (which described the EPI mechanisms in different EU and non-EU states) was commissioned (Ecologic 1999), to aid lesson drawing, very much in the spirit of the open method of coordination (OMC). Crucially, the workshop was supposed to start the process of creating a network comprising the European coordinating units within the national environment departments. This did not quite work out as hoped; in practice, the network (see Chapter 3) discusses issues related to the work of the Environment Council, and only then depending on the lead shown by the Presidency. Overall, however, the German Presidency's record on EU-EPI was rather modest (Wurzel 2001). The Cardiff process was extended by adding a third wave of sectors (see Chapter 3), but the European Council did not take any major new strategic initiatives. Crucially, the ongoing work of the first two waves was not invigorated in the run-up to the Helsinki Council in 1999.

The environment department tried to take another step forward in March 2001 when it co-organized another workshop with the UK and Austria on the quality of the sector council strategies (see Chapter 3). However, this did not lead to a searching discussion of the sustainability of sector policies in Germany. The national and EU-EPI systems thus continued to plough different furrows. The German departments were not, for example, obliged to develop comprehensive environmental policy integration strategies with clear timetables and indicators (cf. the Dutch environmental action plan). According to officials that we interviewed in different German departments, the Cardiff process has not heightened awareness of environment issues (Unfried 2004).

To conclude, like the UK and the Netherlands, Germany has advocated EU-EPI by pushing for Article 6 and encouraging a wider debate on the outputs of the Cardiff process. But it has done very little to build a national Cardiff-like process which undertakes sectoral reviews at the national level, let alone align it with the emerging EU-EPI system. In other words, the horizontal links in Germany are weak, but the vertical links to EU-level activities are weak to non-existent.

The practical links between national and EU-EPI

As noted in Chapter 5, there is no environmental policy appraisal system for daily policymaking at the national level. Much, therefore, depends on the extent to which individual departments monitor cognate policy fields. In his study of the German environment department, Pehle (1997*b*: 103) discovered that the sector departments have invested more resources in trying to keep an eye on the environment department's activities than vice versa (see also Unfried 2000). This also affects the scrutiny of EU policies. This is partly due to the internal fragmentation in the environment department, which makes it very hard to understand which line units are relevant to which Councils. The new EPI measures in Germany (i.e. the green cabinet and the Council for Sustainable Development—see Chapter 4) have had very little impact on the environmental scrutiny of new EU proposals. Although these new bodies have helped to institution-alize thinking about EPI and sustainable development in national government, they have a questionable relevance to EU-EPI.

As a result, the practical link between national and EU-EPI depends mainly on the horizontal coordination of EU dossiers. For this purpose, it is the combined responsibility of the departments of foreign affairs and finance to look forward. But as discussed in Chapter 4, this ambition hardly lives up to its potential. Domestic coordination has normally barely begun at the point when most Commission proposals are sent to the Council. At this stage there is normally no review committee. The obligation to send an official position to the Bundestag is often treated more as an aspiration than as a formal requirement. According to the official manual of distribution (*Geschäftsverteilungsplan*), the department of finance must send new EU proposals to the lead department and any others which may have an interest. Hence, discussions are left to the normal arena of intra- and interdepartmental conflict. This makes discussions dependent on the initiatives taken by the lead department (note the influence of passive information).

The coordination of EU environmental policy in the environment sector is done by the European affairs unit and by two attachés in the German Permanent Representation. The European Affairs unit (which is part of the Directorate for International Cooperation) has one unit head and two desk officers, with some support staff. It is primarily responsible for:

- Information gathering and dissemination to the line units in the environment department;
- Strategic planning of the departments involvement in EU policymaking;
- Preparing for the Environment Council;
- Giving advice on infringement procedures/implementation problems;
- A multitude of horizontal dossiers (e.g. the Cardiff strategies, liaising with the EEA, intergovernmental conferences, etc.).

Given its size, it cannot devote much time to national or to EU-EPI. Therefore, it is primarily up to the line units in the environment department—rather than the EU coordinators—to be alert and ready to search for opportunities to influence sectoral EU policies. However, the line units are hamstrung by a lack of information (again, note the disruptive influence of passive information), and in any case their focus tends to be on their primary objective (i.e. national environment policy), not EU-EPI, let alone other departments' EU policies.

In addition to this EU unit, there are monitoring units (for Mintzberg, *liason roles*) in the departments of agriculture, economy, energy, and transport. These have experts to monitor their relevant Councils. However, these units are very small and have very little time to monitor EU affairs in these areas. The exceptions are the climate change-related units—such as energy—which have devoted more staff members to monitoring. Various suggestions for improving coordination have been discussed within the environment department, for example through task forces, but with little effect thus far.

Finally, as discussed in Chapter 5, the German Permanent Representation is a potentially important player in the case of environmental proposals especially with regards to its role in screening future policy agendas. However, it cannot be relied upon to push EPI at EU level. The environment attachés' primary focus is on dossiers destined for the Environment Council. They do not see it as their job to liaise with other policy areas.

The national coordination of EU-EPI

Our assessment of the level of coordination achieved by the German system at the various stages of the policy process is summarized in Table 6.1.

Initiation

INTERDEPARTMENTAL COORDINATION

From the very first phase, German coordination suffers from the conflict between the general expectation to coordinate (Derlien 2000) and the principle of departmental autonomy. The EU Manual of the German Government is very brief on the very early phases of policymaking (*Bundesministerium de Finanzen* 2004). It indicates that the different departments are responsible for the contacts with the Commission in all the phases before the proposal is presented, but there is no further explanation as to what this might entail (hence, even the achievement of Level 2 is uncertain). It is up to the lead department to decide when to start to coordinate (note the pronounced lack of *bureaucratic procedures*). The department of foreign affairs is supposed to have organized the forward planning process, including early developments in the initiation phase, within the different coordination fora. The 'early warning report' of the Permanent Representation also focuses on dossiers in the Council phase. All in all, the typical routine of event coordination predominates in practice. In particular, the coordination of the COREPER instruction meeting normally focuses on dossiers in the Council phase. Whatever coordination takes place in the early Commission phase is entirely dependent on informal cooperation and the willingness of the lead department to involve others. This passive event coordination is not a sturdy basis for

Table 6.1. Germany: levels of inter-departmental EU policy coordination

	Commission phases						Council phases				
	Initiation of new proposals	Work plans	White & Green papers	Drafting of proposals	Inter-service consultation	Presentation of proposals	Presidency agenda	Working parties	COREPER	Council	Conciliation
Coordination level											
9 Strategy											
8 Margins											
7 Arbitration										+/–	
6 Conciliation									+/–	+/–	
5 Consensus								+/–	+/–	+/–	+/–
4 One voice			+/–			+/–		+/–	+/–	+/–	+/–
3 Consultation			+	+/–		+		+/–	+	+	+
2 Communication			+	+/–		+	+	+	+	+	+
1 Independent policy making	+	+	+	+	N/a	+	+	+	+	+	+

	Initiation of new proposals	Work plans	White & Green papers	Drafting of proposals	Inter-service consultation	Presentation of proposals	Presidency agenda	Working parties	COREPER	Council	Conciliation
Coordination capacities											
Hierarchical											
Bureaucratic		+	+			+		+/–	+	+	+/–
Specification of output											
Horizontal											
Informal relations	+/–			+/–				+			
Liaison roles			+	+/–		+	+/–	+/–	+	+	
Task forces			+			+/–		+/–	+	+	
Teams						+		+	+	+	
Weak integrator						+		+	+	+	
Strong integrator								+	+	+	
Mission statements											
Role of the EU coordinating units	Deals with horizontal dossiers (e.g. Cardiff, SDS)										+/–

Explanation:

+ = coordination capacity at this level exists and is used.

+/– = the coordination capacity at this level exists to some extent, but may not always be used.

(+/–) = the coordination capacity at this level exists, but is only used in exceptional cases.

building sustained coordination (cf. Ostrom's preconditions for voluntary coordination in Chapter 2).

INTRADEPARTMENTAL COORDINATION IN THE ENVIRONMENT DEPARTMENT

In the absence of sound interdepartmental capacities, the *liason roles* in the sectors are important to consider. However, these are too small and fragmented to monitor the relevant sectors, or to pick up information on initiatives in the Commission or other member states. They hardly have time to conduct a simple screening of topics in this early phase. Due to the often highly competitive nature of interdepartmental coordination, environment officials cannot expect colleagues from cognate departments to inform them about the EPI dimensions of each and every dossier. Hence, the environment department's involvement is normally delayed until the Council phase. This is not such a problem for the more prominent and most obviously environmental initiatives in the sectors where the alarm bells are ringing very early, and intradepartmental coordination between the unit of EU and the expert unit is possible. But many dossiers in agriculture, transport, or energy have environmental implications which are less obvious. When external political interest (particularly by pressure groups and parliamentarians) is lower, the alarm bells do not ring and important opportunities to pursue EU-EPI are easily lost.

Commission workplanning

INTERDEPARTMENTAL COORDINATION

One recent innovation has been the introduction of 'early warning reports' written by the German permanent representation. These are discussed three times a year by the Group of Departmental Director Generals for EU affairs. These reports, however, are more focused on the later Council phase, with respect to possible conflicts between member states and between departments. As regards the Commission's workplan, this material is passed routinely across by the department of foreign affairs using the normal information channels (i.e. there is a *bureaucratic procedure*). However, it does not appear to have much of a bearing on the eventual shape of policy outputs.

INTRADEPARTMENTAL POLICY COORDINATION IN THE ENVIRONMENT DEPARTMENT

The workplan is mainly used by the EU-coordination unit as a source of information with respect to the environment field. Whether the workplan of other DGs is monitored within the national environment department depends on its monitoring and expert units. In general, officials normally know about the workplan, but the focus in mainly on DG Environment (i.e. leaving coordination at Level 1 on the scale). There is no procedure to undertake a comprehensive screening of other policy sectors. It is up to the monitoring units to evaluate the work programmes, for which they hardly ever have the time.

White/Green Papers and Communications

INTERDEPARTMENTAL POLICY COORDINATION

White and Green papers are treated in much the same way as Commission proposals. Therefore, the standard but simple *bureaucratic procedures* (i.e. to inform the Bundestag (parliament) and the Bundesrat (regional chamber)) have to be followed. Coordination of the national position is organized by the lead department, in cooperation with departments that have interests at stake. This is usually a first and superficial position mainly aimed at Level 4. Due to the sectorization of the EU system, the lead department has an advantage because it will normally have already had ample contacts with the lead DG in the Commission. The asymmetric power relations appeared, for example, in the case of the White Papers on chemicals (in which the department of economic affairs played a very active role) and on energy security (where the monitoring unit responsible for energy policy within the environment department was little more than a bystander).

INTRADEPARTMENTAL COORDINATION IN THE ENVIRONMENT DEPARTMENT

White Papers and, to a lesser extent, Green Papers are prominent dossiers at the EU level. Therefore the EU unit and the respective expert units follow events carefully when they concern environmental matters, but pay much less attention to documents in other policy fields. Even the energy monitoring unit in the environment department—which is comparatively big—reports that there is hardly enough time or resources for this sort of horizontal task.

This is not simply a problem of ownership, since the officials in the environment department do feel responsible. Neither do they naively assume that the environmental dimension of the dossier will be adequately taken into account by other departments. This is strikingly different to the UK and the Netherlands, where environment officials emphasized that the other departments should 'own' environmental objectives. Apparently, the German environment officials are much less inhibited about publicly stating their mistrust of colleagues than their opposite numbers in the other two states. Clearly, they are suffering from the perverse effects of passive information.

Drafting of proposals (expert meetings)

INTERDEPARTMENTAL POLICY COORDINATION

This phase is not formally coordinated, but when working relations are cooperative, officials may try to consult one another. The extent to which this happens in practice, however, varies enormously. Attempting to speak with one voice (Level 4) is just as possible as no coordination at all—depending on the desk officer and on the interests of the environment official. In the more openly political cases, the relevant unit in the environment department will monitor this phase (i.e. they have a *liaison role*).

The invitation to send experts can often be made quite informally by the Commission. This makes it exceedingly difficult for the environment department to monitor the work of national experts. The culture of passive information means that a member of a Commission working group only spreads information if he or she thinks there is an urgent need to do so, or when a cognate sector specifically asks for details. Even when the environment department is aware of EU-level activities, it requires a lot of work to exert influence at this stage. The desk official certainly has to be confident enough as well as have the internal support to pick up an issue or to involve the Chancellary, let alone to write letters to the Commissioners. One example where this did occur was in relation to the environmental guidelines for state aid (2001). In the negotiation process with the Commission, DG Environment gained the lead instead of finance or economic affairs. Although this was an exception, it does illustrate the opportunities that can flow from knowing about (and possibly even influencing) the EU policy process before the Commission takes an internal decision.

INTRADEPARTMENTAL COORDINATION IN THE ENVIRONMENT DEPARTMENT

The EU unit does not scrutinize the expert committees in the sectors. The information flow goes not via the EU unit, but by informal contacts between the expert units in different departments. Monitoring interservice negotiations in the Commission is an extra task that the environment department's expert units do not regard as a high priority.

Interservice consultation within the Commission

INTERDEPARTMENTAL COORDINATION

This phase is characterized by virtually no coordination (i.e. Level 1 on the scale). Lobbying activities are normally undertaken by the lead department. The non-circulation of information is by no means exceptional. If disputes on a dossier in the Commission phases are crucial and not solved, it is hardly possible to change the lobbying efforts of another national department. In order to respect the rules of procedure of the federal government, the onus should fall on the lead and not a cognate department, thus limiting the environment department's scope for advancing EPI. Hence, the environment department is normally very careful about lobbying individual Commissioners in others sectors. On the other hand, there have been environmental dossiers where sector ministers directly lobbied the Commission by sending letters. Existing studies have shown how diverse the positions adopted by German federal departments in the EU can be (Deubner and Huppertz 2003: 32).

INTRADEPARTMENTAL COORDINATION IN THE ENVIRONMENT DEPARTMENT

This step is hardly monitored by the department. We know of no attempts, such as existed in the Dutch environment department, to secure a better overview of the agenda of the meetings of the College (cf. Chapter 7).

Presentation of proposals

INTERDEPARTMENTAL COORDINATION

The presentation of a proposal triggers a structured procedure within the German government through which the Bundestag and the Bundesrat are informed about the national position to be taken. There are also procedures with respect to the evaluation of the subsidiarity principle and any financial implications, which are laid down in the rules of procedures of the government (*Gemeinsame Geschäftsordnung*, Articles 70 and 85). As indicated in Chapter 5, there is no environmental policy appraisal applied to Commission proposals; this is viewed as the Commission's responsibility. It is the lead department's task to coordinate the dossier with the relevant departments when preparing the first position for the German Bundestag. This requires a written statement according to a given time-frame (normally five working days of the Bundestag).

However, the system is not required to go beyond Level 4. As there is rarely any systematic assessment of new proposals from different sectors in one interdepartmental working group, the coordination system struggles to achieve early agreement. It may be simpler for all concerned to delay the (dis-)agreement until the COREPER stage. The low level of coordination achieved at this phase corresponds to the rather weak involvement of national parliament in EU affairs (Unfried 2004). As there is no need for the government to get a formal mandate from the Bundestag for the positions it takes in the Council, there is little pressure to agree a cross-government position.

INTRADEPARTMENTAL COORDINATION IN THE ENVIRONMENT DEPARTMENT

According to formal distribution of tasks in the department (*Geschäftsver-teilungsplan*), a specific unit normally gets the lead on a dossier. However, there is no discussion about items that span two or more Councils. Much, therefore, depends on the willingness of the lead department to involve the environment department. This will usually not be a problem when it concerns major and clear issues (as in the case of green taxes or environmental aid guidelines). But more technical dossiers (e.g. in the field of agriculture) where the environmental dimension is less obvious, have tended to escape the notice of environment officials.

The Presidency agenda

INTERDEPARTMENTAL COORDINATION

In 2000, the group of the EU division heads was given a new role of screening, among others, the Presidency agenda. Nevertheless, the Presidency agenda still has no special priority. Insofar as coordination occurs, it is only limited to information exchange (Level 2 on the coordination scale). The new early warning reports have only highlighted key dossiers on the Presidency agenda. According to several officials, the early warning reporting system needs to be better utilized at interdepartmental level and within individual departments.

INTRADEPARTMENTAL COORDINATION IN THE ENVIRONMENT DEPARTMENT

The EU coordination unit focuses most of its energies on the Environment Council. This is usually accompanied by informal contacts with its opposite numbers in the other member states. Contacts with the new Presidency are very important to get first-hand information on its priorities and objectives. However, at the moment, this is mainly seen as an opportunity to improve the early coordination of dossiers destined for the Environment Council, *not* to promote EU-EPI.

Monitoring the Presidency agenda in other policy sectors has to be done by the environment department's monitoring units. Thus, there is no systematic *liaison role* during this phase. In our interviews, officials from the line units said they regarded monitoring as the EU-coordination unit's job.

Council working party negotiations

INTERDEPARTMENTAL COORDINATION

The coordination during the Commission phase barely reaches beyond Level 3. During the negotiations in the Council working groups, coordination varies considerably. In order to maintain a sense of harmony, departments will often try to find a consensus (Level 5) to prevent problems appearing at later stages. There are some general rules that lay down the obligation to coordinate, but as noted above, these conflict with the tradition of departmental autonomy. However, there are also strong incentives to search for agreement, as the same officials will often be involved in continuous and ongoing rounds of EU policymaking. The willingness to consult or achieve consensus is often determined by the nature of the individuals involved.

Coordination may include mediation in the layers of *teams* described in Chapter 4 (e.g. in the two-weekly meeting of the heads of division). Conflicts among departments are addressed bilaterally, without involving the interdepartmental EU-coordination mechanism (except in the major controversial cases where even the Chancellery can be involved; see

Derlien 2000). Again, the quality of the interdepartmental information flow is very much dependent on the personal contacts made by the sector officials involved. It is always possible for an official to gain information by requesting his or her own minister to intervene, but this requires a lot of effort for an uncertain outcome, and is therefore only used *in extremis*. Therefore, the overall position of the government on dossiers often remains unsettled for a very long time; it can even change drastically in the endgame of an EU negotiation. This was also clear from our interviews with officials from other member states who explained that if there is no coherent German position, they take what the German officials are saying with a large pinch of salt.

In addition to this bilateral exchange, there is the layered system of meetings of division heads, secretaries of state, and cabinet (i.e. *teams*), in which the departments of foreign affairs and finance act as *integrators*. These are, however, likely to suffer from the collective decisionmaking trap that characterizes German interdepartmental relations (Deubner and Huppertz 2003: 25–7). Finding consensus is therefore usually postponed until the Council phases. The more controversial dossiers can easily suffer from *bureaucratic politics*, in which case information and coordination tend to be used in a strategic rather than a collegial way. The extent to which this occurs also depends on the personal chemistry between the respective ministers, which is not a sturdy basis for coordination.

The coordination during this phase is also shaped by the size of the monitoring units (*liason roles*). Clearly, larger and better resourced departments tend to do better in this respect than smaller ones like environment. According to environmental officials, the finance and economic affairs departments have the resources to attend the environment working group meetings in Brussels (*watchdogs*). The environment department is less endowed and lacks similar *liaison roles* to participate frequently in the working parties attached to other Councils.

INTRADEPARTMENTAL COORDINATION IN THE ENVIRONMENT DEPARTMENT

A lot of effort is normally required to make sure that officials from other departments are aware of the environment department's position and that they stick to any coordinated positions in Brussels. The lack of coordination capacities to monitor this phase (exacerbated by the incentives *not* to coordinate), make it difficult for the EU affairs unit to stimulate environment officials to be involved. In fact, the climate of mistrust between departments is sometimes so bad that environment officials have no other option but to make direct contacts with sector officials in the Commission's DGs and in other member states to push EU-EPI.

The working party phase is crucial in the formulation of new policies. As Table 6.1 (the 'input' side) shows, the German coordination capacities are considerable. However, the *teams, integrating roles,* and *bureaucratic politics* are not sufficiently strong coordinating capacities to generate consensus. Remaining informed of the negotiations, having *ex ante* influence, and monitoring results from meetings in Brussels, are all very time consuming. The inefficiency of the system leaves environment officials with little alternative but to monitor the lead department every step of the way. In other words, seen from the perspective of a department (like environment) with a horizontal responsibility, the system may offer ample opportunities to exert influence, but the transaction costs (information costs, ensuring influence, etc.) are normally prohibitively high due to the prevalence of passive information.

COREPER

INTERDEPARTMENTAL COORDINATION

This is the central coordinating point in the system. This meeting is supposed to be a forum to exchange views on dossiers in the pipeline and identify emerging conflicts at the interdepartmental level (*Bundesministerium der Finanzen* 2004). The responsibility for the instruction lies with the lead department, which is obliged to coordinate the content with the others involved. The ambition is to reach at least Level 5. There is a special form (i.e. a *bureaucratic procedure*), which has to be used. There is a special COREPER instruction meeting every Tuesday morning, where the EU coordinators of all departments feed their instructions into a common list for the COREPER meeting the following day (Wednesday). Finance and foreign affairs departments act as *integrators* in this *team* meeting. This meeting is also the place to mediate (Level 6). Even though this happens very often, the mediating capacities of the two coordinating departments are debatable; in fact, the lead department can often delay mediation as much as it wants. Moreover, in case of lasting differences—and because of the limited arbitration rights of the Chancellery—it is possible that problems are not solved at all, leading to either a silence from the German delegation in the COREPER or the German Ambassador stepping in at the last minute to hammer out a consensus.

There are a number of problems associated with this *team*. First of all, the meeting is overburdened with all the technical details that were bottled up at previous phases. These overload the agenda and make the whole system slow, inefficient, and reactive. The changes in 2000 were supposed to allow more strategies and earlier discussions about agendas and thus identify potential problems. Most officials, however, feel that the discussions are still technical and that the meeting is not sufficiently forward-looking. Second, in view of the strong position of departments, the coordinating departments for COREPER I items (i.e. financial or foreign affairs) are *weak integrators* that can do little more than act as chairs. If a problem is not solved bilaterally before the meeting, it will normally be translated into a weak COREPER instruction rather than be solved. Only on matters of high political salience (if time limits before COREPER allow) can dossiers be referred to the cabinet (e.g. when Franco-German relations are concerned). Third, it is inherently reactive. Despite the efforts to change the focus of this meeting, it is primarily occupied with reviewing COREPER instructions. A general problem is the lack of *bureaucratic procedures* that force departments to formulate positions earlier in the process. With the lack of power behind the Tuesday meeting—the monthly meeting of the heads is simply too infrequent and hamstrung by excessively strong departments—it is hardly surprising that there are continuing pressures to upgrade its decisionmaking capacity.

INTRADEPARTMENTAL COORDINATION IN THE ENVIRONMENT DEPARTMENT

The lead department will normally inform the relevant unit in environment about the COREPER instruction. If the unit is unhappy, it can deal directly with the lead department; otherwise the EU-affairs unit will have to intervene during the COREPER instruction meeting. If this does not work, the matter may have to be taken to cabinet—but this means that there is no instruction for the next COREPER. In any case, it is often too late at this stage to make fundamental changes to the overall instruction, thereby forcing the minister to get involved (which can only be done in exceptional cases).

Council meetings

In principle, the German cabinet—chaired by the Chancellery—is a *strong integrator* and is thus best placed to settle any remaining difficulties before the Council itself meets. Contending issues normally travel via the meeting of heads of divisions (see Chapter 4) to cabinet. However, during our interviews, this phase was hardly ever mentioned (Unfried 2004). The Chancellery, it seems, is hardly used for mediation at this stage (apart from the most highly politicized issues—see Derlien 2000).

Some officials indicated that the environment minister avoids picking political fights with his or her colleagues before a Council meeting due to the strength of the sector departments. Moreover, the department of foreign affairs struggles to act as a *strong integrator* in the higher team meetings (see above). Instead, civil servants prefer the informal influencing of positions until the last moment, despite the labour intensity required. Initiating a conflict in the highest coordination body (the Group of Secretary of States) is not really regarded as a viable option except in the most exceptional of circumstances. Hence, the system attempts to reach Level 6 but often fails to go beyond Level 4 in view of the information and power imbalances. The Chancellery plays a modest role in EU coordination as it can only mediate—let alone arbitrate—in exceptional cases. As already mentioned, the establishment of a 'green cabinet' (see Chapter 5) under the lead of the Chancellery is unlikely to change this situation dramatically, since it is only focused on national sustainability questions and is not involved in the daily coordination of EU proposals.

Co-decisionmaking and conciliation

The national position with respect to conciliation is formally subject to interdepartmental coordination. Again, the lead department is responsible for this. Our interviews showed that the environment department's EU affairs and monitoring units hardly ever think about the importance of influencing dossiers in cognate policy sectors during this phase. One general problem is the need for flexibility in what are often very fast moving and fluid discussions. But this also means that the German member of the Council delegation cannot undertake a full coordination with other departments when a decision has to be made within the Council group. To some extent, one can therefore speak about coordination up to, but not beyond, Level 2 or 3 (information/consultation). The Council instructions that were agreed in the previous step nowadays act as a sort of *mission statement* for the negotiators, but the extent to which the sectors abide by them can vary considerably. Overall, this phase remains very much in the hands of the lead department.

Improving the German System

The current situation

As discussed in Chapter 1, it is particularly important to ensure that coordination is efficient, proactive, and effective (i.e. leading to solutions). Currently, the German system does not meet these coordination requirements as regards EU-EPI. The defining characteristics of the German system are its openness and the dependence on informal, non-proceduralized relations between individual actors. Coordination greatly depends on the input made by officials in the lead or those who are affected.

Of the five actors studied, Germany is probably the most internally and openly competitive system. The advantages of this reliance on *bureaucratic politics* are not insignificant. The competing interdepartmental relations allow access and—with that—flexibility right up to the final moment. But these strengths are equally also weaknesses, especially if you are not in the lead. They create mistrust and allow departments to play tactical games. More importantly, they impose very high transaction costs on officials that are not in the lead (i.e. environment in the case of many aspects of EU-EPI). Even Level 4 on the coordination scale is difficult to attain. Thus the system is highly ineffective as well as inefficient. Influence comes at a high price. This may not be as problematic in the case of salient political issues (e.g. see recent developments in climate change policy and energy policy). However, it is quite conceivable that with more and more interdependent EU policies, it is less possible—for example—for the environment department to monitor other Councils, let alone routinely influence their activities.

In addition, the German system is reactive and there is only weak support given by interdepartmental coordinating committees. Although consisting of several layers, the various *teams* mainly build on the Tuesday COREPER meetings. In theory, the higher-level *teams* discuss EU policies independent of the policymaking phase. But they meet infrequently and in practice often rely on the material submitted by the unit heads in the COREPER instruction meetings. The departments of foreign affairs and finance chair the *teams*, but they have not been accepted as *strong integrators*. Hence, problem-solving works best in those limited numbers of cases in which the Chancellery steps in or when the heads of the most involved departments make bilateral interventions. However, this makes the system even more cumbersome to operate for the more routine policy proposals.

In the terminology of Chapter 2, Germany therefore relies on passive coordination and is highly event-oriented. This means that problems are not identified at lower levels, but instead are bottled up until the Tuesday COREPER meetings. But at this point the die of most policies is already well on the way to being cast. These inefficiencies put huge burdens on environment officials seeking to pursue EU-EPI. They have to: monitor agendas; prepare for working parties; and throughout, ensure timely feedback. To make matters worse, the environment department's monitoring and EU affairs units are too small to spend much time pursuing EU-EPI. As a result, the extent to which officials are involved in other Councils depends on the time the sector experts invest in them. However, given their workloads and incentive mechanisms, monitoring other departments only happens in major cases.

Options for reform

The main objective of any change package should be to increase the efficiency and effectiveness of coordination. There are several adaptations (related to interdepartmental relations, the role of the apex, and the environment department) that deserve closer scrutiny.

First, in the current set-up, coordination depends heavily on the input from those departments that want to ensure input. Any other structural changes would be hard to implement, so the environment department is the obvious place to start. Enlarging its monitoring capacities is needed to reach the political objectives of EU-EPI. As we will see when discussing the other actors, environment ministers and their staffs are in favour of EPI in general, but they are not keen on becoming involved in the nitty-gritty of the sectoral department's core work.

Second, what is most needed at the interdepartmental level is a switch to a more active form of coordination, by laying (as in the UK) the burden of coordination squarely on the lead department. This presupposes a precise definition of what this would require from the lead department in the various phases of EU decisionmaking (see also the Dutch case in Chapter 7). Without this switch, coordination of a horizontal policy like EU-EPI will be highly inefficient and very laborious for the German environment department.

In addition, interdepartmental coordination now centres on the Tuesday COREPER meeting and is therefore both event-related and reactive (see Chapter 2). Instead, issue coordination is needed to emphasize environment in earlier phases and to settle disputes as and when they arise. Hence, coordination needs to be more strongly attached to arising problems. This in turn requires a stronger emphasis on the Presidency agenda and the heads of unit meeting that is currently very weak (cf. the Grant–Darroch meeting in the UK—see Chapter 8).

Moreover, to give the *team(s)* the power they require to coordinate would require a significantly greater chairing role for the Chancellery. This, however, raises the vexed question of whether and how to involve the highest political level as horizontal interdependence becomes more important (Deubner and Huppertz 2003; Schout 2004). Deubner and Huppertz (2003), for example, argue for a stronger role for the Chancellery, but this is not a simple step for coalition governments to take. However, it remains to be seen whether countries, like Germany, that have coalition governments can continue to operate in this way in a world of growing policy interdependence. One reason for a higher-level involvement is to be able to force a proactive agenda on team meetings and to force cooperation and to arbitrate when problems arise (issue coordination). After all, it is much easier to ignore a colleague than it is to ignore a *primus inter pares*. Moreover, due to its responsibility for collective decisionmaking in cabinet, the Chancellery is able to mediate in the case of protracted disputes.

This package of options is very different from the reforms that Germany has implemented thus far. These include intensifying the existing team meetings by organizing two-monthly meetings of division heads, and holding additional meetings of the EU coordinators better to anticipate new proposals (*Bundesministerium der Finanzen* 2004). In addition, there have been attempts to increase forward-looking capacities within departments and in the German permanent representation. These suggestions have, however, not been very successful, and it is doubtful whether they ever will be. The current system already sucks up the modest resources which the environment department has invested in coordination. The new reforms risk making coordination even more, not less, demanding and inefficient, as more and more time risks being spent in unproductive coordination meetings that do not have the capacity to arrive at coordinated solutions. This is because these suggestions fail to tame the *bureaucratic politics*. Most importantly, the proposed changes would leave the workload of coordination squarely on the shoulders of the departments that are not in the lead. With horizontal policy interdependence increasing, this seems a very inefficient and outdated way to organize EU affairs.

Conclusions

Germany's support for EPI in EU policies is very clear. Despite sidelining the environment department and favouring industry interests in recent debates (e.g. on the new chemicals policy), the German government is generally still committed to stronger environmental measures (Wurzel 2004a). This support can be seen in relation to renewable energies, green taxes, and environmental guidelines for state aid. However, the coordination capacities to push EPI in daily policymaking within the EU remains relatively weak. There is, as yet, still no national environmental policy appraisal system that can be linked to EU policy processes, and the recent creations of the green cabinet and the Council for Sustainable Development have almost no influence upon Germany's ability to support EPI in day-to-day EU policymaking. Germany does not even appear to have recognized (unlike the UK and the Netherlands) that EU-EPI requires sufficient coordination capacities to be in place *nationally* as well as in the EU. In 2002, the re-elected green minister, Jürgen Trittin, believed his top priority was to wrest the competence for renewable energies from the department of economic affairs. However, adapting his own department to the needs of EU-EPI was not high on his agenda.

In fact, there is not even much to report in terms of developing new coordination capacities for EU policy coordination more generally. Passive information and a lack of mediation and arbitration powers make it difficult for environmental interests—supported by the national environment department—to be adequately integrated into EU negotiating positions. Consequently, coordination remains highly labour-intensive. If (and *only* if) sufficient effort is put into monitoring each and every phase, the system is capable of being open and flexible. But only the most well-resourced departments will benefit from this. The inefficiency and the reactive nature of the German system make our assessment of the capacities needed for EPI much less sanguine than those of Derlien (2000) and Maurer (2003), who conclude that politically important topics are normally well coordinated. EPI requires an across-the-board efficiency that is alien to the German system.

That said, these deficiencies in internal coordination work both ways. That is, they support the environment department (and hence EPI) with respect to the development of new EU dossiers in its own domain (this being a feature of German environmental policymaking in the EU that does not receive the recognition that it perhaps deserves). However, sector departments are better resourced to defend their interests in interdepartmental battles. One explanation for this is that they have fewer areas to monitor so their resources are spread less thinly (see the reference to football teams at the start of this chapter). Because of the lack of early and reliable common positions on dossiers (in the Commission and Council phases), the administrative burden on departments that do not have the lead (i.e. environment in relation to many aspects of EU-EPI) is large. The German environment department also lacks the efficiency of the UK system with more open information flows, active information, and earlier conflict-solving. Therefore, the German system works to the advantage of bigger departments such as economic affairs or finance that have the resources to police the work of cognate departments by organizing 'control trips' to Brussels.

To conclude, the German environment department still operates with a set-up that is to a large extent focused on its environmental policymaking tasks. It has not accepted ownership of horizontal tasks like EU-EPI nor invested in sufficient additional coordination capacities. Also, its EU affairs unit continues to operate with a focus on the Environment Council. It only really claimed ownership in the field of climate/energy policy. Then (and only then) did it undertake the necessary capacity building to achieve EPI in EU policies. This is far less true for the agriculture, transport, and economy people in the environment department. Here, monitoring EU dossiers in cognate policy fields is simply not seen as a priority. This is partly a function of having too few resources. But it is also due to an unwillingness to accept ownership for EU-EPI. The department did not easily come to terms with the single challenge arising from the Europeanization of national environmental policy (Pehle 1997*a*; 1997*b*; Wurzel 2004*a*). Another round of significant changes is now needed to get to grips with the 'double challenge' of EU-EPI.

7

THE NETHERLANDS: FROM EVENT TO ISSUE COORDINATION?

> We are all overworked, so why should we become involved in policies
> for which other ministries are responsible? We have to be selective
> otherwise they [the sectors] will never take their environmental
> responsibilities seriously.
>
> (Dutch environment official on intervening in EU policies led by other
> departments)

Introduction

It is not immediately clear what to expect from the Netherlands in terms of
its ability to respond to the challenge of EU-EPI. On the one hand, it has
always been very supportive of both European integration and EPI.
The Netherlands has always sought to work with the grain of EU
environmental policies (Liefferink 1996; 1997), as it is too small and
too interconnected with neighbouring countries to solve environmental
problems on its own (Liefferink and van de Zouwen 2004). Crucially,
industry and the economic affairs department have generally been in
favour of a pan-EU approach to environmental protection to ensure a
level playing field. The Netherlands has certainly been one of the front
runners in introducing EPI at EU level and supporting its implementation
via the Cardiff process.

On the other hand, Dutch EU policy coordination has struggled for a
long time to manage the overlaps between policy fields (Schout 1999*a*).
These difficulties can be traced back to, among others, the difficulties
of having a collegial and coalition government, and a pro-European
parliament that has not always critically appraised Commission proposals.

Besides, EU policy coordination in the Netherlands has been characterized as reactive (VWS 2003) and event-dominated (Schout and Metcalfe 1999). Environment officials face an uphill battle to pursue EPI in this setting because the passive approach to coordination makes them heavily dependent on cooperation from their sectoral colleagues. Following a number of major crises, new mechanisms were introduced in the 1990s to make the Dutch system more proactive and to improve problem-solving (see Chapter 4)). With this in mind, this chapter tries to assess how well prepared the Netherlands is for dealing with the challenge of EU-EPI.

The links between national and EU-EPI

Advocating EPI in the EU

The Netherlands is well known for being one of the most environmentally ambitious member states in the EU (Liefferink 1996: 244–5; 1997). The most widely known feature of Dutch environmental policy is the system of national environmental policy plans (NEPPs) (see Chapter 5), the first of which was published in 1989 (Bressers and Plettenberg 1997: 123–4). This long-term, goal-directed approach 'presupposes a full integration of environmental considerations into other policy areas and close cooperation with target groups in society, such as industry and consumers' (Liefferink and van der Zouwen 2004: 138). The Netherlands is also equally well known for 'marketing' its ideas to shape EU environmental policymaking (Liefferink 1999). However, it did not take the lead in pushing for the incorporation of EPI in the founding treaties. Although it supported the inclusion of EPI in the Single European Act, most of the running was apparently done by DG Environment and the Danish government (Moravcsik 1998: 374; Haagsma 1989: 335). As regards Article 6 of the Amsterdam Treaty, here the Netherlands (together with Germany) also supported a much stronger reference to EPI, but only after preparatory work had been done by the post-1995 member states (ENDS Ltd. No. 255: 41; McDonagh 1998: 88–9). Together, they fought for strong reference to be included in each and every chapter of the new Treaty, but failed to secure sufficient political backing (Calster and Deketelaere 1998: 18).

Nonetheless, the Dutch have been consistently in the vanguard of states pushing for the implementation of Article 6. The Netherlands has given strong political support to the Cardiff process, particularly in its more difficult recent phases, when less environmentally minded states started to switch their attention to the Lisbon strategy. At the start of its 2004

Presidency, the Dutch government promised to reintegrate environment into the EU's overall push for growth, competitiveness, and sustainability—that is, the Lisbon strategy. It also promised to give the Cardiff process a new lease of life, following the publication of the 2004 Cardiff stocktake by the Commission (see Chapter 3). It did so by emphasizing a key aspect of the NEPPs, namely the search for synergies between environmental and economic policy goals. An informal Environment Council meeting in July 2004 was devoted to discussing the whole issue of environmental competitiveness. Discussions centred on a report entitled 'Clean, Clever and Competitive' which was produced by a high level advisory panel, which included Catherine Day, the then Director-General of Environmental Protection in DG Environment. The Dutch have also sought to pursue EPI at the EU level by pushing the Commission to adopt its 'target group policy' of entering long-term commitments with polluting industries (i.e. voluntary agreements) (see Chapter 3) (Hanf and de Gronden 1998: 168; Zito et al. 2003).

The most visible evidence that the Dutch have shaped EU thinking in relation to EPI is to be found in the Commission's Fifth EAP, which is very closely modelled on the Dutch approach to long-term planning. The similarity is not coincidental: the Dutch environment department seconded one of its officials to DG Environment to write it (Kronsell 1997). But the department's attempts to flesh out the programme with sectoral strategies and long-term targets (*specification of output*—very much following the national environmental policy planning approach) failed to secure sufficient support, leaving it as a rather empty shell (Liefferink 1996: 245).

Finally, the Dutch are committed to linking EU and national approaches to EPI. A recent Green Paper remarked that '[national] policy should primarily be oriented towards assessing the environmental implications of EC-policy and EC-legislation' (VROM 2001: 31). In 1999, the environment department commissioned a study of national coordination capacities for EU-EPI (Schout and Metcalfe 1999). In late 2001, it organized an informal meeting of national EU environmental coordinators to discuss (apparently for the first time) what could be done at the national level to support the implementation of Article 6.

The practical links between national and EU-EPI

Given the many and varied ways in which the Netherlands has sought to advocate environmental integration nationally (Chapter 5) and in the EU, one might have expected it to have done a great deal to strengthen the practical links between national and EU-EPI systems. In practice, however, very little has been done. Previous studies show that the process of building sufficient coordination capacities at the national level since the early 1990s has been slow and patchy (Schout 1996). The environment department has a good reputation as far as the management of its 'own' EU policies are concerned (e.g. *Algemene Rekenkamer* 2004), but it suffers from a number of inefficiencies which largely arise from the prevalence of passive information flows (Chapter 4). As a result, the past decade has seen an almost constant search for more proactive mechanisms to ensure that the environment department has earlier access to Commission proposals in 'non-'environmental fields. The problem with such suggestions is that they make an informal system more regulated and in so doing reinforce the event-driven style of coordination in the Netherlands.

Because of system-wide inefficiencies, the department's global affairs unit is forced to do a lot of additional legwork. Of the thirty officials working in it, only around five deal with EU matters. Their primary task is to coordinate EU policy in the department and to represent it in interdepartmental coordination meetings. A lot of their time is devoted to chasing their colleagues to ensure they adapt to the Europeanization of national environmental policy. Any remaining time is devoted to monitoring developments in other sectors and the work of the Commission, the Parliament, and the Council. It is quite impossible for five people to complete all these tasks, so workloads and working patterns tend to be dictated by key events, such as upcoming Environment Councils or interdepartmental coordination meetings. EPI, at both national and EU levels, is seen as an additional task rather than an immediate priority. As EU-related activities are strongly event-related, any greening of EU policy proposals that the unit manages to achieve, tends to be reactive and partial.

In an attempt to improve this situation, in 2000 the EU environment unit established a weekly 'international VROM[1] meeting' (IVO) that provides an earlier warning of new proposals entering the policy pipeline. This committee, which is prepared and chaired by the EU environment unit, aims further to Europeanize officials in the various policy divisions in the environment department. Even though it was meant to play a role in pursuing EU-EPI, the IVO is also too understaffed to make much of an impression. The EPI-related topics that have figured most regularly on its agenda are EU enlargement and the Cardiff strategies—that is, very broad policy developments, not individual policy proposals. Apparently, the IVO does not look in detail at emerging agendas in other EU policy fields; it mainly addresses dossiers destined for the Environment Council.

Environmental policy appraisal (or e-testing) (which is a *bureaucratic procedure*, backed up by *skills development and training*) has the potential to be an effective coordinating capacity. However, as we noted in Chapter 5, very few new policy proposals are fully appraised. Those are that tend to be done superficially and far too late in the legislative process to have much effect (Verheem 2004). The links between national e-testing and the EU's IA system are also underdeveloped. Formally, the national e-testing regime only covers national legislative proposals (van Ruiten 2002; VROM 2003: 23). Furthermore, the scope of the regime was streamlined to ensure that national legislation which directly implements EU requirements is exempt from the e-test regime (VROM 2003). Interestingly, the general assumption seems to be that EU policy proposals are already effectively assessed under the EU's IA procedure (cf. the Commission's perception; see Chapter 9).

Finally, it is worth remembering that the environment is a special case as far as the interdepartmental coordination of EU business is concerned, because it is coordinated by the department of foreign affairs, whereas the sectoral departments coordinate their own EU policies (see Chapter 4). This means that the other departments can easily monitor preparations for the Environment Council, whereas it can be difficult for the environment department to influence negotiations in other Councils. This problem is accentuated when officials work informally (i.e. without written instructions). One way that the environment department could overcome this limitation is, as in Germany, physically to accompany colleagues to EU meetings in large football-sized teams. However, the environment department does not have the resources to shadow the sectors in Brussels, so this option is not really a viable one.

The national coordination of EU-EPI

Our assessment of the level of coordination achieved by the Dutch system at the various stages of the policy process is summarized in Table 7.1.

Initiation

INTERDEPARTMENTAL COORDINATION
The first phase of the process is hardly coordinated. Agendas of high-level meetings are normally not distributed or discussed. The lobbying activities of sector experts are sometimes coordinated between different

Table 7.1. The Netherlands: levels of inter-departmental EU policy coordination

	Initiation of new proposals	Work plans	White & Green papers	Drafting of proposals	Inter-service consultation	Presentation of proposals	Presidency agenda	Working parties	COREPER	Council	Conciliation
	Commission phases						Council phases				
Coordination level (OUTPUT)											
9 Strategy											
8 Margins			+|−			+|−					
7 Arbitration								+|−	+|−	+|−	+|−
6 Conciliation			+|−			+|−		+|−	+	+	+
5 Consensus			+|−			+|−		+|−	+	+	+
4 One voice			+			+|−		+|−	+|−	+	+|−
3 Consultation			+	+|−		+|−		+	+|−	+	+
2 Communication	+|−	+	+	+|−		+	+|−	+	+	+	+
1 Independent policy making	+|−	+		+		+	+|−	+	+		
Coordination capacities (INPUT)											
Hierarchical							+				
Bureaucratic		+	+			+		+	+	+	+
Specification of output								+|−	+	+	+|−
Horizontal											
Informal relations	+|−		+	+|−		+	+	+		+	+
Liaison roles			+			+		+|−			
Task forces			+|−			+|−		+|−			
Teams		+|−	+|−			+		+	+		
Weak integrator			+|−			+|−	+|−	+	+		
Strong integrator											
Mission statements											
Role and resources of the EU coordinating units			Pushes for strategy papers to be taken more seriously			Coordinates input from the environment department			Coordinates input from the environment department	Coordinates input from the environment department	Coordinates input from the environment department

Explanation:

+ = coordination capacity at this level exists and is used.

+/− = the coordination capacity at this level exists to some extent, but may not always be used.

(+/−) = the coordination capacity at this level exists, but is only used in exceptional cases.

departments, but not in any consistent or formal way (for example, VWS 2003). So, even achieving Levels 1 and 2 on the scale is sometimes a problem. Our interviews showed that officials are unaware of the existence of high-level meetings in other policy areas and there are no rules about distributing future agendas.

One reason why these activities are so rarely coordinated is that officials prefer to have free-flowing discussions with like-minded experts about common problems and possible policy innovations, without being constrained by having to agree to a national negotiating position. Not discussing EU-EPI issues from the start does, however, have real disadvantages. Environmental factors need not necessarily trump sector considerations right at the start of a negotiation, but not considering them at all may mean that opportunities to implement EU-EPI are lost forever.

At this stage there is no role for the department for foreign affairs. Hence, there is no overview of new initiatives entering the pipeline within other sectors. Opportunities to select priorities and discuss possible environmental implications are therefore lost.

INTRADEPARTMENTAL COORDINATION IN THE ENVIRONMENT DEPARTMENT

Environment department officials are often not aware of the existence of high-level meetings in other fields. Moreover, there is little information available about lobbying activities and emerging new policies in other sectors. The passive way in which departments exchange information (see Chapter 4) means that many potential spillover effects are not adequately picked up and acted upon.

Commission workplanning

INTERDEPARTMENTAL COORDINATION

The workplan of the Commission is hardly used at all as a formal focus for coordination. Increasingly, ministers look at the plans for their 'own' policies, but that is often as far as it goes. Standard internal *bureaucratic procedures* specify that the department of foreign affairs should pass the workplans around to the interdepartmental liaisons and refer them to the next meeting of the BNC (Committee to Assess New Commission Proposals; see Chapter 4). The BNC is an example of a horizontal coordinating mechanism (a *team*). However, our interviews revealed that little is done with the workplans at this stage (i.e. Level 2 on the scale).

Consequently, important opportunities to integrate an environmental dimension in the work of sectoral policies are not exploited.

INTRADEPARTMENTAL COORDINATION IN THE ENVIRONMENT DEPARTMENT

The EU affairs coordinator in the department who is responsible for the BNC, looks at new workplans and the detailed lists of the DGs. The lists are then presented to the IVO, but they do not normally provoke many reactions. That is, there is a *bureaucratic procedure*, but it is not always effective. Due to the level of detail and uncertainty as to when new policies will actually emerge, few officials show much enthusiasm for picking up workplans in other fields. The weaknesses of passive coordination are very obvious: if environment officials were to track every proposal at this very early stage, it could add up to a huge amount of unnecessary work. Therefore, pragmatism dictates that it is better to wait until negotiations are more advanced—that is, to see what the Commission comes up with, or better still, wait until the final proposal goes to the COREPER.

White/Green Papers and Communications

INTERDEPARTMENTAL COORDINATION

White and Green Papers are treated the same as new Commission proposals and are therefore routinely sent to the *liaison* officers for EU affairs in the departments. The title of the relevant paper is also put on the list for discussion at the next BNC team, together with any other new Commission proposal. However, the BNC only facilitates an exchange of information; it offers little room for strategic discussions on new Commission proposals (Level 2 on the scale). Nevertheless, White and Green Papers are increasingly the basis for more strategic debates between departments. Parliament now takes more interest in the *fiche* (or policy appraisal) that has to be filled in (*Algemene Rekenkamer* 2004). This forces the government to coordinate away the most obvious divergences (i.e. Level 4 on the scale). But as the Dutch audit office recently concluded (*Algemene Rekenkamer* 2004), the information in this brief assessment is often far from complete. The discussions are mainly informal, although some White Papers have led to the creation of task forces and to conciliation in the Coordinating Committee (CoCo) (see Chapter 4) (i.e. Levels 5 and 6), although this rarely happens. Despite this, the officials that we interviewed felt that the environment department should make greater use of White Papers, for example to indicate the broad environmental boundaries within which a dossier should develop (implying a move up to Level 8).

INTRADEPARTMENTAL COORDINATION IN THE ENVIRONMENT DEPARTMENT

The environment department puts very little effort into monitoring the production of Commission papers outside the realms of environment policy. White Papers in other policy fields are often discussed between the EU-coordinating unit in the environment department and the relevant sector experts. These discussions are needed because the environment department is involved in the discussion of the BNC's *fiche* and (if necessary) in the discussion in CoCo (see below). With some exceptions, White Papers are mostly discussed at a much higher level of abstraction (the aim being to 'speak with one voice' (Level 4) on major points of policy).

Drafting of proposals (expert meetings)

INTERDEPARTMENTAL COORDINATION

The Netherlands has a tradition of respecting the Commission's formal right of initiative. Therefore, officials who are invited by the Commission to give expert advice are normally treated as independent experts. This 'hands-off' attitude does not, however, rule out the possibility of seeking informal coordination. Personal contacts are very much based on the initiative of the lead department; those that work, tend to build on a long history of good working relations between officials. Due to the pressure of heavy workloads, experts tend to eschew formal coordination (i.e. up to Level 3 on the scale) (e.g. see VWS 2003).

In principle, the foreign affairs department is ideally placed to gain a good overview of future developments in expert committees, because invitations are also copied to the Dutch Permanent Representation in Brussels. However, trying to monitor each and every expert committee would be a true *mer à boire*. Therefore, day-to-day responsibility is normally devolved to the sectoral departments. The downside is that no one has a good overview of the precise membership or agendas of the myriad expert meetings (Schout 1999a; VWS 2003; *Algemene Rekenkamer* 2004). Consequently, no one (other than the sectors) has a real idea of what is coming over the hill in the form of new policies.

INTRADEPARTMENTAL COORDINATION IN THE ENVIRONMENT DEPARTMENT

There is a paradox in the way in which environment officials describe how expert committees are followed. On the one hand, our interviewees commented to the effect that 'we never hear anything from other departments about what happens in the Commission'. On the other hand, they all do their best to stick to their core (i.e. sectoral) tasks to avoid 'information overload'. As a consequence, the amount of information shared about potential spillover effects differs sharply between the various policy fields.

Interservice consultation within the Commission

INTERDEPARTMENTAL COORDINATION

This stage does not warrant a detailed discussion because it only gets limited attention. The names of those responsible for environment in the relevant *cabinets* of Commissioners are hardly known.

INTRADEPARTMENTAL COORDINATION IN THE ENVIRONMENT DEPARTMENT

The environment department experimented with a new mechanism to anticipate Commission decisions. Before 2000, information about Commission decisions would arrive via the foreign affairs department and/or the BNC. However, the BNC only forwarded information at the last minute, and valuable time was lost. Therefore, in 2000, a junior position was created to track agendas of the College of Commissioners so that the EU coordinators and the experts would have more time—two weeks at most—to examine proposals. But when this failed to have an immediate impact, the position was removed.

Presentation of proposals

The BNC's involvement is strongest at this stage. Initially, it was supposed to be a *team* made up of more senior officials. In practice, it is actually a junior committee that does little more than exchange information and write the *fiche* for the national parliament (i.e. it hardly qualifies as 'team' according to the definition offered in Chapter 2). Any remaining differences of view can be raised at the senior CoCo team. In order to strengthen the BNC, it has recently been linked to a new *team* that looks in detail at the legal implications of new proposals (the *Interdepartementale Commissie Europees Recht*). However, this body has been unable fully to discharge this task (Haersolte and Oosterkamp 2003). This underlines the fact that more teams do not necessarily lead to better problem-solving.[2]

INTERDEPARTMENTAL COORDINATION

The BNC provides the first opportunity to hold an interdepartmental discussion about a new proposal. On average, it meets once every fortnight on Wednesdays under the chairmanship of the department of foreign affairs. Its agenda lists the Commission proposals, White and Green Papers, and Presidency papers. The BNC reviews the *fiches* from the lead departments on the new Commission proposals. These are then forwarded to the cabinet via the CoCo. A selection is also sent to Dutch MEPs. The role of the department of foreign affairs is mainly administrative (i.e. it is a *weak integrator*). It collects and distributes titles of new Commission proposals, chairs the meeting, and indicates which department should write the *fiche*. These draft policy appraisals are passed around on the Friday or Monday before the BNC meetings. It is up to the lead department to ensure that any differences of view are solved. However, problem-solving is usually postponed until negotiations evolve in the Council; departments are often insufficiently aware at this stage of the precise implications of a particular proposal. The BNC therefore mainly serves to distribute information and allocate primary responsibilities.

When they arise, there are various ways of resolving interdepartmental differences. Usually, the initial position is along the lines of: 'this is an interesting proposal, but some aspects need further attention.' Hence, neither problems are solved nor fresh priorities set. They are simply delayed, pending a more detailed analysis. In exceptional cases—for example, an important White Paper—more effort is invested to avoid divergences (among others, with a view to informing the Dutch Parliament). Sometimes, *task forces* are created to hammer out broad agreement (i.e. Levels 3–5). When necessary, difficulties can be raised in the CoCo or in cabinet (i.e. Level 6—conciliation). Occasionally, CoCo establishes broad limits that serve as a *specification of output* for the working party phase. However, this does not happen very often; when it does, the specifications are flexibly interpreted in subsequent phases. However, most *fiches* go through without causing much upheaval because officials mainly economize on their input by waiting until the proposal is ripe for decision-taking later (see below). Hence, coordination at this stage generally resides at Level 2.

INTRADEPARTMENTAL COORDINATION IN THE ENVIRONMENT DEPARTMENT

The international environment unit coordinates the BNC. It goes over the list of titles forwarded by the foreign affairs department and scrutinizes any draft *fiches* produced by the lead departments. A junior official subsequently contacts officials in the sector directorates to draw up the *fiches* connected to the Environment Council or to look at those drafted by cognate departments. However, the short time between the arrival of the Commission proposal and the BNC allows little room for detailed analysis.[3] Problems encountered in this process include the difficulty of finding an appropriate expert who can look at an EPI-related file. A second problem is that the environment expert may not be sufficiently interested to give the proposal a detailed look at this stage; showing an early interest may create extra (and, depending on how the negotiations go, unnecessary) work.

The Presidency agenda

The department for foreign affairs distributes Presidency agendas. These are used for setting priorities and proactive problem-solving when the Dutch are at the helm of the EU. However, when its Presidency ends, this phase is no longer used as a formal coordinating point.

Council working party negotiations

INTERDEPARTMENTAL COORDINATION

National officials that serve in working parties represent the national government as a whole and are therefore expected to arrive with a coordinated position. The way in which this phase works in the Netherlands differs sharply between topics. Officials in working parties can be career diplomats from the foreign affairs department or technical experts seconded from sectoral departments. Some work with formal instructions; others do not. Some write reports and send them to all departments, whereas other officials limit reporting to colleagues who were involved in the preparation of the meeting. One general feature of all this activity is its informality. This limits information overload, but also has its dangers. It is, as explained in Chapter 2, not necessarily conducive to EU-EPI. Another general feature is the predominance of passive information flows. This makes life easier for officials in the lead department, but it increases the costs incurred by cognate departments that want to exert influence (e.g. the environment department with respect to EU-EPI).

Most departments are responsible for servicing the working parties in their field. The major exception is environmental policy, which is coordinated by the foreign affairs department. Environmental negotiations are coordinated in an interdepartmental committee that meets every week (*Coördinatie Commissie voor Internationale Milieuvraagstukken*—CIM). The involvement of foreign affairs makes it easier for the sectors to monitor EU environment policy because foreign officials are supposed to be neutral. Indeed, they will often go out of their way actively to involve other departments by pointing out the implications of a particular proposal (i.e. more active coordination). Developments in the Environment Council are therefore more transparent than in other councils. The sector departments of course appreciate this arrangement, but the environment department regards it as being inherently unfair. By contrast, the environment department is denied a similarly early opportunity to integrate an environmental dimension into the work of the sectors (i.e. pro-EU-EPI). To address this imbalance, the environment department has repeatedly asked for this arrangement to be extended to all Council areas. Not surprisingly, this has not received much support amongst the sectors.

In general, the foreign affairs department follows all the meetings. A fairly junior official normally follows each Council. He or she attends coordination meetings, and gathers the reports from the negotiators and from the Council Secretariat. However, the role of the foreign affairs department is principally to remain informed; at this stage, it does not seek to detect or solve horizontal coordination problems.

Overall, interdepartmental relations during this crucial negotiation phase are dominated by *bureaucratic politics*. There is nothing inherently wrong with this—it builds on a long tradition of *informal relations* (that is, *bureaucratic politics*) between departments (Rosenthal 1988)—but it puts a lot of pressure on the environment department. Many environment officials are happy with the informal culture of the Dutch system. However, there have been cases in which coordination has been more difficult, problems cannot be solved, and sector ministers have defended positions that were inconsistent with the environment department's wishes. As a result, complaints persist about insufficient information and poor cross-sectoral involvement.

In terms of coordination capacities, there is a general willingness to look for consensus between departments (i.e. Level 5). In theory, topics can be sent to the CoCo for discussion at a higher level (Level 6—conciliation), but this is normally avoided until the proposal is sent to COREPER (i.e typical event coordination). Nevertheless, there is no guarantee that Level 5 will be reached due to information problems, either because the lead department makes little effort to inform the environment department or because the appropriate environment expert has no time.

INTRADEPARTMENTAL COORDINATION IN THE ENVIRONMENT DEPARTMENT

As far as EU-EPI is concerned, the extent to which working parties are followed in other Council fields is the responsibility of the relevant experts. Their involvement has differed greatly over time. In 1999, EU energy policy hardly achieved attention, whereas in 2001 it was carefully monitored with respect to EU-EPI. Similarly, agriculture has not been a priority for the department, even though it is an established area of EU competence. This varied picture can be explained by the workload required to service the national policy agenda and the weak interest in EU policies shown by senior officials and ministers.

COREPER

INTERDEPARTMENTAL COORDINATION

COREPER instructions are coordinated in a meeting chaired by the department of foreign affairs on Tuesday mornings. This meeting also monitors the instructions for conciliation procedures. After the BNC, this is where topics resurface. It offers an opportunity to review the outcomes of the working parties. Each department prepares the draft instructions for COREPER in its field. These drafts are distributed by the foreign affairs department on Friday—or sometimes Monday—so that everyone can arrive fully prepared.

This is the meeting in which the environment department can check the status of EU-EPI. It analyses whether environmental dimensions have been adequately included in the negotiations thus far. Environment officials are structurally disadvantaged in these meetings, too, because the sector departments will have been able to follow all the instructions for the environment working parties in the CIM (see above). The COREPER instruction meeting is therefore less likely to lead to surprises as far the Environment Council is concerned. Because working parties in other

Council areas are less transparent, the environment department's ability to spot upcoming issues in other sectors (and thus pursue EU-EPI) is not nearly as strong. Even though the coordination system is stacked against the environment department, it can be frustrating for the sector departments to hear an environment official flagging issues at this relatively late stage in the negotiation. The environment official will of course often respond that they should make more effort to keep him or her informed of any possible environmental spillovers. This is part of the paradox noted above.

The department of foreign affairs' role increases as proposals move to the end of the policy cycle. In addition to administering this meeting, it will keep an eye on more general themes and monitor whether instructions are in line with national priorities. Moreover, it will mediate when conflicts arise between departments (i.e. up to Level 6 where necessary), even though in practice there is little that can be done because the Dutch Permanent Representation cannot wait for instructions for the COREPER meeting the next morning.

The strengths of this committee are its transparency and its ability to make one final check on the national position. However, it has three weaknesses that reduce its scope for consultation and conciliation. First, it is quite reactive. Many interstate negotiations will have already taken place when it meets. The officials from most member states—including the Netherlands—will have already presented their national positions, and may even have reached outline agreement. Second, the time pressures under which it operates tend to be very tight. This also restricts what can be done in terms of mustering support for EU-EPI from other member states. Third, agriculture is not a theme for the COREPER, but is discussed in the special COREPER for agriculture (the *Comite Agriculture Special*), which reports directly to the Agriculture Council. Because agricultural matters are not systematically discussed in the COREPER instruction meeting, the scope for the Dutch to achieve EU-EPI in this sector is very much reduced.

INTRADEPARTMENTAL COORDINATION IN THE ENVIRONMENT DEPARTMENT

An official from the EU-coordinating unit in the environment department receives the draft instructions the day before the meeting. The staff in this unit have a broad understanding of the developments in their fields, and can detect quickly whether there is scope for tightening environmental objectives. However, there are limitations on the extent to which drafts can be reconsidered at this stage, because member states are not expected fundamentally to reopen discussions in the COREPER.

Council meetings

INTERDEPARTMENTAL COORDINATION

The negotiating lines for Council are approved in the cabinet meeting on Fridays. These are normally prepared on Tuesdays in the CoCo which is chaired by the secretary of state for EU affairs. CoCo is the central body in which the official and political levels overlap.[4] This committee is also the main conciliation body. Problems can be referred to the CoCo in each of the phases. Hence, strictly speaking, the CoCo is not at the very end of the policy cycle as Table 7.1 suggests. However, in practice, its core business is to approve national negotiating positions before each Council meeting. There is a limit to the extent to which upstream issues are discussed, because much of the proposal will still be unclear and officials prefer to solve problems themselves.

The department of foreign affairs writes the draft instructions for each council to ensure that they reflect the interdepartmental consensus. These draft briefs are subsequently sent to the departments—usually on Friday or Monday. The junior minister for EU affairs sits in the chair and has considerable power to resolve any remaining controversies (i.e. up to Level 7 on the scale). But mostly, his or her power is counterbalanced by the powers of individual departments. This committee therefore has a fairly strong integrating role (also because the junior minister can forward remaining problems to the cabinet).

Nevertheless, officials from departments that have not succeeded in the CoCo can urge their minister to reopen conclusions in the cabinet meeting on Friday. Alternatively, ministers may persist in their views. This is possible in the Dutch system, which is very collegial and lacks strong political leadership. This also explains why ministers may sometimes go beyond their formal briefs (i.e. a failure at Level 2 on the scale) when appearing in the Council. EU-EPI has suffered because of this on several occasions.

The main problem with the CoCo is that it is preoccupied with the very end of the decisionmaking cycle. This focus reinforces the reactive nature of Dutch EU policymaking. It also means that scarce resources for coordinating EU policy in the departments are used up in preparing for the Council, rather than in undertaking more proactive coordination at earlier phases (see above).

INTRADEPARTMENTAL COORDINATION IN THE ENVIRONMENT DEPARTMENT

CoCo conclusions are examined by the EU-affairs coordinators and experts from the sector directorates in the same way as the COREPER instructions.

Co-decisionmaking and conciliation

The instructions for this phase are coordinated in the same way as COREPER instructions.

Improving the Dutch System

The strengths of the Dutch system stem from its informality and flexibility. The main weakness from the perspective of EU-EPI is that it requires a lot from environment officials, who have to monitor and exert influence at each step of the process. Moreover, the system as a whole is inefficient— it takes more than seventy persons just to maintain it (Chapter 4). Furthermore, the system is reactive, and not particularly good at identifying and solving problems in advance.

The Netherlands is continuously struggling to upgrade its coordination capacities, while maintaining this culture of flexibility and informality. The BNC is a constant focus of discussion, particularly as regards improving the coordination of the early stages and deepening the discussion of the *fiches*. Possible steps here might include trying to arrive at more profound discussions on proposals and to scrutinize proposals through a more rigorously applied national e-test (the current environmental policy appraisal system in the Netherlands is not very consistently applied—see Chapter 5). As regards the working parties, suggestions have been made to create weekly coordination committees for each Council and to include more environment officials in national delegations. Similar suggestions have been to achieve other horizontal objectives (e.g. deregulation and implementation) (Schout 2004).

However, these and many other suggestions share a number of problems. First of all, they aim to make piecemeal rather wholesale changes.

The danger with further incremental steps is that they may reduce the very flexibility of the system if they simply introduce more procedures and committees. Second, greater information exchange at interdepartmental level means even more work for environment officials. Therefore, suggestions for change have irritated other departments as the environment department cannot live up to its current coordination requirements. Moreover, if the environment department invested more resources in picking up more work, this would lead to more interdepartmental controversies and increase the workload of officials in the foreign affairs department. Hence, incremental changes could pile even more work on to an already overloaded system.

A set of more drastic changes could be imagined, which draw inspiration from the UK's system (see Chapter 8). The UK system is based on active information, does not work through fixed coordinating committees, and sets priorities and determines positions proactively on the basis of the Presidency agenda. Active information would force officials from other departments to arrive earlier at coordinated positions and oblige them to get feedback from the environment department. The workload of keeping environmental aspects on board through the various phases would thus shift to the lead (i.e. sector) department. Moreover, it would help to shift the Dutch system from event to issue coordination.

With active information, the formal coordinating committees (BNC, the COREPER instruction meeting, and the CoCo) could be abolished. Instead of running around trying to identify EPI-relevant negotiating positions in all these meetings, the EU coordinators in the environment department could devote more of their time to identifying strategic issues and scrutinizing upcoming agendas from the Commission and the Presidency. Abolishing these committees would also change the work of the department of foreign affairs, from that of supporting meetings to actively solving horizontal coordination problems. There would, of course, need to be new coordination capacities to handle strategic tasks (e.g. problem-solving, selecting priorities, and ensuring rules are effective) at higher levels in the Dutch government. Using the Presidency agenda to set priorities and identify differences would, as in the UK, require new interdepartmental meetings to discuss the agendas of the various Councils. To make this work, the EU affairs unit in the environment department could examine the agendas in consultation with sector experts and then select priorities for EPI. Finally, the link between national and EU-level appraisal systems could be greatly reinforced (see Chapter 8), by refocusing the Dutch e-test system (see Chapter 5).

How realistic are these changes? Is it possible to mix the current passive system with active coordination? As long as the COREPER instruction meeting and the CoCo remain, they will continue to monopolize the attention of officials, who will continue to say (as they do now) 'let's see what happens in the COREPER'. Hence, there are doubts as to whether active coordination can be introduced while continuing with the current system. This calls for structural rather than incremental changes.

Conclusions

The Netherlands has a long tradition of integrating an environmental dimension in the work of the EU. The importance of adding a suitably robust international dimension to national-level EPI activities has been underlined in countless policy statements. This creates high expectations as regards the way in which the Dutch manage the challenge of EU-EPI. However, we have shown that there are a number of characteristics of the Dutch system that facilitate EU-EPI, and some which undermine it. It is probably best to divide these into two dimensions—inter- and intradepartmental.

Interdepartmental coordination

Here, coordination appears to be working quite well, in the sense that information is regularly exchanged and problems are solved informally. When there are intractable controversies, CoCo steps in to take discussions to a higher level on the coordination scale. In other cases, information flows less efficiently because officials are not aware of the relevance of topics for each other (i.e. there is a failure at Level 1), or because insufficient effort is made by the sender to inform and/or the receiver to offer feedback. Failures can therefore happen at any level on the coordination scale.

One major element of Dutch EU policymaking is its reliance on a series of collegial bodies. In such colleges no one has the authority to take a decision or to overrule others. For difficult cases, Level 6—conciliation—is the highest level that the system can effectively achieve. Arbitration can be difficult as it involves sending a topic from one conciliation committee to another without the threat of an authority (strong *integrator*) that can force a decision. As a result, interdepartmental problems regularly persist until they are well inside the Council. In order to provide support for

EU-EPI, the system should demand that Levels 7 and 8 are also reached (i.e problem-solving and agreeing margins). The interdepartmental committees deal with a proposal when it is sent to the Council and the European Parliament (BNC), when it reaches COREPER, and when it goes to the Council (CoCo). This makes coordination highly event-driven. The second major feature is the informal nature of the Dutch system. Even though this is in one sense efficient, it makes it very difficult for the environment department to monitor EPI in cognate sectors. The third feature is the reliance on passive information. This puts huge pressure on the environment department to ensure that EPI is incorporated in the work of the sectors.

Intradepartmental coordination

Integrating environment into other EU sectors is not very popular in the sector directorates of the environment department. It is labour intensive and adds to existing workloads. The EU affairs unit in the environment department is the only real champion of EU-EPI in the Dutch system, but it needs the cooperation of other departments and directorates to achieve its goals. It also needs to be better resourced, and to overcome the structural weaknesses in the interdepartmental coordination system. Currently, the unit devotes most of its meagre budget to getting the instructions ready for various EU environment policy meetings, such as the Environment Council. Achieving EU-EPI will demand a significant reinforcement of this unit, allowing it to refocus its work towards agenda setting.

Applying the coordination scale to intradepartmental coordination of EPI shows that there are problems already at Level 1. Some officials seem to expect the EU coordinators in the environment department to 'own' the problem of EU-EPI, but this is not based on mutual agreement. Sector directorates are in general less eager than the EU affairs coordinators to examine EU policies which lie largely in the domain of other departments. There is no system for selecting priorities or monitoring progress in the selected files. The newly created IVO could start to play a role in achieving this, but has so far focused on developing new policies in the Environment Council. If the Dutch are really serious about doing something about EU-EPI, they will need to make considerable changes both in the national environment department and at an interdepartmental level, as well as do more to connect national and EU-level EPI activities.

Notes

1. VROM is the national environment department (see Chapter 5).
2. For example, the Netherlands still has a relatively poor record on implementing EU laws (see Chapter 4).
3. If necessary, the environment department can ask for a two-week delay in the BNC meeting so that a proposal can be analysed.
4. CoCo meets at (deputy) director level. The CoCoHan (see Chapter 4) meets less frequently and discusses topics of strategic importance such as enlargement. CoCo can also set up special working parties which look at major EU policies (e.g. Kyoto protocol on climate change).

8

THE UNITED KINGDOM: STRONG ADMINISTRATIVE COORDINATION MECHANISMS BUT WEAK POLITICAL AMBITIONS?

The UK is more than a 'taker' of regulation from Brussels, [the environment department's] fate is not as a simple transcriber of European law... We strongly recommend that [it] adopts a much wider programme of conversation with EU institutions and other member state ministries... with the specific aim of influencing at an early stage other EU partners. This will require additional resources which will need to be targeted for maximum effect.

(A recommendation made by a Better Regulation taskforce)

(DEFRA 2004: 51)

Introduction

On paper, the UK appears to be on track to meet Prime Minister Blair's aspirations to be an international leader in the implementation of EPI (Jordan 2000; 2002c). In 2002, the OECD (2002b: 141) praised the UK for the 'extensive institutional framework, and numerous inter-agency policy initiatives' that it had put in place to achieve EPI in the UK (see Chapter 5 for details). It concluded that 'substantial progress in policy integration has been achieved' in the UK (ibid.: 27).

There are four reasons to believe that the OECD's rosy assessment can also be extended to the UK's contribution to EU-EPI. First, EPI has been a long-standing domestic policy priority since the early 1990s, and the UK has done a great deal to upload this positive experience to the EU (i.e. to inform the creation of the Cardiff process). Second, the UK has made important contributions to the technical debate about how to achieve EPI both domestically and in the EU. For instance, British economists helped to pioneer tools of environmental policy appraisal like cost-benefit analysis (Pearce 1998). British environmental organizations such as the Institute for European Environmental Policy (IEEP) have played an equally important part in creating the intellectual case for building EPI requirements into the Treaties and reviewing implementation processes such as Cardiff (Jordan 2002c). Third, the UK is widely recognized as having one of the strongest and most effectively coordinated systems of any member state (Wallace 1997: 687). Moreover, better horizontal coordination is a major political priority of the Blair government (Perri 6 et al. 2002; Bevir and Rhodes 2003). Add to these Blair's personal determination to make a more positive contribution to EU affairs than most of his predecessors (Bache and Jordan 2006; Bulmer and Burch 1998; 2006), and the UK does seem to be very well placed to make a strong contribution to any EU level EPI network.

In this chapter we assess how far these factors have helped the UK manage the problem of growing policy interdependence in the EU. More specifically, we investigate how well the UK's very actively coordinated 'Rolls Royce' administrative system (Bulmer and Burch 1998; 2000) has responded to the double challenge of EU-EPI.

The links between national and EU-EPI

Advocating EPI in the EU

The UK environment department has been an enthusiastic advocate of EU-EPI since the early 1980s. The British, it is often argued, have a reputation for championing and implementing 'good governance' in the EU (Jordan 2004). They are especially strong advocates of the Better Regulation initiative now being implemented by the Barroso Commission at EU level. Because of this, they have tended to 'translate issues of [environmental] policy... into questions about policy process and the machinery of government' (Weale et al. 2000: 180). This tendency has been further exacerbated by sustained political pressure from the UK's extensive and very well-resourced system of environmental pressure groups, which have fought long and hard for environmentally damaging EU sectoral policies (such as the Common Agricultural Policy) to be systematically overhauled.

The UK has always been slightly perplexed that the EU is capable on the one hand of producing large quantities of environmentally progressive legislation, while at the same time nurturing sectoral policies that systematically negate environmental progress. William Waldegrave, an environment minister in the mid-1980s, remembers having been 'goaded' by British environmental NGOs into:

> boring our colleagues silly in the Environment Council by making long speeches at 6 o'clock in the morning about the importance of the integration of agricultural and environmental policy. When we started doing that, people did rather rush for their aeroplanes home...
>
> (HL 135 Session 1986–7: 92)

Building on these early, if somewhat ad hoc, interventions at national level, in the early 1990s the environment department started to pursue EPI at EU level. EPI was, for example, on the UK's list of demands during the 1991 Maastricht Treaty intergovernmental conference. The UK suggested that all new Commission proposals should receive a UK-style environmental policy appraisal. It also encouraged DG Environment to go one better than existing UK practice (established by the 1990 Environment White Paper; see Chapter 5 for details) and establish an environmental appraisal unit to audit the environmental performance of the other DGs (ENDS Ltd. No. 194: 3). The fact that these two ideas failed to make the final text of the Treaty (Jordan 2002*c*) does suggest that the UK was some way ahead of the other member states in its thinking about EPI at this time. During its EU Presidency in 1992, the UK again sought to revive interest in EU-EPI. However, the discussion, which was informed by a document specially prepared by the IEEP (1992), failed to generate sufficient political impetus and the opportunity was lost.

Shortly after entering power, Blair's Labour government overhauled the national EPI system, which it dubbed 'Greening Government'. In 1998 it sought to export some of the principles and practices of this initiative to the rest of the EU when it made environment a key priority during its 1998 Presidency of the EU. It was during this Presidency that British officials clinched a political deal on the Cardiff process (Jordan and Lenschow 2000) (Chapter 3). Although other member states had prepared the ground, the UK deserves a lot of credit for this achievement. Specifically, it succeeded in uploading a variant of its own national system of EPI to the EU, and extending ownership of it to the Council. Since then, the national environment department has worked with partners in Germany and Austria to maintain a focus on EPI (see Chapter 3). For instance, it has published well-timed reports on the performance of the Cardiff process (Fergusson et al. 2001) and the new EU IA regime (Wilkinson et al. 2004*b*) to maintain political support.

The practical links between national and EU-EPI

Given this history of supporting EPI at national and EU level, one would expect to find strong practical links between the two levels. There are certainly some links. According to the environment department's 'best practice' guidelines for undertaking environmental policy appraisals in Whitehall (see Chapter 5), *any* policy (either UK or EU derived) that is likely significantly to affect the environment should undergo an environmental appraisal, regardless of whether it is a national or an EU policy. In practice, environment was the only department which consistently produced them (see Chapter 5). Moreover, the number of EU proposals that underwent an environmental policy appraisal was generally very low, across *all* departments, including environment (Jordan et al. 2003). The only body that routinely appraised new EU policies under the scheme was the Forestry Commission, but most of the ones it reported were not environmental policy appraisals at all but environmental impact assessments required by an EU Directive. Consequently, there was actually very little practical integration between the national and EU appraisal systems.

Time will tell whether the recent shift first to a regulatory impact assessment-based system and then integrated appraisal (see Chapter 5), succeeds in building deeper connections between appraisal at national and EU levels (see below). This is not to suggest that EU proposals were never appraised: all EU environmental proposals were supposed to undergo an RIA as part of the standard parliamentary scrutiny process (they are normally referred to in the Explanatory Memoranda submitted to Parliament) (see below). However, traditionally, RIAs have concentrated on the potential impacts on business, charities, and the voluntary sector. Until the relatively recent shift to integrated appraisal (Eales et al. 2005), they have not explicitly focused on environmental impacts.

These findings jar with the widespread perception that the UK has an excellent administrative coordination system. Peters and Wright (2001: 157) go as far as to describe it as a 'first class integrated national machine' (see also Kassim 2000; 2001). If active information was indeed normalized across Whitehall, then the sector departments would produce and disseminate many more environmental policy appraisals than they are at present. On the contrary, when pushed by the Parliamentary environmental audit committee to explain the performance of the environmental policy appraisal initiative, the sustainable development unit in the environment department had to hunt around Whitehall to find sufficient policy appraisals to include in its annual report to the committee of green ministers (Russel 2004). Evidently, those departments that did undertake environmental policy appraisals (the majority did not) felt no strong compunction to disseminate them actively to other departments and third parties. When asked by the Parliamentary committee to account for the very low number of appraisals produced (only eight departments, covering fourteen to twenty-five separate policy issues, could actually list the appraisals they had undertaken in the preceding year), the sectors tried to claim that their policies were not environmentally significant enough to warrant them. In response, the Committee remarked that:

the limited list... of appraisals cannot reflect the full extent of [departments'] relevant policy work and must reflect either a very different, more limited, interpretation of whether they have undertaken appraisals or indicate that environmental impacts have not been addressed where they might have been expected.

(HC 426-I Session 1998–9: para. 49)

More worryingly, the committee discovered clear evidence that appraisals were being used as 'after the event justification and mitigation of environmental impacts—the "green proofing" of policy decisions already taken' (HC 426-I Sixth Report Session 1998–9: para. 54). Clearly, this does not accord with the interpretation of EPI offered in Chapter 3.

To conclude, the national EPI system is not performing nearly as strongly as Blair promised it would when he came to power in 1997 (Jordan 2000). Furthermore, the national EPI system is not very strongly tied into EU policymaking, even though the UK is, in most other respects, a comparatively strong champion of EPI in the EU. One contributory factor is political—the environment department has never been put under significant external political pressure to strengthen the links between the two levels. The national parliamentary environmental audit committee (see Chapter 5) has certainly not investigated the extent to which EU environmental proposals are formally integrated into the national EPI system. In fact, recently, it has shifted its focus from auditing the national EPI system, to more publicly and politically visible topics such as road fuel taxation, genetically modified organisms, litter, and environmental crime.

Institutional factors have also played a part. Crucially, EPI at national level is overseen by one part of the environment department (namely the Sustainable Development Unit—SDU), whereas the UK input to EU-EPI initiatives such as Cardiff is directed by another (i.e. the EU-coordinating unit). Moreover, Whitehall officials do not seem to appreciate the need to link EU coordination and national level EPI to facilitate EU-EPI (i.e. the 'double challenge'). Despite many pleas from the Commission to think and act more holistically (see Chapter 5), UK officials still prefer to argue that it is not terribly meaningful to undertake detailed appraisals of Commission proposals when EU environmental policymaking is so dynamic and uncertain. There is an equally strong perception (even within the environment department—see the quotation at the beginning of Chapter 1) that in spite of countless Europeanization initiatives, the primary responsibility for anticipating, appraising, and shaping new EU policies rests primarily with the *Commission*. The Cabinet Office is, however, trying to overturn this perception by pointing out that much national policy is EU-derived, and that new EU policies should therefore undergo a RIA (see below). Evidently, the UK is still getting to grips with the first element of our 'double challenge', let alone moving to deal with both elements simultaneously.

The national coordination of EU-EPI

Our assessment of the level of interdepartmental coordination achieved by the UK administrative system at the various stages of the EU policy process is summarized in Table 8.1.

Initiation

INTERDEPARTMENTAL COORDINATION
Although Cabinet Office guidance recommends that work on an RIA should begin as soon as possible (Cabinet Office 2003: ch. 5), the UK does not formally coordinate policy at this early and somewhat speculative stage unless an individual department has an obvious and strong interest in doing so, or the UKREP believes the national interest demands it. Environment officials argue that if they tried to coordinate every possible policy proposal at this stage, the national coordination system would grind to a halt in a blizzard of paper and emails. Civil servants say they

Table 8.1. The UK: levels of inter-departmental EU policy coordination

	Commission phases						Council phases				
Coordination level	Initiation of new proposals	Work plans	White & Green papers	Drafting of proposals	Inter-service consultation	Presentation of proposals	Presidency agenda	Working parties	COREPER	Council	Conciliation
9 Strategy											
8 Margins			+/−	+/−	+	+	+	+	+	+	+/−
7 Arbitration			+/−	+/−	+	+	+	+	+	+	+/−
6 Conciliation			+/−	+/−	+	+	+	+	+	+	+/−
5 Consensus			+/−	+/−	+	+	+	+	+	+	+
4 One voice			+/−	+	+	+	+	+	+	+	+
3 Consultation	+/−	+/−	+	+	+	+	+	+	+	+	+
2 Communication	+/−	+	+	+	+	+	+	+	+	+	+
1 Independent policy making	+	+	+	+	N/a	+	+	+	+	+	+

Coordination capacities	Initiation of new proposals	Work plans	White & Green papers	Drafting of proposals	Inter-service consultation	Presentation of proposals	Presidency agenda	Working parties	COREPER	Council	Conciliation
Hierarchical											
Bureaucratic	+	+	+	+	+	+	+	+	+	+	+
Specification of output	+/−	+/−	+/−	+/−	+/−	+/−	+/−	+/−	+/−	+/−	+/−
Horizontal	+	+	+	+	+	+	+	+	+	+	+
Informal relations											
Liaison roles	+/−	+/−	+/−	+/−	+/−	+/−	+/−	+/−	+/−	+/−	+/−
Task forces											
Teams	+/−	+/−	+/−	+/−	+/−	+/−	+/−	+/−	+/−	+/−	+/−
Weak integrator	+/−	+/−	+/−	+/−	+/−	+/−	+/−	+/−	+/−	+/−	+/−
Strong integrator	+/−	+/−	+/−	+/−	+/−	+/−	+/−	+/−	+/−	+/−	+/−
Mission statements	+/−	+/−	+/−	+/−	+/−	+/−	+/−	+/−	+/−	+/−	+/−
Role of the EU coordinating units	Backup service for tactical advice (i.e. a *liaison role*) if policy divisions ask for it. But may also be called into settle disputes.										

Explanation:

+ = coordination capacity at this level exists and is used.

+/− = the coordination capacity at this level exists to some extent, but may not always be used.

(+/−) = the coordination capacity at this level exists, but is only used in exceptional cases.

would also feel slightly inhibited if they knew that they had to communicate the existence of every new policy development to sector departments in Whitehall (i.e. the perceived benefits of active information in the UK system are not, it appears, limitless).

The overriding objective at this early stage is to differentiate active policy developments from more inactive ones (e.g. those unlikely to be taken up by the Commission and worked up into legal acts). The UK's EU-coordinating system (and specifically the EU-coordination unit in the environment department) tries to respond to 'active' issues by informing the relevant policy divisions that are likely to be most directly impacted (*watchdog*). If we look at the flow running in the other direction (i.e. national to EU), the EU-coordinating unit in the environment department will expect to be informed of proposals for new EU legislation generated by the policy divisions (*gatekeeper*). In this sense, the unit tries to fulfil at least two distinct *liaison roles*. The EU-coordinating unit in the environment department also tries to work with UKREP (see Chapter 4) to identify important upcoming items of legislation destined for the Environment Council. In practice, however, our interviews suggest that the individual policy divisions in the environment department are better placed to perform this particular task because they are 'closer to the ground'. Indeed, the expectation is that wherever possible, the policy divisions should 'think (and act) European' for themselves (Jordan 2001; 2002a; DEFRA 2004: 51). These divisions do, on occasions, rely upon informal links with their opposite numbers in other member states, but tend not to have direct links with officials in other countries' sectoral departments. Meanwhile, UKREP works with the Cabinet Office and the UK's embassies to help the EU-coordinating unit in the environment department anticipate environment-related developments in other Councils. The system also attempts to anticipate proposals/initiatives made by other member states and the EU institutions.

The EU coordinators in the environment department perform a *liason role* in the environment sector, but they do not formally coordinate dossiers destined for other councils (i.e. formally, they are not cross-sectoral *watchdogs*). As a general rule, the relevant policy divisions are expected to liaise directly with one another (note, the principle of subsidiarity). The EU-coordinating units may, however, be consulted and/or copied papers if and when necessary. They may also try to arbitrate if intersectoral conflicts emerge, but this is not a routine part of their work. The potential flaw in this arrangement is that it is heavily reliant on the presence of active information; that is, the willingness of the sectoral departments to 'inform and consult' their colleagues in the environment department. If the EU-coordinating unit is not involved, it may be difficult to take a holistic view of a proposal from the outset, thereby reducing the scope for achieving EU-EPI at later stages. Therefore, the aspiration is, where possible, to consult (Level 3 on the scale), but in specific circumstances (e.g. a fast-moving situation, lapses into passive information, deliberate strategies not to forewarn cognate departments), simply achieving Level 1 can sometimes be a challenge.

INTRADEPARTMENTAL COORDINATION IN THE ENVIRONMENT DEPARTMENT

The environment department does not formally coordinate policy at this early and somewhat speculative stage unless there is an obvious need (see above).

Commission workplanning

Generally speaking, this stage is treated in exactly the same manner as the previous one; the workplan of the Commission with its detailed annexes is hardly used at all as a formal focus for coordination. On the whole, the EU-coordinating units in the departments normally only look at the workplans produced by 'their' sectoral Commission DG; that is, items destined for the Environment Council would mainly be coordinated by the EU environment-coordinating unit and the relevant policy divisions in the environment department. Even then, coordination tends to be quite informal; that is, the EU-coordinating units do not formally circulate every plan to their respective policy divisions (unless, of course, there are serious cross-departmental implications). Following the subsidiarity principle, policy divisions are therefore expected to do their own intelligence gathering. Consequently, any cross-sectoral coordination that occurs will take place at a fairly low level in Whitehall (i.e. not involving the core—corresponding to Levels 1–3 on the scale). However, the biannual high-level meetings to discuss Presidency agendas (see below) are increasingly used to anticipate upcoming Commission agendas (in view also of the increasing importance of interinstitutional agenda setting in Brussels). This in itself creates a higher level of collective awareness of major new issues which are already heading down the policy pipeline.

White/Green Papers and Communications

These are generally afforded the same importance as a Commission proposal. Because of the legal and political importance of White Papers,
coordination within the UK system generally aspires to solving problems
in the case of intractable interdepartmental disagreement (Level 7) and
defining the room for manoeuvre for the negotiators (Level 8—broad
level of agreement on the direction). However, this can only be achieved
when individual policy divisions actively inform one another of possible
spillover effects. The pressure for early coordination may also grow if a
national parliamentary committee decides to undertake a detailed scrutiny of a particular EU initiative. The need to inform Parliament forces the
government to coordinate away the most obvious divergences (i.e. Level 4
on the scale). Normally, though, the environment department uses White
Papers as a cue to undertake a wide-ranging discussion with cognate
departments about the broad direction of current and future policy (i.e.
is the 'environment' part of their thinking?). They are not normally used
to determine the specific aspects of a policy, or what might be required to
implement EU-EPI.

Drafting of proposals (expert meetings)

INTERDEPARTMENTAL COORDINATION

In the past, experts were regarded as independent and hence 'non-political',
but now the UK regards this phase as an important opportunity to
shape EU policy to reflect national interests (e.g. Cabinet Office 2003: 40).
All departments now recognize the importance of uploading UK ideas
during these early, formative stages. According to the environment department's guide to negotiating in the EU:

> The meetings of national experts... should be taken very seriously.... Commis-
> sion officials... are often under-resourced and short of practical information...
> [T]his should mean UK practice is taken into account by Commission officials...
> and could even lead to the UK system becoming the model for parts of it.
>
> (Humphreys 1996: 93)

Given this general expectation, Whitehall aspires to speak with 'one voice'
(Level 4) when there are intractable cross-sectoral differences. Like its
opposite number in the Netherlands, UKREP is well placed to form a
good overview of upcoming developments in expert committees because
the invitations to individual experts are copied to it. However, everyone in

the system accepts that trying to monitor each and every expert committee would be an administrative nightmare, hence the emphasis on only actively distributing information to relevant actors. The environment department's EU-coordinating unit will certainly not be directly involved in shaping the UK's input to the sectoral councils, as the initiative rests with other departments. Unless there are intractable intersectoral conflicts, the 'core' of the system (i.e. the Cabinet Office—*a strong integrator*) will not get involved until much later in the policy cycle (i.e. the Council phases).

INTRADEPARTMENTAL COORDINATION IN THE ENVIRONMENT DEPARTMENT

In general, the EU-coordinating unit does not formally coordinate the UK's input at this particular stage, though much depends on what is being discussed and by whom. Policy divisions led by experienced negotiators who know how to 'play the European game', will not normally need its assistance. The head of the negotiating team on the proposal will be expected to follow the department's well-established checklist (i.e. *a bureaucratic procedure*) for handling EU legislation (Humphreys 1996: ch. 13). In policy divisions where the EU's involvement is less routine, the EU coordinator(s) will expect to have to intervene more directly; for example, by providing advice and identifying the necessary consultative/coordination links with other divisions (i.e. a *liaison role—watchdog*). Administrative subsidiarity is also achieved in other ways. For instance, less politically salient issues tend to be coordinated bilaterally by the relevant policy divisions, whereas politically more important matters (e.g. a proposal for a new Directive) will usually involve a much greater input from the EU-coordinating unit in the environment department.

Interservice consultation within the Commission

This stage is not regarded as a legitimate focus of UK activity as, formally speaking, it falls within the Commission's sphere of influence. Civil servants are therefore strongly discouraged from contacting Commissioners or their private offices directly (and only then after consulting UKREP). Of course in reality, the environment department will want to ensure that it maintains a watching brief on what the Commission is doing, using more informal means if necessary (see the quote at the beginning of this chapter). If contact has to be made other, more legitimate avenues will be utilized (i.e. via UKREP or through the minister's private office). In this respect, UKREP is regarded as a very good storehouse of advanced information, but in practice it is so overloaded that it can only maintain a watching brief over a relatively small number of strategically important dossiers. Hence, the day-to-day responsibility for following EU affairs normally rests with the individual policy divisions. These points notwithstanding, we can broadly conclude that this stage is not particularly relevant to the UK.

Presentation of proposals

INTRADEPARTMENTAL COORDINATION IN THE ENVIRONMENT DEPARTMENT

Once a proposal has been formally issued as a COM document it will be fed into the national coordinating system by UKREP. From there, it will be passed on to the lead department as well as any other relevant departments, with the EU-coordinating units advising as and when necessary. If the coordinating system has worked properly thus far, the proposal should not contain any nasty or unforeseen surprises. Sometimes, the EU environment coordinators' main task is simply one of ensuring that the whole process runs according to the schedule dictated by the EU (i.e. that policy divisions feed the right information into the national coordinating system at precisely the right time). When intractable conflicts arise between different policy divisions, the EU-coordinating unit will intervene directly to suggest a new or amended policy position to the division in question. In such circumstances, it tries to be the department's own, internal 'honest broker' (i.e. *a weak integrator*).

INTERDEPARTMENTAL COORDINATION

If serious conflicts emerge between departments at this stage they may be left to ride out until much later in the EU policy process. In these circumstances, coordination may only achieve Level 5 on the scale (consensus). But if Parliament decides to undertake a more detailed scrutiny (e.g. prepare a select committee report) the need for a resolution of key conflicts may have to be brought forward, in which case the Cabinet Office's involvement may be needed (i.e. Level 7 on the scale). At this stage the lead policy division will send a draft of the RIA[1] to the UK Parliament as part of the Explanatory Memoranda (see above). The deadline for submitting these documents is extremely tight (ten days from receipt of the proposal), which greatly curtails what can be achieved in terms of spotting environmental impacts and/or coordinating with cognate departments (hence the pressure to start drafting the RIA as soon as possible—see Chapter 5). The EU environmental coordinating unit is always on hand to provide advice, but its services are not always called upon. In the case of controversial or strategically important proposals, the Memoranda should be cleared with UKREP or the relevant departmental EU-coordinating unit in advance. Then, wider, cross-departmental coordination can take place. Another potential trigger for deeper cross-sectoral interaction is the public consultation stage of an RIA (ideally, this should commence as soon as the proposal is formally published) (Cabinet Office 2003: 44). If sectoral officials decide not to reveal some aspects of their thinking about the RIA to the public in order 'to retain the confidentiality of a negotiating position' in the EU, they should inform their departmental RIA unit[2] (Cabinet Office 2003: 44). This unit will then contact the Cabinet Office European Secretariat or UKREP.

Before 2004, there was an expectation that all EU proposals with 'significant' environmental impacts would be formally appraised (see above). However, the decision about whether or not to follow this rested with the respective policy divisions/sectors. The sustainable development unit in the environment department could ask to be consulted, but it had neither the resources nor the political clout to force other departments to undertake appraisals. Not surprisingly, very few EU proposals were ever subjected to an environmental policy appraisal in the UK (see above). Since April 2004, all new EU proposals are supposed to be subjected to an extended RIA, including an assessment of any relevant environmental effects (see Chapter 5).

In theory, therefore, the various policy divisions within the environment department should be fully informed in advance of any environmentally relevant dossiers emerging from other Councils. But in the past, this was somewhat limited by the refusal of the sectoral departments to produce adequate environmental policy appraisals and the inability of the EU-coordinating unit in the environment department to take on 'sectoral' coordinating tasks such as EPI. Time will tell whether the new RIA system leads to a fuller exchange of information between departments about possible environmental impacts of new EU proposals.

The Presidency agenda

A key feature of the UK system is the central role played by the Presidency agendas in shaping interdepartmental coordination (Schout and Metcalfe 1999; Schout 2004). The key actors are the Cabinet Office and the foreign affairs department, but the UK embassy in the country hosting the Presidency will normally play a strong supporting role. The preparations start when the upcoming chair is preparing its agenda, to avoid surprises later on (i.e. more than a year in advance). On arrival of the (six-monthly as well as annual) agendas, interdepartmental meetings are organized to find out whether there are disagreements between departments on cross-cutting issues such as EU-EPI. Again, the relevant policy divisions are normally left to iron out any disputes. However, in the case of more persistent disagreements, the Cabinet Office may be called upon to arbitrate, but as discussed in Chapter 4, its involvement is normally very minimal. The results of their meetings are reported to the relevant cabinet committees.

Because of these activities, there is normally sufficient agreement at the start of each new Presidency to avoid significant coordination problems later. The purpose of these preparations is to reach a general agreement on the broad direction in which the negotiations should move (defining the initial room for manoeuvre, Level 8). Details on the national positions can subsequently be taken in the course of the working party discussions. Adopting this proactive approach is actually amazingly simple. It is also much more effective than (as the Netherlands and Germany are now trying) simply focusing on Commission proposals and workplans.

Council working party negotiations/COREPER/Council meetings

By these stages, the UK system will have identified a cross-governmental position, using the Cabinet Office (*a strong integrator*) to broker disputes as and where appropriate (i.e. up to Level 7 on the scale). The Cabinet Office is continuously supported in this role by the core of the system—namely the UKREP, the weekly Grant–Darroch meeting, and the foreign affairs department (see Chapter 4). The objective is to achieve (as quickly as possible) general agreement on the overall direction of the negotiation, while leaving the negotiators as much leeway as possible (i.e. Level 8). Monitoring is principally organized through the well-established *bureaucratic procedure* of same-day reporting (with a wide distribution) via UKREP, which follows all negotiations. Ideally, this should prevent departments from destabilizing the negotiation by suddenly introducing new demands during the endgame. During these stages, the UK permanent representation is primarily responsible for ensuring that the coordination system works smoothly and effectively. If it has not already done so, by this point the environment department will struggle significantly to win a rearguard battle to (re)integrate some environmental thinking into an environmentally damaging proposal.

Co-decisionmaking and conciliation

At this relatively late stage, the environment department's input is usually highly reactive. The turnaround times are normally so tight as to reduce new coordination efforts to the very minimum. The job of coordinating a response to last-minute developments in the Parliament across Whitehall should not, however, be unduly onerous if a cross-governmental position has been agreed upon in advance. There may be last-minute opportunities for the environment department to push EU-EPI at this late stage, but they tend not to be that predictable in advance.

Improving the UK System

Although there has been no comprehensive, official evaluation of the entire system (Bulmer and Burch 2000: 55; 2006), the general perception is that the UK's coordination works well. Imperfections inevitably arise (for some examples of poor coordination in the environmental sphere, see Sharp (1998)), but many informed commentators regard it as being 'second to none' in the EU (Wallace 1996: 64). When it is functioning properly, the UK system is 'tight' but sufficiently flexible to anticipate and respond to unforeseen changes in a dossier. The culture of issue coordination and active information means that information is moved relatively quickly and efficiently around the system. As regards Mintzberg's six coordinating mechanisms, the UK is heavily reliant on *bureaucratic politics* (i.e. active information informed by policy appraisals, etc.), various *liason roles* (specifically the EU coordinators in each department), and *informal relations* (most departments recognize the benefit of 'speaking with one voice' in the EU). The Grant–Darroch meeting (*team*) and various standing cabinet committees (*teams*), and even the foreign and cabinet offices themselves (*strong integrators*), are available to broker compromises if need be. *Skills development and training* in environmental policy appraisal is in theory always available, but very few sector officials attend courses run by the civil service college (Russel 2004).

The UK system has a number of strengths (Humphreys 1996: 38–9). First and foremost, once the environment department has secured a cross-governmental position on a particular dossier, the other departments are normally bound to support it throughout the remainder of a negotiation. Unlike some of its opposite numbers in other, less well-coordinated member states (e.g. of Germany), it does not have to invest in monitoring units or undertake 'control trips' to Brussels. This can pay dividends particularly at the implementation stage (the UK does have a very good (but not entirely unblemished) record in this respect) (National Audit Office 2005). Second, it allows for the early identification and consideration of all relevant sectoral interests (Bulmer and Burch 2000; 2006). In theory, this should mean that the environment department receives an early warning of EU proposals in the sectors that have the potential to subvert EU-EPI. Again, its opposite numbers in other member states find themselves in a much weaker position vis-à-vis their sector departments. Moreover, because the UK will normally have thought about issues proactively on the basis of Presidency agendas, it is likely to be more informed than other states about possible cross-sectoral impacts. Consequently, it should be more than capable of playing a strong role in any EPI network at EU level.

However, the British system also suffers from a number of well-known weaknesses (Kassim 2000; 2001; Bulmer and Burch 2000; 2006). There are at least two which impact on the scope for pursuing EPI. The first arises from the tendency for the British to 'overprepare' for EU negotiations. Being the first country to adopt a negotiating position can, it has been claimed, reduce the room for tactical manoeuvring during the endgame of an EU negotiation. So, for example, this may limit what the environment department can do to influence the activities of cognate departments in the sectoral Councils. Secondly, there is a price to be paid for active information and issue coordination, which is that officials with horizontal coordinating ambitions (e.g. EU-EPI) have to mobilize very early, as negotiating positions become solidified much earlier in the UK than they do in the other actors. Departments that do not 'think and act European' will therefore lose out, as did the UK environment department throughout the 1970s and 1980s (Jordan 2002a). By contrast, Dutch and German environment officials can step in and open a national negotiating position at any time (sometimes unilaterally), whereas this option is not normally available to UK environment officials. The corollary is that UK environment officials must be especially alert to what is going on during the very early stages of policy development in the EU policy sectors.

How well does the EU coordination system work in the environment department? As with the national-level system, there have been surprisingly few comprehensive assessments (but see DEFRA 2004). One of the first (in 1992–3) concluded that policy divisions do not consult the

EU-coordinating unit enough (DoE 1993: 13–14). Since then, the department has tried to improve its handling of EU business (Sharp 1998), by increasing the profile of European work in the policy divisions and disseminating advice. Nowadays, the feeling within and outside Whitehall is that the environment department is one of the most Europeanized departments (Jordan 2002a; 2003) and hence capable of meeting the first part of the double challenge of EU-EPI.

How could the present arrangements for handling EU-EPI be improved? First and foremost, the Rolls Royce coordination system should, in theory, work in favour of cross-sectoral coordination, by, for example, making it difficult for a sectoral department to pursue secretly an environmentally destructive path in the EU. In comparison to the Netherlands and Germany, it provides the environment department with a much earlier opportunity to integrate environmental considerations into other policy sectors before the die of the UK's national negotiating position is cast. And once that position has been brokered across Whitehall, the EU-coordinating system should ensure that it is maintained throughout the course of the negotiation (hence, no need for monitoring units and 'control trips' to Brussels). In one sense, this puts the environment department at a huge advantage over its opposite numbers in Germany, the Netherlands, and DG Environment. However, the UK system only ever presents pro-environment departments in Whitehall with an *opportunity* to achieve EPI in the EU. In order to exploit it, the environment department must muster sufficient political support for integration within and outside Whitehall, bearing in mind that other departments will simultaneously be seeking to pursue their own sectoral concerns.

This leads to a second possible improvement: the environment department is doing a lot more to adopt a proactive relationship with the EU system (see the quote at the beginning of this chapter), but it could do a lot more to seize the coordination opportunities provided by the UK system to pursue EU-EPI. At present, its EU-coordinating unit is too small and it has not sufficiently re-evaluated its tasks to address the challenges posed by EU-EPI. Consequently, the environment department as a whole is not able to ensure that dossiers negotiated in the sectoral councils take account of the environment. This may (as discussed above) require a more explicit interface with the formal administrative guardian of national level EPI, namely the SDU. Although these two units are in a constant dialogue, by separating their functions, the environment department gives the strong impression that EU-EPI and national EPI are functionally separate, when our evidence suggests that the opposite is true. In 2004, the environment minister created a Better Regulation Unit to coordinate the production of advice on the new, more integrated policy appraisal system and generally promote the principles of better regulation in the department (DEFRA 2004: 50). It is still not clear how this new unit will interface with the sustainable development and EU-coordinating units.

Third, the links between the systems of national and EU-level EPI could be strengthened. Nowhere is this need more apparent than in relation to policy appraisal. For a country which proclaims to be a champion of EPI, it is very strange that so few Commission proposals since 1997 have received an adequate environmental policy appraisal in the UK. The Cabinet Office has made it clear that *all* EU proposals should be subjected to a full RIA under the new regime. Moreover, it expects the preparatory work to begin as soon as possible (and certainly by the time the Commission begins to draft a legislative proposal) (Cabinet Office 2003:10). Although the Cabinet Office's involvement is helping to drive up the number of new EU proposals that are subjected to an RIA, doubts have been expressed about their environmental content (see Chapter 5). The Parliamentary environmental audit committee recently suggested that RIA is 'ill-suited' to the multifaceted challenge of sustainability (HC 261 Seventh Report Session 2004–5: para. 10). It would prefer to incorporate RIA into a 'meta-'system of sustainability impact assessment (SIA), overseen by a dedicated 'sustainable development unit' in the Cabinet Office (HC 261 Seventh Report Session 2004–5: para. 11, 17). At the time of writing, the government does not appear inclined to accept this.

Conclusions

With its network of green ministers, green cabinet committee, and long-established environmental policy appraisal regime, the UK should be very well placed to address a complicated cross-sectoral challenge such as EPI. Having noted the presence of these features, it is not entirely surprising that the OECD made such a positive assessment of the UK's response to EPI. The OECD's optimism is consistent with textbook descriptions of how Whitehall supposedly coordinates EU policy. In fact, the system appears to be so well designed that for many of the policy stages, we found it very difficult to distinguish between inter- and intradepartmental coordination.

However, the UK's very well-oiled administrative machine struggles consistently to extend EPI into all aspects of national and EU policymaking.

On reflection, the OECD's glowing assessment probably stems from a rather cursory check that the various coordination capacities are present, rather than a much more detailed analysis of how they actually function on a daily basis. There are at least four factors that can account for this omission. The first is that while the UK is undoubtedly the most internally coordinated of the three states in our sample (Kassim 2000; 2001), the UK system was not set up to achieve EPI, agricultural policy integration, transport policy integration, or any other sectoral integration/coordination objective. On the contrary, it provides a more or less neutral venue in which the differences between different departments can be aired and, wherever possible, resolved. In the absence of a stronger, more directed push from the centre of government, the fate of sectoral coordination targets like EPI is strongly determined by relatively non-hierarchical *informal relations* (i.e. *bureaucratic politics*). The problem here is that such an arrangement only presents pro-integration departments with an opportunity—and only an opportunity—to achieve stronger coordination, but the environment department has still not invested in the resources to exploit them. Moreover, important opportunities to strengthen the links between EPI initiatives at EU and at national level, are not being identified or exploited by the environment department. Many officials that we interviewed implied that they should concentrate on national level EPI, leaving EU-EPI to the Commission. These beliefs could only have been strengthened by comments made by ministers like Michael Meacher (see the quotation at the beginning of Chapter 1). To make matters worse, no one else in the domestic political system (most notably, the national parliamentary audit committee) seems to be aware that EPI is a multilevel coordination challenge that requires coordination networks to be established.

Second, support for stronger environmental protection is not sufficiently strong across Whitehall to guarantee EPI via *bureaucratic politics* alone. According to a former senior DoE official:

at its heart the British establishment is not very green, as is reflected in the [environment department's] pecking order among Whitehall [departments]. There are many environmental assumptions, right or wrong, that have to be argued within the UK Government machine that simply appear to be self-evident in the German or Dutch context. (Sharp 1998: 55)

One way in which the prime minister could overcome this systematic downgrading of environmental arguments, is to deploy coordinating capacities with greater hierarchical force. For example, clear environmental limits could be determined across government and applied *ex ante* (e.g. in public service agreements or in the implementation of the national sustainable development strategy) (i.e. *specification of output*). In this chapter we have shown that most of the existing targets have little hierarchical force, being more akin to *mission statements* than *specifications of output*. Similarly, the Cabinet Office could be given a much stronger remit to champion EPI and sustainability across government. At present, it acts as the 'honest broker' as regards EU policy coordination; it is not the guardian of EPI in Whitehall or even (in spite of recent demands made by the parliamentary environmental audit committee—see above) of better environmental policy appraisal. In fact, its environmental unit was transferred to the environment department in 1970, where it has remained ever since (Jordan 2002*a*).

Third, the likelihood of the centre of government giving EPI a stronger hierarchical push remains quite low *inter alia* because the political pressure on the administrative system remains low, especially in the pro-jobs and-growth climate typified by the Lisbon process. At heart, Blair is not personally committed to environmental issues, despite many protestations to the contrary (Jordan 2000; Humphrey 2003). With the exception of the Green Alliance and the IEEP (Jordan 2002*c*), national environmental pressure groups do not take an active interest in the functioning of the national or the EU's EPI systems, let alone the connections between the two. Even the parliamentary audit committee appears to have shifted its focus to more high-profile environmental challenges. The combination of strong administrative mechanisms but weak political ambitions goes a long way to explaining why the UK finds itself 'in the middle range of EU or OECD countries for many environmental indicators' (OECD 2002*b*: 136).

Notes

1. The RIA is not completed (i.e. 'signed off' by the relevant Minister) until the implementing legislation is laid before the UK Parliament (Cabinet Office 2003: 45).
2. Each department has a regulatory impact or 'better regulation' unit, whose job it is to promote the principles and practice of 'better regulation'.

Part IV

European Union Institutions

9

THE EUROPEAN COMMISSION: AN ORGANIZATION IN TRANSITION?

[Preventing] a damaging gap between the Commission's roles and the Commission's functioning... will be the real test of the effectiveness and durability of reform. I am confident that the Commission will pass that test. The irony will be, of course, that no-one will notice it because operational efficiency rarely attracts attention and even more rarely generates news.

(European Commissioner Neil Kinnock, 9 February 2004) (Kinnock 2004)

Introduction

The Commission has a poor reputation for internal and external management. In Chapter 2, we noted Metcalfe's claim that the Commission is insufficiently active in managing networks, although we also identified some issue areas in which it plays a more hands-on role. Previous chapters have concluded that the three member states in our sample have not done much to stimulate EPI-related networks at EU level, or connect them to effective coordination capacities at the national level. Building on Chapter 5, they also noted that the coordination capacities at national level are also weak in a number of important respects.

This chapter looks at the issue of EU-EPI from the Commission's perspective. It is important to spend some time looking at the Commission because it plays a number of special roles in the context of this study. It is *inter alia* the formal initiator of EU policy, the guardian of the treaties (including Article 6), and a mediator between states and EU institutions.

As noted in Chapter 1, a Commission proposal and the documents attached to it frame subsequent negotiations in the Council and the European Parliament (see also Chapter 2) to such an extent, that the battle for greater EPI can very often be lost at this early stage. Moreover, the increasing practice of planning agendas and work programmes between the Commission, the Parliament, and the Council (Presidencies) has underlined its special position even more.

So, how well positioned is the Commission to act as the champion and manager of EU-EPI? There is, at least on paper, abundant political support in the Commission for more policy integration. It has made countless high-level promises dating back to the 1970s to reconsider its own internal procedures and has been instrumental in pushing the rest of the EU to commit to EU-EPI (Chapter 3). In addition, the renewed emphasis put on Better Regulation has emphasized the importance of systematically testing all new proposals against subsidiarity and proportionality guidelines (see e.g. CEC 2005*d*) and subjecting them to IAs. This has helped to make Commission proposals more solid and credible. But as already noted in Chapter 4, the Commission has a history of weak planning and internal coordination. Dinan (1999: 213) goes as far as to suggest that it is an intrinsically 'uncollegiate' organization. Furthermore, a succession of previous reform efforts have failed to deliver what was expected of them (Dinan 1999: 222–3; Cini 2005). What, therefore, can we say about the internal reforms made by the Commission in pursuit of EU-EPI? This is an important question to pose given the (apparently widely held) view that the Commission should take the lead in pursuing EU-EPI.

The Commission and EU-EPI

Advocating EPI in the EU

The Commission—or at least its DG Environment—stands out as having been the most consistently forceful advocate of EPI in the EU. Bringing together observations made in Chapters 3 and 5, we can say that it has contributed by: embedding EPI in the EU's constitutional system; initiating reform processes that adapt its internal coordination capacities better to foster EU-EPI; organizing benchmarking exercises to enhance national sustainability; building external links and networks; and calling attention to the administrative requirements of EPI.

EMBEDDING EPI IN THE TREATIES

The Commission's thinking on EPI had already begun to crystallize as early as 1980 when it issued a report on the implementation of the Second EAP. This report noted the need for new 'measures designed to give greater consistency between the exigencies of environmental policy and those of other policies... by dovetailing environmental policy into those policies more effectively' (quoted in Haigh 2002: section 3.1–1). Soon after, the Commission succeeded in inserting a much fuller reference to EPI into the Third EAP, covering the period 1983–7 (Official Journal C46, 17 February 1983, section I: 8). Thereafter, the Commission played an instrumental part in ensuring the inclusion of EPI in the environmental part of the 1987 Single European Act. It also worked with other like-minded actors to push for this commitment to be strengthened in the Maastricht and Amsterdam Treaties. Finally, as discussed in Chapter 3, DG Environment also played a hugely important part in first initiating, and then stocktaking, the Cardiff process. The Lisbon process is, of course, also handled by the Commission's Secretariat-General.

INTERNAL CAPACITY BUILDING

The Commission has made several internal changes to facilitate greater EPI (see Chapter 5). It also produces general frameworks for policy development (e.g. EAPs and the SDS), although these do not specify many concrete targets and tasks.[1] Similarly, in its first five-year mission the Barroso Commission argued that 'the environmental challenges facing Europe need a coordinated, EU-wide response' (CEC 2005e: 7). However, in recent years, Barroso has demonstrated on a number occasions that his main priority is jobs and growth (i.e. the Lisbon agenda), Better Regulation (read, the simplification of the *acquis* and, where possible, deregulation to enhance economic competitiveness), as well as generally improving the administrative capacity of the Commission. In 2004, he famously compared himself to the father of a sick child—the economy—that urgently needed his special attention.

ORGANIZING BENCHMARKING EXERCISES

The Commission has tried to overcome its weak influence over national administrative arrangements, by developing and employing 'new governance' type tools. For instance, in 2004 it published a benchmarked summary of national sustainable development strategies, which highlighted the need for greater information sharing on 'horizontal measures and policy guidelines that... increase policy coherence across sectors' (CEC 2004f: 21).

BUILDING EXTERNAL LINKAGES AND NETWORKS

Chapter 3 discussed and assessed the various administrative innovations pushed by the Commission to improve policy coordination at various levels of governance. These include the Strauss–Kahn round-table negotiations and the EPRG. However, neither of these have done much to advance EU-EPI in daily policymaking.

URGING OTHER INSTITUTIONS TO BUILD CAPACITIES

As well as enhance its own internal coordination capacities, the Commission's SDU has enjoined other actors to work together in a 'partnership' (or network) for integration. It has also repeatedly (but as yet unsuccessfully) requested that the European Parliament and the Council of Ministers to subject substantial amendments to a policy appraisal.

The Commission's coordination capacities supporting EU-EPI

Since 1970, the Commission has undertaken a trial-and-error search for new coordination capacities to pursue EU-EPI. However, the steps taken by the Commission to alter its own internal organization have been more successful. These are summarized in the following subsections.

DG ENVIRONMENT'S MANAGEMENT MEETINGS

Decisions in DG Environment on activities (including which topics to monitor in other DGs) are taken in meetings of directors on Monday mornings. Each unit within DG Environment is responsible for pursuing EPI in its own field. In general, the emphasis is very much upon their work in the Environment Council. There is little capacity at a high level in DG Environment to champion EU-EPI or take a synoptic view of events.[2] The unit for sustainable development and integration (SDU) is the most directly responsible, but as discussed below, it has to supervise a wide range of other tasks. Currently, it does not receive sufficient political support from the apex of the Commission or even DG Environment.

THE UNIT FOR SUSTAINABLE DEVELOPMENT AND ECONOMIC ANALYSIS[3]

The unit was created in the wake of the Fifth EAP (see Chapter 5). Broadly, its tasks are: to support the use of environmental policy appraisal in the DGs; assist the environmental correspondents (see below); and facilitate an exchange of information about EU-EPI between DGs. With respect to EU-EPI, it has also, *inter alia*, coordinated the production of EAPs; led the writing of the Cardiff stocktakes (see Chapter 3); liaised with the EPRG; and coordinated DG Environment's input to the preparation of the annual 'synthesis reports' delivered to each spring council as part of the Lisbon process. This is a long and very varied list of tasks for a unit that (in 2004) employed just nine policy officials and eight support staff. This explains partly why it does not do more to monitor day-to-day policy developments in the other DGs.

Secondly, our interviews echo widespread doubts about the political support it receives from the apex of DG Environment (see Chapter 3). The upper echelons of DG Environment do not appear to favour a 'policing' role as they see their primary task as one of producing new environment policy (or, more recently, defending existing environmental policies from various deregulation and simplification initiatives). EPI requires frequent intervention by the apex in the work of other DGs, but this goes against the tradition of respecting 'turf' boundaries in the Commission. Finally, guiding such a horizontal unit requires the incumbent to have a good overview, a strong network, and a secure position. However, this unit has never enjoyed consistent leadership—there have been frequent changes of director and head of unit.

ENVIRONMENTAL CORRESPONDENTS IN OTHER DGS

A network of environment experts from each DG was created in the early 1990s to reinforce the coordination capacities of the DGs and facilitate greater information flows. These environmental correspondents (or *liaisons* in Mintzberg's terms) were expected to champion EPI. But the way in which the various DGs incorporated them into their work differed quite significantly. Thus, some merely added environment policy to someone's job description (e.g. DG Internal Market and Services), whereas the former DG Transport created a specific unit for environment policy and positioned officials with environment tasks throughout its organization.[4] However, most of the correspondents were too junior, or simply too peripheral, to have a long-lasting impact. In practice, they often acted more like *gatekeepers* than environmental *ambassadors*. Their function was supposed to make the organization more transparent and reduce coordination costs, but they never actually defended EU-EPI in the daily battles between different DGs over individual items of policy. Hence, political support for EU-EPI had to come from elsewhere.

THE SECRETARIAT GENERAL

Over the past decade, the Secretariat has increased markedly in terms of its prestige and powers, due *inter alia* to the internal crises of the late 1990s (see Chapter 4). Currently, its roles include: planning and reporting on progress; keeping an overview on policy development and ensuring consistency where necessary; and monitoring procedures and facilitating coordination. Before a proposal is passed to the interservice committees and College, the Secretariat General checks that all steps in the planning process have been taken, that relevant parties have been heard, and that the necessary forms have been completed.[5] It also monitors conciliation and coordinates the Lisbon process.

In spite of its central position, the Secretariat General's influence has tended to be rather limited (see Chapter 4). The Commissioners have traditionally had a strong role in the Commission (Dinan 1999: 222); the President of the College is no more than a *primus inter pares* (*strong integrator*) (but see Devuyst 2004: 18). The Secretariat General therefore has neither the time nor the political muscle systematically to pursue better coordination across the entire organization (Schendelen 2004: 65), especially in relation to relatively technical (i.e. sectoral) issues such as EU-EPI. For example, it was supposed to monitor the application of the environmental policy appraisal procedure ('green star') introduced in 1992–3 (see Chapter 5), but it saw this as being the responsibility of individual DGs, notably DG Environment. Lacking support from the Secretariat General on this important initiative, DG Environment failed to make much progress. Our interviews suggest that the Secretariat General resembles less the coordinating 'cabinet offices' that exist in some member states, and more an administrative postbox—a function which is commonly performed by the foreign affairs departments in the member states (cf. Hocking 1999; Schout and Metcalfe 1999).

In the 2000s, the tasks of the Secretariat General's SPP unit were widened and its position was upgraded under the Secretary General. Consequently, the Secretariat General now plays a much stronger role in policy planning (see Chapter 5). All planning and drafting phases are now much more visible due to the rolling planning process and the 'roadmaps' produced under the new IA system (see Chapter 4). Nevertheless, during our interviews, staff repeatedly complained that the Commission still produces far too much new policy (see also Lodge 2005).[6] Time will tell whether the current drive for Better Regulation has a long-lasting impact. The jury is also still out on whether the Commission's Secretariat has sufficient prestige and power to plan better as well as supervise a rapidly increasing number of IAs (compare also Hertin, Jacob, and Volkery 2007).

OFFICIALS WITH ENVIRONMENTAL RESPONSIBILITIES IN THE *CABINETS* OF OTHER COMMISSIONERS

Each Commissioner shares responsibility for Commission policy and has an official in his or her *cabinet* to cover other policy fields. Each DG's primary task, however, is to make sure that Commission policy suits the profile of his or her Commissioner (cf. Spence 1994). This makes them 'gatekeepers' of the (national) interests of the Commissioner and his or her policy objectives, rather than green ambassadors (i.e. they are weak rather than strong *liason roles*).

SUBGROUPS OF COMMISSIONERS RELATED TO ENVIRONMENT POLICY

Another possible coordination capacity for facilitating EU-EPI is to create a subgroup of EPI Commissioners. The list of subgroups of Commissioners is, of course, ever-changing. Significantly, the subgroups created by Barroso are strongly related to the Lisbon agenda, to economic competitiveness, external relations, fundamental rights, and better communications and programming (CEC 2005*f*). However, the effectiveness of these groups can vary enormously. The group of green Commissioners that existed during the 1990s (see Chapter 5) hardly ever met due to the workload of those involved and the political commitment of those selected to participate.

The Coordination of EU-EPI

Our assessment of the level of interdepartmental coordination achieved by the Commission's administrative system at the various stages of the EU policy process is summarized in Table 9.1.

Initiation

Most ideas for new policy proposals stem from outside the Commission. Estimates of so-called 'own Commission' proposals vary from 5 to 15 per cent of the total (Peterson 1999: 59). Most proposals in fact originate in response to requests from the Council (following a crisis such as the

Table 9.1. The European Commission: levels of inter-departmental policy coordination

	Commission phases						Council phases				
	Initiation of new proposals	Work plans	White & Green papers	Drafting of proposals	Inter-service consultation	Presentation of proposals	Presidency agenda	Working parties	COREPER	Council	Conciliation
Coordination level											
9 Strategy											
8 Margins											
7 Arbitration											
6 Conciliation			+	+|–	+				+	+	+
5 Consensus			+	+|–	+			+	+	+	+
4 One voice			+	+|–	+			+	+	+	+
3 Consultation		+	+	+|–	+			+	+	+	+
2 Communication	+|–	+	+	+|–	+		+|–	+	+	+	+
1 Independent policy making	+	+	+	+	+	Not relevant	+	+	+	+	+
Coordination capacities											
Hierarchical											
Bureaucratic	+|–	+	+	+	+				+	+	+
Specification of output								+	+		
Horizontal											
Informal relations				+							
Liaison roles	+|–	+|–					+|–	+	+	+	
Task forces		+			+						
Teams			+	+							
Weak integrator		+	+	+|–	+			+|–	+		+
Strong integrator		+		+|–					+	+|–	
Mission statements											
Role of the EU coordinating units	The sustainable development unit is mainly oriented towards strategic policies (Cardiff, the EAPs and the SDS), not so much the day-to-day policies)										

Explanation:

+ = coordination capacity at this level exists and is used.

+/– = the coordination capacity at this level exists to some extent, but may not always be used.

(+/–) = the coordination capacity at this level exists, but is only used in exceptional cases.

sinking of an oil tanker), the European Parliament, individual member states, industrial bodies, or pressure groups. Also, international agreements, rulings by the ECJ, and reports by the EEA and the OECD all help to trigger initiatives. Otherwise, many items on the agenda comprise revisions of existing legislation or concern the implementation of existing White Papers. Regardless of the precise origin of a proposal, it goes through many internal and external consultations before being adopted by the College of Commissioners. In terms of the coordination scale, most policy proposals originate from within individual policy fields (i.e. Level 1).

If officials know each other and have a history of working well together, they may want to discuss the need for a new proposal informally (hence the +/− at Level 2 in Table 9.1). A first priority is to get the idea put on the workplan of the relevant DG. However, there are many things that are explored in DGs that are not listed in the workplans—because they either are too premature or are not liked by other DGs. Except for an increasing number of references in internal rules of procedure and other internal handbooks to work 'in close cooperation and in coordinated fashion' (e.g. Article 21), there are no formal coordination capacities at this stage; indeed, examples of poor coordination are not difficult to find.

Commission workplanning

Workplanning has increased in the last few years in response to repeated criticism that decisionmaking in the Commission was too opaque and incoherent. It has helped to make the Commission's activities more visible, and has given member states and interested third parties more time to prepare. All the Commission's activities are set out in an annual workplan. Within the DGs, there are *liaison roles*—such as assistants to the DG—whose job it is to pass on indicative lists of new legislation to the Secretariat General. The draft workplan then follows the same route (i.e. via the *cabinets* and college—both examples of coordinating *teams*) as regular Commission proposals. The Secretariat General coordinates the preparations of each workplan to ensure that deadlines are kept and proper procedures are followed (i.e. a *weak integrator*).

Putting items on a workplan is one thing, but starting to draft a proposal is another entirely. Among other things, this hugely important step depends on workloads, political demands, and of course the ease with which they go through internal procedures. Planning has, however, become more structured because of rolling programmes like Lisbon, interinstitutional cooperation, multi-annual presidency programmes, and the shift to team Presidencies (but see Schout 2006).

The first step in the planning process is the development of an indicative list of proposals presented by each DG. Until recently, these lists were still quite long—the list for 2000 contained 257 legislative proposals and 176 White Papers, Communications, and reports, as well as seventy Commission acts. These numbers vary: seventy-three new proposals were scheduled in 2004 and fifty-three were still on the agenda from 2003 (see also CEC 2003a: 31–3; CEC 2005d). Nowadays, there is a much stronger push from the President and powerful member states for the Commission to 'do less but better'. Hence, the length of new indicative lists is declining.

The college discusses the workplan in October so that it can be presented to the European Parliament in December and enter into force in January. The Commission normally presents a shortened version to the Parliament at the end of each year. Therefore, the planning process is a relatively bottom-up process through which officials and heads of units indicate what they intend to work on. On the other hand, it also contains an element of top-down steering because the Commissioner and his or her senior staff will often try to use it to stamp their mark on the direction of future policy.

Table 9.1 shows that workplanning—despite being routinized—is still mainly an independent activity dominated by the DGs with little inter-DG cooperation. The Secretariat General and the other DGs are constantly informed (i.e. Level 2 on the scale), but higher levels of coordination are difficult to achieve due to lack of resources and a residual tendency to avoid early coordination. Information flows are therefore still relatively passive. As discussed more fully in Chapter 5, the Commission is supposed to subject each workplan and individual proposals to an IA (i.e. *a bureaucratic procedure*). Some hope that the new system will create a spirit of learning (like a *mission statement*) that eventually produces a a new 'sustainable development culture' in the Commission. But so far, the initial outcomes have been quite disappointing (Wilkinson et al. 2004b).

In theory, the new workplanning process should make it much easier for DG Environment to see what is emerging in the other important fields. However, as officials explained, it has little time to act on the information it receives at this very early stage. As a result, agreeing collective priorities with the sectors is very hard to do as it involves coordinating across administrative and sectoral boundaries, which inevitably sucks political and staff resources from DG Environment's 'core' environmental work.

3.3 White/Green Papers and Communications

Before embarking on the drafting process, the need for the policy is first discussed in the College and the objectives are presented to the relevant Council. New measures have to be placed in the context of Commission strategies and objectives as set out in Green and White Papers, strategic programmes, and communications, which set out the major policy objectives for the medium term. In 2003, the Commission published six Green Papers and one White Paper (although two were planned). These strategic papers are usually well coordinated. DGs will make strong efforts to arrive at consensus before the paper is presented to the College. There are several mediation mechanisms in the policy formulation process, such as informal level mediation at higher level and involvement of the Secretariat General if necessary (i.e. up to Level 6). Arbitration is more difficult due to the strong position of DGs and Commissioners.

The President is no more than the *primus inter pares* of the College (i.e. there is an *integrating role*, but not a strong one). Arbitration is particularly difficult when there are highly sensitive topics, for example when particular Commissioners come under intense pressures from (their) national governments. Coordination, therefore, sometimes reaches Level 6, but normally no higher. But even Level 6 (conciliation) can be very difficult to achieve if Commissioners have a strong personal attachment to a particular proposal.

Drafting of proposals (expert meetings)

This phase is highly regulated by *bureaucratic procedures* and coordination is also supported by various *horizontal mechanisms* (see Table 9.1). However, the hierarchical control exerted by the DGs or Commissioners may easily frustrate them. Generally, one DG is in charge and appoints a file officer. This *rapporteur* is formally expected to consult with colleagues (see, among others, CEC 2005c: 5), giving the impression that information flows actively. But whether and how this happens varies. Mostly, officials will have internal Commission networks, which are regularly consulted. Sometimes, the *rapporteur* will first discuss the issues—and how to handle the process—with his own management before consulting other DGs. Consultation is highly dependent on the person involved, the working culture of particular DGs, the instructions received from the lead DG, and the political sensitivity of the topic in question (hence the '+/−' in Table 9.1).

Openness between DGs is usually not a problem. During the writing process, the lead DG may gather several advisory meetings with national officials and European sectoral bodies. However, the more sensitive and controversial the topic, or the stronger the personal preferences of a Commissioner, the more he or she will be inclined to restrict preparatory discussions with cognate DGs. For example, during our interviews, DG Environment officials regularly complained about other DGs producing Green and White Papers of which they had no prior warning. As a result, they struggle to respect the tight deadlines for reacting when the documents eventually go to the *cabinet* (see below).

The management of the lead DG examines the developments of the proposal at regular intervals and decides when to refer a proposal to inter-DG discussions. If necessary, the Commissioner can be consulted through the relevant *cabinet* member. The Commissioner may have asked to be kept abreast due to expected sensitivities within the Commission or his or her national government (Spence 1994; Nugent 2001: 251). Any controversies that arise between DGs can be discussed bilaterally between unit heads, directors, DGs, or Commissioners. Alternatively, they can also be discussed in interservice committees (or *task force* in the terminology of Table 9.1) convened by the *rapporteur*. These comprise colleagues from other DGs and allow an informal discussion to take place. However, due to time constraints, consultation is often limited to experts in the same field, thereby reducing the scope for EU-EPI. If necessary, EU-EPI-related conflicts can be raised in the weekly meetings of DGs and their deputies, and in the College of Commissioners. However, the normal workload carried by the College means this does not occur routinely. Finally, the Secretariat General is in theory available to deal with disputes; for example, to ensure that horizontal Commission objectives are respected (i.e. up to Level 6). However, as noted above, it will only make this check when the proposal is finally submitted.

In summary, deliberations on EU-EPI are quite ad hoc during this vital stage in the Commission's preparation. Much depends on the working style of individuals in the Commission and the passive efforts made by DG Environment to raise the profile of EU-EPI. The Commission is very much an organization in transition—see, for example, the new workplanning system supported by roadmaps, the IA regime, and the efforts to achieve wider consultation. However, the actual extent of cross-sectoral cooperation thereby achieved continues to depend heavily on the work put in by individual officials and the shifting inclinations of their managers.

Interservice consultation within the Commission/presentation of proposals

The route to the College runs directly through the Secretariat General. When a DG has agreed on a proposal, it is sent to the meeting of DGs. The proposal is subsequently put on the agenda of the management meetings in the various DGs, who have just ten days to react.[7] It is not unusual for a proposal to arrive a few days before the weekly meeting of *cabinets* (on Mondays) or the weekly meetings of the *chefs* (on Fridays). This leaves very little time for a DG to assess the different—and possibly conflicting—environmental effects of a proposal or resolve differences that undermine the pursuit of EU-EPI. Commitments to present proposals to Parliament or the Council—for example, because it was promised to the Presidency—may accentuate these time pressures even more. The jury is still out on whether the new roadmaps provide sufficient respite.

After the interservice consultation, the proposal is put on the agenda of the College. The Secretariat General checks whether the annexes are complete, including the IA. *Cabinet* meetings discuss the proposal before it reaches the College.[8] If necessary a meeting of the 'special chefs' (i.e. lower-level *teams* of *cabinet* members from specific fields) can examine it first. The College is prepared by the Hebdo (a *team* of Cabinet *chefs*—see Chapter 4). The Hebdo may send proposals back to the *rapporteurs* and marks those that can proceed as A-point on the agenda of the College (i.e. without discussion). If there are severe controversies, the Secretary General can call in the contending parties and conciliate (i.e. Level 6 on the scale). The Secretary General has strong formal and informal powers but he cannot arbitrate—the final decision rests with the College. Officially, it may decide by majority (Article 8, Rules of Procedure, CEC (2000*b*)) but unanimity is the preferred way of working. The College—the highest and strongest *team* in the Commission—benefits from the *integrating role* of the President of the Commission. But despite his powers, he generally only ever conciliates.

The Presidency agenda

The Presidency agenda is not a point in the process that is intensely coordinated between DGs. The Secretariat General is involved in the annual agenda setting in cooperation with the upcoming Presidencies, but this mainly concerns the overall shape of the agenda, not the detailed content of topics. This information is widely shared between

DGs. Individual DGs will, of course, liaise with their sectoral counterparts in the Council and the European Parliament about the work programme for the coming months and year. This can happen quite independently (hence '+/−' at Level 2). During these discussions, they will have the Commission's overall priorities and objectives in mind. The assistants to the Directors General will scrutinize the agendas in other fields (resembling a *liaison role*), but the emphasis remains on 'their' sectoral Councils.

Council working party negotiations

The Commission continues to be a key player during the subsequent negotiations (it remains responsible for the content of a proposal until adoption or conciliation) and Commission officials will negotiate continuously with the member states and Presidency in and outside formal meetings. As a general note, the way in which EU-EPI is pursued differs strongly within and between different DGs. Some DG Environment officials will make an effort to track a proposal through cognate DGs whose support is specifically needed to ensure EU-EPI. Others, however, find it harder to perform this task because of the sectorization of the Council and Parliament. The Parliament's BSE inquiry showed the extent to which Councils are fragmented and how this affects intra-Commission coordination (European Parliament 1997). Therefore, the prospects for EU-EPI often depend on other actors—for example, national environment departments, MEPs, and environmental pressure groups. Some officials within the lead DGs will make an effort to keep DG Environment posted, but often only on an informal and ad hoc basis. *Task forces* may be organized and all officials formally have the right to call meetings, but because of the ever-present time pressures and the large workloads that everyone is carrying, this does not regularly happen.

During the working party stage, the lead DG is able to work independently because the objective is to defend the proposal agreed by the College. But of course the Council and Parliament will often want to suggest changes that may or may not preserve the integrity of what the College has agreed. In general, Commission officials will try their utmost to respond with one voice (i.e. Level 6), relying mostly on *bureaucratic politics*. Where necessary, the Secretariat General can mediate; difficulties can also be discussed informally between DGs or *cabinets*. However, the search for solutions is often postponed until the Commission is formally required to reconsider its proposal. If there is time, the sector units in DG

Environment follow the major developments in each of the phases and give feedback, but they have to be very selective about what they track.

COREPER

The political pressure to achieve effective mediation reaches its zenith during the COREPER, where the DGs have to agree a common line. The Commission's Rules of Procedure (*bureaucratic procedures*), state that the draft instructions should be circulated to all those with a legitimate interest. COREPER positions are coordinated by the Group for Interinstitutional Relations (GRI), which meets every week. This *team* is prepared by a pre-GRI at a slightly lower level. The meetings discuss positions for COREPER as well as for Council and any conciliation. The GRI team consists of *cabinet* members (i.e. *liaison roles*) and is chaired by a member of the President's *cabinet*. If necessary, the Secretary General or the relevant *cabinet* members can be called in to conciliate (i.e. an *integrating role* bringing the coordination up to Level 6). Whether this is effective depends on the preferences of individual Commissioners, the time available, and the extent to which DG Environment is prepared to take on other DGs. The challenge it faces here is deciding how best to influence the strongest DGs. Our interviews suggest that the Barroso Commission's strategic focus on growth and jobs leaves DG Environment in a rather weakened position.

Council meetings

These meetings are prepared in much the same way as the COREPER. A rough estimate is that 10 per cent of all files go beyond the GRI and are discussed in the Hebdo and the College (or also in the meeting of special *chefs*). The rest can be handled as 'A-points' in the College. Points of disagreement are summarized by the chair of the GRI and presented to the College. As any problems can therefore easily be foreseen, there will often be continuous informal negotiations at all levels well in advance of meetings of the College—that is, unless officials call upon their Commissioner to lend a hand in the College.

Co-decisionmaking and conciliation[9]

The role of the Commission changes when the proposal goes into conciliation. As suggested in the European Parliament's co-decision report from 2004, the Commission is the main mediator during this phase. Bringing the 'two co-legislators' closer together demands a 'great deal of impartiality' (EP 287.644: 19). Together with the sector DGs, the conciliation unit in the Commission's Secretariat acts as an honest broker (*strong integrator*). It also tries to coordinate the positions within the Commission to bring the negotiations between Council and the Parliament to a close.

Improving the Commission's coordination system

Despite some of the skeptical remarks noted above, our interviews revealed that the Commission has responded well to the challenge set by Commissioner Kinnock during his term of office. The Commission seems to be moving towards active information by lowering some of the 'Chinese walls' that the former UK environment minister Michael Meacher complained about at the very start of Chapter 1. Apart from the formalization of active information obligations (i.e. *bureaucratic procedures*), the past few years have witnessed a real improvement in terms of forward workplanning. And if implemented fully, the new IA system could make it much easier for environment officials to monitor cognate policy fields.

This does not mean that the organization is now fully fit for EU-EPI. First of all, the political attention seems to be fading as the administrative ideology of the Barroso Commission moves towards the competitiveness dimensions of the Lisbon agenda. Secondly (and because of this), DG Environment has been forced to protect its previously hard-fought gains (e.g. the Thematic Strategies created under the Sixth EAP) (ENDS Ltd. No. 366: 3–4; 367: 43–4) by arguing that existing environmental measures do not undermine economic growth and competitiveness (e.g. CEC 2005i). In consequence, it appears to have less appetite for integrating environment into the other sectors than it did, say, five years ago (see Chapter 3).

Conclusions

All the actors in this study have a role to play in implementing EU-EPI, but the Commission's position is arguably more central and hence more critical than the others. It has the right of initiative, member states expect it to guard the quality—including the environmental integrity—of proposals, and it is the hub of EU decisionmaking and policy implementation in the first pillar. The previous chapters showed that there is a widespread assumption, particularly at member state level, that the Commission should take the lead in delivering Article 6. This translates into a leadership role (see Chapter 1), which involves creating expectations, and organizing common tasks such as network audits. In this chapter we have examined how well DG Environment pushes EPI externally within the Commission and the rest of the EU. Does it have sufficient coordinating capacities to respond to the demand for greater EU-EPI emanating from within and outside its formal structures?

The internal (EPI) capacities

Politically, the Commission has arguably been the most forceful and consistent advocate of EPI in the EU. However, the political mood in the Commission has changed in recent years, so that it seems that DG Enterprise and the President, among others, are more concerned with 'reverse integration'; that is, ensuring that environmental measures do not interfere with economic growth and the drive for greater competitiveness (i.e. the Lisbon agenda). Therefore the question has to be asked: how much pressure is DG Environment able and willing to put behind EPI? This is a political and an administrative issue relating to political objectives and mechanisms through which influence can be secured in the bureaucratic–political context of intra-Commission decisionmaking.

It should not be forgotten that EU-EPI is a very demanding objective that places heavy requirements on the Commission's still relatively fragile internal coordination capacities. The existing literature and our own interviews point to severe coordination problems within the Commission. Impediments to integration include the French style of bureaucracy based on strong sectors headed by powerful heads of departments (i.e. Commissioners), the political pressure for various non-environmental priorities arising from various member states, the traditionally weak internal planning mechanisms, and weak central leadership (see also Nugent 2001; Chapter 3). However, this chapter presented some reasons for guarded optimism. A wide range of initiatives have been taken over the past decade to improve internal coordination in general and to embed EPI in particular. There are now, among others, new strategic planning procedures (SPP), a renewed emphasis on early consultation and rigorous policy assessment, a renewed interest in ensuring policy consistency, and a growing culture of active information. In addition, the stronger involvement of the Secretariat General in tasks such as workplanning and the writing of

Lisbon synthesis reports, is expected to increase the Commission's contribution to EU-EPI and to stimulate officials to think beyond the easy satisfaction of short-term sectoral interests (see also CEC 2003b: 6). These improvements are illustrative of a shift towards a more subsidiarity-based approach to coordination. Even though some officials have decried these reforms as creeping centralization, in reality they are not. Both central and decentralized coordination mechanisms have been upgraded. In terms of our definition of coordination capacities (Table 9.1), the changes imply that internal coordination in the Commission now benefits from a more elaborate system of *bureaucratic procedures*, which create the basis for more active forms of coordination.

But, there are still limits related to political sensitivities and the fact that officials often need the approval of management to consult colleagues in cognate sectors. Moreover, the Commission's coordination capacities are strongly attached to the phases and thus lead to event coordination and reactive policymaking. This also retards the shift to active coordination. In combination with the layered system of decisionmaking in teams, political controversies still tend to be bottled up (i.e. delayed) until a proposal hits a particular stage (or 'event'). As with the Netherlands and Germany, a further shift towards a more UK-like system of information exchange could reap dividends. Furthermore, *specification of output* is not applied top-down: there are no overall targets formulated for individual DGs, and certainly not environmental ones.

We can also see major developments in terms of *horizontal coordination capacities*. There have been countless pleas for more informal coordination, and informal exchange has been greatly supported by the publication of the roadmaps (IAs) on the website. Moreover, the Commission can now rely on several *liaison roles* (e.g. assistants to the DG and *cabinet* members with dedicated coordinating tasks), *teams* (e.g. the special *chefs'* meetings, GRI, and Hebdo), and *task forces*.[10] Finally, there are some general policy principles that can be regarded as *mission statements*. These include the general expectation to formulate more sustainable proposals (see Chapter 3).

In view of these mechanisms, how can the Commission's overall performance be characterized? On the whole, the recent upgrading of coordination capacities has been complemented with a wider desire to improve internal coordination. The reforms have clearly had an impact. Our interviews revealed that knowledge about what each part of the organization is doing and the awareness of the importance of working across boundaries have increased. Nevertheless, this new pattern is not guaranteed and all kinds of omissions and lack of information can still be found. Moreover, coordination can still be highly passive. Crucially, putting something on the website and listing it in workplans may not be complemented by actively involving others or safeguarding values from colleagues. One official likened workplanning to 'going to mass on Sunday—it means little for what you do during the rest of the week'. Hence, coordination still remains a matter of individual choice, rather than organizational routine. Also, political sensitivities, a strong atavistic urge to score a quick political 'hit' by developing one's 'own' policies, and pervasive time constraints, all enhance the power of individual Commissioners and Directors General. These fly in the face of attempts to achieve greater horizontal integration.

The role of DG Environment

To some extent, the new coordination capacities in the Commission are a better starting point to pursue greater EU-EPI than was the case even five years ago. However, as is the case with most overloaded organizations hamstrung by passive coordination, DG Environment will require a lot of energy to track dossiers in cognate sectors to ensure they do not undermine EPI. Hence, the extent to which these opportunities are used depends on the willingness of DG Environment's (middle) management to invest resources in scrutinizing other sectors and, where necessary, modulating them. History suggests that the sectors will not easily acquiesce to DG Environment's demands. Importantly, DG Environment has not invested much in achieving this thus far. As noted above, the SDU lacks staff to oversee the complex and expansive set of tasks which it has been given. The other units in DG Environment are already overburdened with their own (environment) policies and can only devote a limited amount of time to 'policing' other sectors.

Unless there is a stronger basis for active coordination (due to, among others, the internal *bureaucratic procedures* of roadmaps and IAs), upgrading internal coordination will require at least two things. First, new investments (in terms of personnel) in the SDU to facilitate overall priority setting and in the various sector units of DG Environment. Secondly, active coordination demands high level political support for a more interventionist role. However, shifting resources towards EPI could easily mean achieving less political visibility in relation to new environment policy. Pursuing EPI may also involve picking political fights with other, much stronger Commissioners and their DGs. In the current political climate, this may not be something that DG Environment would want to do.

Given the resources needed to coordinate in a passively coordinated organization, it is not surprising to hear DG Environment pleading the other DGs to share in the 'ownership' of environmental protection problems. The ownership assumption is to be found throughout DG Environment. Our interviewees accepted that there is an element of convenience in this for all. It relieves DG Environment of having to police others and it gives the other DGs the leeway they crave to go off and do what they wanted to do all along (hence, no coordination).

DG Environment as an external capacity builder

The Commission has also invested to improve EPI capacities in the other actors and in nurturing the Cardiff partnership (or 'network') for EPI (see Chapter 3). However, DG Environment has not been able to exert much pressure on the member states, through bodies such as the EPRG. Important as these activities have been, our analysis of the member states already shows that the Commission needs to do more by way of network management. But the Commission cannot possibly achieve this on its own; it needs the political support of the member states. Our analysis reveals that EPI would be a lot less ad hoc if the member states put more concerted pressure on the sectoral DGs in all phases of EU decisionmaking. In other words, they have to operate in a more interdependent manner.

All this points to the need for a system-wide audit of existing coordination capacities (see Chapter 2). There are at least two reasons why this has not yet occurred. According to insiders, questioning the capacity of national administrations is extremely sensitive. Worse still, our interviews revealed that many of the administrative questions identified above are not even on the many Commission officials' 'mental map'. Apart from a general commitment to EPI, we found little interest in how the Commission might be redesigned to facilitate greater EU-EPI internally—apart from pushing 'ownership'—or externally. The Commission emphasizes, for example, the role that the member states must play, particularly in faithfully applying and transposing EU legislation (CEC 2003*b*: 13–14; 2005*d*). It does not, however, address the importance of working with the Commission on ensuring horizontal objectives like EU-EPI in the early phases of the EU policy process.

To conclude, many developments within the Commission have greatly improved the prospects for implementing EU-EPI, but real doubts remain about their ultimate success. The remark made by Spence (1994: 105–7) in relation to the wider running of the Commission applies equally well to the vexed question of EU-EPI: 'despite the many procedures and fall back provisions, the routines are not without difficulty'. As regards EPI, much now depends on whether or not DG Environment's management is willing to invest in taking a systems perspective. This asks a lot from it in the current political climate.

Notes

1. Consequently, these are best thought of as fairly broad *mission statements*, which apply to the entire organization.
2. There is, for example, no one at senior management level within DG Environment with a specific responsibility for EU-EPI.
3. The structure of the Commission is—as in most organizations—continuously changing. Hence, we do not employ the precise name(s) of the units in DG Environment.
4. It may only be a coincidence that the EPI strategy produced by the transport sector is generally regarded as being one of the very best (see Chapter 3).
5. These include an IA and the explanatory memorandum listing—among other things—any dissenting opinions (e.g. Article 21 in the Commission's Rules of Procedure) (CEC 2000*b*)
6. See, for example, President Barroso's recent complaint that two-thirds of the Commission's legislative output is still not listed in its work programmes (CEC 2004*c*: 5).
7. Twenty days for major policy proposals.
8. Minor cases are handled through a written procedure.
9. There used to be a special committee coordinating the relations with the Parliament (*Groupe des Affaires Parlementaires*—GAP). It was composed of *cabinet* members and was chaired by the *cabinet* member from the Commissioner responsible for relations with the Parliament. But it recently merged with the GRI.
10. *Strong integrating roles* have been much more difficult to create due to the Commission's collegial style of operation.

10

THE EUROPEAN PARLIAMENT: A PARTIALLY DISENGAGED PARTNER?

It is very difficult to influence the work of another committee... We
do not normally look at what they are doing
(an official from the European Parliament's environment committee)

Introduction

The European Parliament is an important actor in our multi-actor, multi-level study of policy coordination in the EU. Among other things, it provides one of the more obvious sources of political pressure needed to push other actors to collaborate in pursuit of greater EPI. It exerts itself directly through the EU policy process (where it now enjoys the power to co-decide policy with the Council in many policy areas), as well as indirectly through a variety of other routes. More importantly for us, it has undoubtedly been a very important player in environmental policymaking, going back to the dawn of EU environmental policy in the early 1970s (Judge 2002; Burns 2005). The advent of co-decisionmaking has given a huge boost to its ability to green individual policy proposals, both with the environmental sector as well as in cognate sectors.[1] The environment committee finds itself in a particularly strong position in this respect, as it covers one-third of all co-decision processes in the Parliament.

However, as highlighted in Chapter 4, there are very many reasons why the European Parliament's struggles to provide a coordinated input to all the policy activities it is involved in. Not surprisingly, its day-to-day involvement in actively promoting EU-EPI at the level of daily policymaking has tended to be rather uneven (Chapter 3). In Chapter 4, we noted the importance of understanding the contribution made both by the Parliament's administrative *and* political activities to the fulfilment of EU-EPI. In this chapter, we take a closer look at how the Parliament has adapted its internal coordinating capacities to meet the challenge of EU-EPI. Recently, a number of more general reforms have been initiated which seek to provide better administrative support to MEPs and facilitate greater cross-sectoral coordination (European Parliament 2002*b*). The Parliament seems to be broadly satisfied with what they have delivered thus far (European Parliament 2005). In this chapter, we focus on whether they have put the Parliament in a stronger position to contribute to the delivery of a specific policy coordination objective, namely EU-EPI. The obvious danger is that if these and any future reforms do not work, the Parliament's ability to contribute to EU-EPI will fail to match its widely acknowledged reputation for being the EU's 'environmental champion' (Burns 2005).

The European Parliament and EU-EPI

Advocating EPI in the EU

The Parliament is widely regarded as one of the—if not *the*—most environmental of all the EU's institutions (Jordan 2002*d*: 6; Burns 2005). Therefore, when the Amsterdam Treaty made co-decision the 'normal' procedure for the environment sector, environmental NGOs in Brussels were delighted.[2] Several explanations have been offered to explain the Parliament's relatively strong stance on environmental issues. One is that in a multiparty system in which there is no permanent majority (Boyce 1995: 148), smaller parties like the Greens can exploit their influence by securing key positions, such as *rapporteurs*.[3] Another is the Parliament's consensus-oriented culture and willingness not to overrule smaller groups (Arp 1992: 36). Moreover, green arguments in the European Parliament were strengthened when green parties became members of coalition governments (e.g. France and Germany) at the national level (e.g. Hey 1998: 93). In addition, environmental issues tend to cut across the dominant left–right cleavage in politics. In the absence of interparty (i.e. interpolitical group) battles, and due to the strong divisionalization of the European Parliament into sectoral committees (see Chapter 4), the environment committee is often able to adopt strong environmental positions (ibid. 55).

Parliament strongly supported the inclusion of Article 6 during the Amsterdam intergovernmental conference, and has since demanded adequate legislative and political follow up (e.g. European Parliament 1998). In subsequent statements, it has regularly complained about the weak environmental outputs of the Cardiff and Lisbon processes respectively (Unfried and Blau 2003). It felt that they should include more concrete targets and timetables. It also underlined the need for improved environmental indicators in the Lisbon process (e.g. European Parliament 2001*b*; 2001*c*). Similarly, the Parliament has called for EPI to be incorporated in EU economic policy. It also asked the Commission to promote green investment strategies (Official Journal C 47E 21 February 2002: 223–30).

The Parliament can also exert its influence on the day-to-day policy process to pursue EPI. As Zito (2000) concludes, however, its influence is very much skewed towards the back-end of the policy process (i.e. decisionmaking in the Council). McCormick (2001: 115) nonetheless explains that it can shape new proposals at the agenda-setting stage. For example, it can submit questions to the Commission, issue resolutions and 'own initiative' reports, and set up special committees of inquiry into alleged breaches of EU law. Also, its opinions can result in higher environmental standards—as was the case in the Trans-European Networks and the Directive on the promotion of electricity produced from renewable energy sources (2001/77/EC). The European Parliament also has the powers to sanction the proposed budget of the EU—a formal power which it used to green the structural funds (Lenschow 1999).

However, in several other respects, the Parliament's response to the challenge of EU-EPI has been decidedly weak. Its limited involvement in a number of EPI-related processes such as Lisbon has also been a continuing matter of concern for some more environmentally minded MEPs (Hinterberger and Zacherl 2003). The Parliament has also been excluded from the development of the SDS and this has 'almost certainly weakened the document at the EU level, and perhaps contributed to its obscurity amongst the general public' (Wilkinson et al. 2004*a*: 20). However, even when the Parliament has been specifically invited to join high-level strategic initiatives (such as the Cardiff process), it has declined. Prior to the 2001 Gothenburg Summit, the Parliament pledged to 'review [its] own method of working with a view to devising working practices which promote sustainable development' (European Parliament 2001*a*: article 52). However, there was little follow-up, aside from the occasional internal discussion about the need for a sustainable development committee and very unspecific calls for 'better' intercommittee coordination. One explanation for this is that the Parliament is geared up to exert itself through the old, Community Method of governing, particularly in those areas subject to co-decisionmaking.

Finally, the Parliament may well be an 'environmental champion', but there are abundant examples of legislation where it could not agree internally on a more sustainable course of action. As documented by Hey (2002: 147), its input at the agenda-setting stage of agreeing environmental taxes for freight transport was weak (see also Pehle and Jansen 1998). We reflect upon the reasons for this rather mixed record in the next section.

The Parliament's coordination capacities supporting EU-EPI

The chapters on the three member states had a strong focus on the role of the environment department, the role of the coordinating units for international affairs and sustainable development, the connection between national and EU level appraisal systems, and the *coordination capacities* concerning the sharing of information. As discussed in Chapter 4, the European Parliament does not have these capacities in quite the same form, nor is it as heavily involved in the early stages of the EU policy process. In fact, towards the end of Chapter 5 we concluded that there is no formal EPI system in the Parliament. Thus, while the Parliament can ask consultants to produce environmental policy appraisals, there is no *bureaucratic procedure* that requires it to produce them routinely for all significant amendments.

However, the differences between the organization of the Parliament and the four other actors in our study go much deeper than this. For instance, its environment committee is fundamentally different to the four environment departments in the Commission, the Netherlands, Germany, and the UK. Instead of policy units being the main players, the Parliament comprises individual MEPs with specialized committee-related interests (notably the environment in our case). It is very much up to them to monitor developments in the environmental policy field. They will normally have a good overview of the most salient issues due to their contacts with national officials and NGOs, etc. However, they are—more so than civil servants working in national departments—more concerned with 'scoring' on environmental dossiers to safeguard their personal visibility and, eventually, secure re-election. For individual MEPs, 'scoring' in other committees is highly labour intensive and often politically unrewarding. Therefore, if EPI is to take root in the Parliament, it is important that the coordination costs borne by individual MEP are relatively low.

Second, the way in which information flows between MEPs in the Parliament differs from that in the other actors due to the simple fact that coordination is much more political—that is, with fewer coordination capacities to support administrative work. In administrations, information exchange is shaped by rules and tradition. Much of the administrative coordination that occurs in and between departments in the other actors is much less important in the European Parliament. As discussed in Chapters 4 and 5, there are team meetings and coordinating roles, such as the meeting of Committee Chairmen, the Group meetings, and the Conference of Presidents. However, these are mainly important in relation to the distribution of dossiers and in deciding on organizational issues (e.g. whether the enhanced cooperation procedure applies), but not in relation to sorting out the content when there are overlapping interests. Planning is also not one of the Parliament's strong points and its overall style of coordination is quite passive. Much of the continuous pulling and hauling that happens in the administrations of other actors throughout the decisionmaking process, is largely absent in the European Parliament.

At the level of daily policymaking, there are other impediments to greater EPI in the Parliament. First, MEPs believe increasingly less in opinions as a way to influence other committees—and hence other sectoral Councils. Our interviews suggest that there is a general belief that a committee that writes too many opinions is unfocused and inefficient. In any case, the workloads are often so great that most committees mainly focus on their 'own' Council.

Second, the lead committee has a monopoly, which gives it a considerable ability to shape the views expressed by the whole Parliament. When it is not in the lead, the transaction costs borne by the environment committee as it tries to track developments in the sectors can be very high. Luck becomes a factor when so much depends on the chemistry between the *rapporteur* and the draftsmen. As a corollary, a useful dialogue between sectoral interests is often lacking throughout the decisionmaking process. There may be opinions and the odd resolution, but there is not the deep cross-fertilization based on intensive cross-sectoral discussion that is needed fundamentally to reorientate a piece of legislation. The opinions given by the opinion-giving committee may only lead to the insertion of two or three points at the end of the first or second reading. Hence, there is often little movement in terms of recalibrating environmental and non-environmental values (i.e. EPI).

Third, intercommittee relations can become very strained and competitive. They are sometimes so bad that opinions are simply shot down by the lead committee or are politely ignored at the second reading stage (when only the lead committee can propose amendments). The enhanced cooperation procedure (Article 47—also known as the enhanced Hughes procedure[4]) suffers from the same problem. The lead committees may simply resist what it perceives to be unwarranted interference from cognate committees.

Finally, the European Parliament's ability to pursue EU-EPI is very much limited by the non-application of co-decisionmaking in environmentally important sectors such as taxation, local planning, agriculture, and fisheries.[5] Hence, important dossiers travelling through these sectoral committees might not get the environmental attention that they deserve.

The coordination of EU-EPI

As discussed in Chapter 4, whether or not co-decisionmaking applies in a particular sector makes a great difference to the extent to which other EU institutions pay attention to the European Parliament's views (Neuhold 2001). However, even without co-decisionmaking, the European Parliament's influence can be substantial due to the exploitation of timetables, budgets, and political pressures (Burns 2005). Our assessment of the level of interdepartmental coordination in the various stages of the EU policy process is summarized in Table 10.1. Because of the series of steps a proposal goes through, this table appears in a slightly different form to that first outlined in Chapter 2. Thus, instead of Presidency agenda, working party, COREPER, and Council, the Parliament stages are divided into three, namely the reading in the lead committee, the first reading, and the second reading.

Initiation

Formally, the Parliament has little direct input into the early Commission phases. After all, until recently its right of initiative was rather limited. In any case, large workloads mean that most MEPs have to limit their attention to the phases for which they are formally responsible. Not surprisingly, the European Parliament's role in the early phases is not really examined in the existing EU literature.

However, as discussed above, MEPs are occasionally highly active in this early phase. The Maastricht Treaty armed them with the right to ask the

Table 10.1. The European Parliament: levels of interdepartmental EU policy coordination

	Commission phases						Council/Parliament phases			
	Initiation of new proposals	Work plans	White & Green papers	Drafting of proposals	Inter-service consultation	Presentation of proposals	Vote in lead Committee	First reading	Second reading	Conciliation
OUTPUT — Coordination level										
9 Strategy										
8 Margins										
7 Arbitration										
6 Conciliation						+/–	+/–	+/–	+	+
5 Consensus						+	+/–	+/–	+/–	+/–
4 One voice						+	+/–	+/–	+/–	+/–
3 Consultation			+			+	+/–	+/–	+/–	+
2 Communication			+			+	+	+/–	+	+
1 Independent policy making	+	+	+	(hardly involved)	(hardly involved)	+	+	+	+	+
INPUT — Coordination capacities										
Hierarchical										
Bureaucratic			+/–			+	+	+	+	+
Specification of output			+							
Horizontal										
Informal relations	+					+	+	+		
Liaison roles		+	+				+	+/–	+/–	+/–
Task forces			+/–				+/–	+/–	+/–	+/–
Teams						+/–	+/–	+/–	+/–	+/–
Weak integrator						+/–	+/–	+/–	+/–	+/–
Strong integrator						+/–	+/–	+/–	+/–	+/–
Mission statements										
Role of the Environment Committee	Draftsmen, committee chair and MEPs can lobby at their respective levels for influence over other committees									

Explanation:

+ = coordination capacity at this level exists and is used.

+/– = the coordination capacity at this level exists to some extent, but may not always be used.

(+/–) = the coordination capacity at this level exists, but is only used in exceptional cases.

Commission to prepare a proposal (Hey 1998: 85; Judge and Earnshaw 2006). Rule 33 of the Parliament's Rules of Procedure now talks about the Commission and the Parliament cooperating on the legislative planning of the EU. Indeed, the governance debate and the attempts to upgrade interinstitutional planning are likely to provide the Parliament with earlier and easier influence (e.g. CEC 2001*a*; 2001*b*). Increasingly, therefore, the Commission and Presidencies consult the European Parliament on the feasibility of new policies especially in relation to agenda setting. In the environmental arena, Burns (2005) emphasizes the importance of the increasingly important informal partnerships between DG Environment and the Environment Committee. However, in other sectors, the extension of co-decisionmaking has made the Commission more receptive to the interests of the European Parliament, typified by a greater eagerness to consult MEPs. Moreover, the European Parliament can use instruments such as the organization of hearings and resolutions to stimulate new policies (see Pehle and Jansen 1998; Héritier et al. 1994; Warleigh 2000; Burns 2005). Judge (2002: 122), among others, argues that during the 1990s, the environment committee used these and other devices proactively to influence the work of DG Environment, rather than simply reacting passively to its proposals.

However, it is very difficult to quantify the Parliament's precise influence on the text of a Commission proposal.[6] Nonetheless, the underlying problem is that the Environment Committee undeniably struggles to monitor dossiers outside its main area—the Environment Council. There are, of course, also hearings organized by other committees, but there is hardly any intercommittee coordination to gather views or initiate discussions. Crucially, there are no *bureaucratic procedures* supporting greater transparency (hence, only Level 1 on the coordination table). *Informal relations (bureaucratic politics)* are mainly between members of the same political group (see Chapter 4). Without procedures for active information, it is difficult to follow new developments or to collect broader political views across committees.

Commission workplanning

Cooperation between the European Parliament and the Commission on legislative planning, is foreseen in Rule 33 of the Parliament's Rules of Procedure. In our interviews, however, MEPs in the environment committee reported that that they do not routinely screen the workplans produced by the DGs for transport, agriculture, and others. Rather, they tend to focus on DG Environment's activities. Moreover, the secretariat of the Environment Committee lacks the manpower to monitor what is going on in the sectoral DGs. Even informal exchanges with the secretariats of other committees in the initiation phase can be highly constrained (i.e. Level 1). The relevant coordinating *teams* (i.e. the Committee of Chairmen, the Conference of Presidents, etc.) do not cover this task either. The shift to better workplanning between the Commission, the Council (General Secretariat and Presidency), and the European Parliament, does give the committee chairperson, the committee's secretariat, or MEPs an opportunity to look at upcoming issues and point to dossiers where opinions may be necessary. However, at this early stage, the detailed aspects of future proposals are generally regarded as internal matters for the Commission to resolve.

White/Green Papers and Communications

As with the initiation of proposals, the European Parliament can support these strategic steps by adopting resolutions. An example was the environmental liability Directive (2004/35/EC), which was initially based on a Commission Green Paper (in 1993) and White Paper (CEC 2000c). Following a joint hearing between the Commission and the European Parliament in 1993, the environment committee adopted a resolution dated 20 April 1994 (Official Journal C128/165) which asked for a directive to be prepared. (Due to internal fights, however, the final negotiation of the Liability Directive was led by the Parliament's Legal Affairs Committee.)

Once published, White and Green Papers normally gain the attention of the Environment Committee. For example, the 2001 Green Paper on the Future of the Common Fisheries Policy stimulated the environment committee to issue an opinion. However, of the sixteen paragraphs of text it adopted, only a limited number were taken up in the Fisheries Committee and, eventually, the final European Parliament opinion of January 2002 (Official Journal, C 107/15, 2002).[7] Overall, the general tone of the Fisheries Committee was not very pro-environment and emphasized that the EU's international fisheries relations should be viewed primarily in financial terms.

According to the Rules of Procedure, committees may consult each other informally and seek opinions (i.e. coordination can reach Level 3). Consultation, however, is not obligatory (Rule 46 of the Rules of Procedure—see Chapter 4). There is no need to speak with one voice and open conflicts are, as in most parliamentary systems, quite normal. We should also remember that the wording of Rule 47 (about 'enhanced cooperation' between committees)[8] is so vague, as to render it very weak. There is also little or no formal mediation. Decisions are taken by the plenary, which is the ultimate arbiter. To anticipate the vote, political groups can create *task forces* to give environmental aspects—launched by the Environment Committee but rejected by the lead committee—a second chance in the plenary.

Drafting of proposals/interservice consultation within the Commission

According to our interviews, the European Parliament does not routinely follow the drafting and interservice consultation phases in the Commission. There may be single officials or MEPs from a committee who have informal contacts with the Commission, but these will rarely be that influential (although the Commission will get an impression of the overall level of political support for its ideas). After commenting on a Green/White Paper, the focus lies on the proposals that are already in the pipeline. MEPs again felt that this is not formally their business. This may change, given that broad stakeholder involvement in the drafting phase is increasingly becoming the norm (see Chapter 9).

Presentation of proposals/the allocation of proposals between committees

The Parliament's involvement normally starts in earnest when proposals are formally issued. This phase is strongly influenced by the internal rules of procedures about deadlines for issuing opinions, for delivering reports in readiness for translation, and the rights of *rapporteurs* and draftsmen (e.g. the enhanced cooperation procedure), etc. These rules have been established to support the efficient management of the negotiations in and between EU institutions.

The first question that has to be decided is, which committee should take the lead? The formal powers and responsibilities of each of the committees are set out in an annexe attached to the Rules of Procedure. Dossiers that span two or more sectors may interest several committees, and competence disputes between them are much more common than is commonly supposed. In the period 1999–2004, there were seventy-three such conflicts, which had to be formally resolved (Corbett et al. 2005: 129). Most of theses were resolved in the Conference of Committee Chairs, whose chairperson acts as an impartial mediator (a *weak integrator*). If agreement still cannot be reached (this occurred on thirty-seven separate occasions between 1999 and 2004) (Corbett et al. 2005: 129), the dossier moves to the Conference of Committee Chairs and eventually to the Conference of Presidents, with the President acting as a *(weak) integrator*.

In recent years, disputes have flared between the Environment and Agriculture/Rural Development Committees on proposals governing food safety (Neuhold 2001: 4). The proposed Directive on environmental liability (proposed in January 2002—see above) was another good example of a contested dossier. This dossier was originally given to the Legal Affairs Committee by the responsible legal service of the Parliament, but this was later challenged by the Environment Committee. The Conference of Presidents handed the dispute to three Vice-Presidents who acted as 'wise men'. They gave it to the Environment Committee but this was not accepted by the Legal Affairs Committee. Finally, there was a vote at a plenary session—which the Environment Committee lost. Similarly, the handling of the Lisbon process has resulted in many battles between committees and political parties. Each of the committees involved claimed the lead. According to our interviews, various suggestions about how to resolve the situation have proved untenable, and as a result, three different procedures have been used to integrate the views of different committees in four years.

What conclusions should we draw from these conflicts? The first point is that in spite of these fights, surprisingly little effort is made to compensate for them in the subsequent negotiations. Second, there is not much belief in influencing committees from the 'outside'—hence the often bitter struggle to take the lead. By claiming ownership, a sectoral committee is effectively restricting the environment committee from having access. Given that information flows passively, this is a very difficult position for the environment committee to operate from, particularly if it wants to push for more EU-EPI.

Vote in the lead committee

The European Parliament has, like the US Congress, weak political parties but strong committees (Hix et al. 1999). To prepare the voting in the plenary, the lead committee first has to produce a report, which is drafted by a *rapporteur*. This task gives the individual concerned considerable influence (see Chapter 4). The major reports are allocated at the start of the legislative term in the meeting of the political group coordinators of a specific committee. The Greens secured over 12 per cent of all *rapporteur-ships* in the year 2001 although they only represented 7.2 per cent of the votes in the Parliament (Maurer 2002: 61). The system benefits EU-EPI as a 'green' *rapporteur* (which may not necessarily be from the group of the Greens) in a sector committee can make a difference (e.g. the Directive on the promotion of renewable energies) (see Chapter 5).

The Environment Committee managed to produce 119 opinions between 1999 and 2004 (see Chapter 4). This may appear impressive, but the Technology, Trade, and Energy Committees all produced more. In this sense, the Environment Committee is more inward-looking than some of the sector committees. Priorities have to be set as resources are limited. There are prominent cases wherein the Environment Committee did not produce opinions, and hence left unused important opportunities to press home the need for EU-EPI. Our interviews revealed, for example, that this has occurred in relation to the opening of entry negotiations with Romania and Bulgaria, the Regulation on air transport slots (led by the Transport Committee), and the multi-annual programme of intelligent energy for Europe 2003–6.

The lead Committee subsequently votes on the reports and opinions. At this stage, the enormous variety in relations between committees becomes even more visible. In theory, this phase is highly regulated by the Parliament's *bureaucratic procedures*; there are even some coordinating *teams* to support it (the Conferences of Presidents and of Committee Chairs, see above). The *bureaucratic rules of procedure* dictate, *inter alia*, that: the lead Committee shall fix a deadline by which the other committees should deliver their opinions; only the lead committee may table amendments in Parliament; the chairman may invite the draftsman to advisory meetings; and that opinions should be attached to the reports (Chapters 2 and 3 of the Rules of Procedure). Moreover, the lead Committee 'shall put' the amendments to a vote.

In practice, our interviews showed that what really count are the informal relations between committees and the votes in the plenary (see Chapter 4). Formal consultation between committees hardly takes place during the writing of and the voting on the opinions/report (i.e. Level 1 between committees is more common than Level 2). The lead committee votes on the draft report of the *rapporteur*, and is free to add or ignore amendments from other committees. The opinions in the annexe are also put to a vote (see Rule 46.2). Crucially, this rule is often interpreted as though it were a suggestion, not a formal requirement. The enhanced cooperation procedure states that the *rapporteur* and the draftsman shall endeavour to agree on the texts they propose to their committees and on their position regarding amendments. This particularly applies to matters that fall under the competence of the committees that are asked to give an opinion, and which do not contradict other elements of the report (Rule 47). But for many of our interviewees, the fact that any proposed amendments can easily be ignored by the lead committee, leaves the enhanced cooperation procedure looking more like a fig leaf to hide poor coordination. Thus, coordination can achieve reach Level 5 (consensus finding) with the enhanced cooperation procedure, but normally it does not even reach higher than Level 3 (consultation) or even stays at Level 2 (information).

The ease with which opinions can be ignored means that it is up to the opinion-giving committee to table amendments in the plenary. In 2003, the Legal Affairs Committee—while leading the environmental liability dossier—ignored all the relevant amendments made by the Environment Committee, thus underlining the importance of poor relations between key players (notably the *rapporteur*, draftsman, and chairmen). However, like the environment departments at the national level, the Environment Committee does not regard itself as a 'green policeman'. If it did, it would quickly grind to a halt under the workload.

To conclude, even though the Environment Committee's responsibilities are very broad, its ability to push EU-EPI during this very important phase is limited *inter alia* by ever-present turf disputes and inefficient cooperation between sectors. Hence, there is little more in terms of coordination beyond that delivered by *informal relations*.

First reading in the plenary

There is no time limit for the first reading. The Council and the European Parliament try to work towards a common timeframe for finishing this phase so that both institutions can adequately plan their work. This allows the committees to set deadlines for giving opinions. The committees present their reports to the plenary—with the opinions from other committees annexed—but only the lead committee can table amendments in the plenary. Once a vote is in sight, the informal contacts between the lead committee and the Commission and the Council increase. The shift to co-decisionmaking has strongly reinforced the search for quick agreements using more informal means (these are known as 'informal trialogues') (European Parliament 2004). Without them, decisionmaking in the EU system would slow down. The committee chair and his or her *rapporteur* have a privileged position in the contacts between the Parliament, the

Council/Presidency, and the Commission. Importantly, this reinforces the other structural advantages enjoyed by the lead committee.

Once the report has been adopted in the lead committee, the draftsman no longer plays a formal role in the first reading vote. She or he is automatically given some time to speak in the plenary after the *rapporteurs*—an important incentive for many draftsmen. Informally, a draftsman (or another committee) can influence the final result in the plenary result, by retabling amendments, which were not adopted by the lead committee. However, this requires the support of a political group or thirty-seven individual MEPs. This was the case in the first reading on the environmental liability Directive, where a series of political groups retabled amendments from the Environment Committee, which eventually defeated the Legal Affairs Committee and the *rapporteur*'s line. Political groups can create a sort of *task force* with a *liaison role* for groups of MEPs in the lead committee (see the discussion of 'intergroups' in Chapter 4). However, lobbying for the adoption of amendments in plenary can be an arduous task and only happens on a limited number of key issues. The ultimate arbiter at this stage is the plenary (*strong integrator*).

Second reading

The second reading is subject to a deadline of three months (although an extension to four months is possible) from the receipt of the common position. Moreover, voting on amendments is now by absolute majority (the minimum threshold being 367 votes). Only the lead committee can present a report. This puts the responsible committee in a very privileged position. Smaller political groups (or a minimum of thirty-seven MEPs) can table further amendments. In addition, informal contacts have emerged and become an important device to smooth relations between the European Parliament and Council (note, any rejection or major amendment by the European Parliament at this stage can trigger a conciliation). Hence, the responsible committee will normally keep in close contact with the other institutions to see what kind of amendments might be acceptable. Using his or her informal contacts, the *rapporteur* will try to maintain political backing and stay in close contact with the chairman and shadow *rapporteur*(s) within his or her committee.

The lead committee tables amendments and searches for an absolute majority in the plenary. In this phase, the other committees are informed but not consulted (i.e. Level 2 on the scale). Therefore, it is more efficient if EPI initiatives throughout this phase come from MEPs in the lead committee, so that their input is part of the lead committee's deliberations. This means that it is—more so than in earlier phases—hugely important to gain the political support of political groups within the lead committee, rather than finding agreement across sectoral committees. The scope for EPI was not that good during the 1999–2004 Parliamentary session in view of the political dominance of the Christian Democrats (PPE–DE) (see also Corbett et al. 2005). Given the average attendance of MEPs, gaining an absolute majority required a split in this party. If not, it could block amendments (as happened, for instance, in the case of the Directive on truck emissions (1999/96/EC)).

Conciliation

To smooth conciliation and stay within the tight deadlines for agreement, informal trialogue meetings (see above) are held, involving participants from the three EU institutions. The Parliament is represented by the vice-president, the chairman of the lead committee, and the *rapporteur*. Within the European Parliament, there is very informal and efficient prenegotiation between relevant committees. Due to the informal contacts around the trialogues, there is potentially greater scope for coordination within the full Parliamentary delegation to the conciliation committee than during the previous readings. The delegation always includes the chairperson and the *rapporteur* from the lead committee. The political groups from the lead committee normally choose a majority of its members. Crucially, there are also members with other backgrounds, including the three vice-presidents (who ensure continuity across all conciliations), as well as members (such as those who have drafted opinions) of other committees. In this phase, the main way to lobby for EU-EPI is through direct contacts with the MEPs who are members of the conciliation committee. Since the discussions are linked to amendments that have already been tabled, there is little or no scope for introducing new (or resurrecting old) environmental dimensions into a dossier at this late stage. This does not, of course, mean that the outcome is effectively signed and sealed; support for EPI must be maintained. After all, the MEPs in a conciliation have to find a consensus, which could require a majority in the plenary (i.e. a third reading). In this case, the vice-presidents may have to be involved if there are major conflicts (Level 6).

Improving the Parliament's coordination system

As noted in Chapters 3 and 5, in spite of repeated requests, the European Parliament has still not reformed itself to respond to the challenges of EU-EPI, or formally joined the partnership (i.e. network) for integration. However, there has been a more or less continuous discussion about the internal organization of Lisbon and of intercommittee cooperation (see the European Parliament's reports—European Parliament 2002*b*; 2005).

Our interviews revealed a mixed picture as regards the need for better internal coordination within the Parliament. Many people working within the European Parliament are generally aware that coordination is rather less than ideal. Some think that the status quo is patently insufficient in the face of increasing policy interdependence. Others feel that MEPs do not want better coordination and prefer the 'divide and rule' principle.

The debate triggered by the Lisbon-based annual reporting procedure has certainly strengthened the hands of those pushing for improved coordination. Others, however, like the autonomy enjoyed by committees, and much prefer the open, freewheeling political battles in the plenary to attempts to engineer 'bureaucratic' coordination in the corridors and committee rooms of the Parliament. However, in our analysis we have tried to point out that the status quo has a number of severe disadvantages, such as high transaction costs, poor horizontal coordination, and weak learning across the successive policy stages.

A number of potential changes have been discussed, including:

- making greater use of standing committees for horizontal policies. The annual reports for the Spring Councils have, however, showed how difficult it is to get existing committees to agree to new horizontal bodies;
- ensuring that lead committees take fuller notice of the opinions received from cognate committees. The current problems with sidelining committees does not, however, make it immediately clear whether or how this should work;
- striving for better coordination within the political groups. The problem with this, as discussed above, is the difference between these groups and national political parties.

As it is, there is very little in terms of discussing cross-sectoral issues and, hence, little support for a mutual learning exercise. This is abundantly clear from the various *Raising the Game* reports (European Parliament 2002*b*; 2005), which mainly address ways of providing MEPs with greater technical back-up in increasingly specialized policy areas. Surprisingly, they barely address how better to manage the increasing horizontal interdependence of policies. They also have not explored what extra steps could be taken to ensure greater collaboration between the European and national parliaments. Maybe the European Parliament could learn important lessons from national parliaments, who have been 'left behind in the rush' to deal with more Europeanized and horizontally interconnected policymaking (Norton 1996: 192). National parliaments have responded by investing in mechanisms to locate and process information about EU policymaking, as well as to safeguard their own participation in it (via parallel committees and meetings at the various levels of government) (Auel and Benz 2004), even though the results have admittedly been rather mixed (Judge 1995; *Tweede Kamer der Staten-Generaal* 2002).

Having stumbled across an important aspect of the Parliament's affairs, which is hardly addressed in the existing literature, we will close simply by noting the need for greater research in this area. However, we suspect that changing the status quo will not be easy. Horizontal cooperation between committees is notoriously difficult to achieve in any parliamentary system. Better sources of predigested information (summaries of the main political sticking points) and a wider dissemination of information across committees, appear to have increased the level of awareness about crosscutting issues, but the challenges identified in Chapter 1 still do not appear to register sufficiently highly on the Parliament's political radar.

Conclusions

The European Parliament has been a very strong supporter of stronger EU environment policies and has exploited a number of pressure points in the decisionmaking system (e.g. budgeting) to advance EU-EPI (see Chapter 5). However, it has been partially disengaged from the EU-EPI debates that have formed around the Cardiff and Lisbon processes. In this chapter, we have shown why it struggles to pursue EPI at the level of daily EU negotiations. This has a lot to do with the difficulties—depending on the case—experienced in working across the sectoral committees. Within the Parliament, the Environment Committee is effectively the guardian of EU-EPI, but it is doing strikingly little to discharge this responsibility. For instance, it still has not found an effective way to monitor and react to dossiers in other committees. There is certainly no special committee that deals with sustainable development matters, nor an environmental audit committee on the UK model. Instead, fragmentation seems to be order of the day. Every committee appears to concentrate on what it perceives to be its 'core' business (which for the Environment Committee is EU environmental policy), while resisting incursions from other committees.

With respect to daily policymaking in the EU, the Parliament's ability to coordinate horizontally depends upon informal contacts, individual volition, and the vagaries of political competition, for example over the allocation of competences for certain dossiers. The allocation of dossiers is especially important, as EU-EPI appears to advance further when a sectoral dossier is placed in the hands of the Environment Committee. However, this is not really a secure basis on which to seek greater EU-EPI. The preparation of reports is very much in the hands of the chairing committee. Other committees are more or less limited to issuing proposals for amendments ('opinions') before the first reading and the adoption of the *rapporteur's* report. Moreover, the Secretariat of the Environment Committee cannot facilitate EU-EPI, as it has its work cut out simply to keep abreast of the dossiers where it has the lead.

The most important formal instrument of cross-sector policymaking is the opinion, but the ease with which it can be ignored must count as a very significant weakness. As a result, of the five actors in this study, the European Parliament is probably the least well endowed with coordination capacities. Most importantly, in the national administrations there is at least a constant struggle among the component parts to interact and to inform one another, which produces some mutual learning. By contrast, this continuous dialogue and rapprochement between MEPs is much less obvious in the Parliament. Moreover, the tendency to *avoid* coordination—which is of course present in the national administrations—seems to be even stronger between Parliamentary committees. What remain, therefore, are *informal relations* (that is, *bureaucratic politics*).

What this means is that horizontal coordination between the committees is at times highly labour-intensive and demanding; the policy agenda is hardly supported at all by sound *bureaucratic procedures* and coordination *teams*. The transaction costs borne by individual MEPs seeking to work across sectoral boundaries are therefore extremely high. More importantly, despite growing awareness of these shortcomings, the Parliament currently has no plans to overhaul its internal procedures to address growing policy interdependence. We are driven to conclude, therefore, that although it may continue strongly to advocate strong environmental policymaking, the Parliament remains partially disengaged from the EU's attempts to pursue EU-EPI via network-based forms of governance.

Notes

1. Several studies have identified the limited impact of the Parliament in the agriculture and fisheries sectors (e.g. Coffey 1999; IEEP 1992; 1995). Lacking co-decision power in these areas, it has had to rely upon softer and more indirect methods to push for EU-EPI, such as initiative reports, conferences, and resolutions. The extension of co-decisionmaking to these two areas was proposed in the (as yet unratified) European Constitution.
2. There are of course also cases where the Parliament—notably its Environment Committee—reduced the environmental ambitions of EU legislation, such as in the negotiations on the end of life vehicles Directive.
3. The appointment of *rapporteurs* is based on an auction system in which each political group is given a limited number of points depending on its size. By concentrating on key dossiers, relatively small political parties like the Greens can maximize their influence.
4. The predecessor of this was the 'Gomes' procedure (for details, see Corbett et al. 2005). Article 47 (building on the Hughes procedure) notes that the two committees have to agree to a timetable. The sensitive issue in this procedure is whether the lead committee has to accept the amendments from the opinion-giving committee without a vote.
5. But this may change, if and when the draft Constitution is ratified.
6. For instance, the Commission may choose to make a courteous reference to a resolution initiated by a member of the environment committee (Judge 2002: 122), even though it does not have to.
7. Crucial issues were accepted in relation to: the integration of environmental requirements into fisheries policy; the importance of ensuring that structural funding supports environmentally sustainable fishing practices; and the importance of the precautionary principle.
8. Notably, 'the *rapporteur* and draftsman shall endeavour to agree...' (see Chapter 4 for further details).

Part V

Comparative Conclusions

11

THE COORDINATION OF THE EUROPEAN UNION: EXPLORING THE CAPACITIES OF NETWORKED GOVERNANCE

[N]ew kinds of policy networks *are* emerging, which . . . act as bridges between national, EU, and international institutions, and policies made at each of these levels . . . [they] facilitate new patterns of policy making [and] change . . . the ways in which national institutions operate.

(Stubb, Wallace, and Peterson 2003: 148–9) (emphasis added)

[E]asy as the new modes of governance may seem at first glance, when they are analyzed in detail, it becomes clear that they are more demanding than expected.

(Héritier 2001: 19).

Introduction

The EU is under growing pressure to act in a more coordinated manner. For various reasons, the Community Method of coordinating by issuing EU legislation no longer seems appropriate or even realistic as the dominant governing tool. This is because 'many of the most critical interdependencies are inter-organizational, inter-sectoral and inter-state in character, and if they can be accommodated at all, they depend on the possibility of "coordination without hierarchy"' (Scharpf 1994: 41). In an attempt to coordinate in an even less hierarchical fashion, the EU has, as we suggested in Chapter 1, begun to explore the promise of new modes of governance, although it continues to rely heavily on legislative instruments (Jordan, Wurzel, and Zito 2005). What many of these new modes have in common is their reliance upon networks. However, scholars disagree about the true extent and utility of multilevel networked governance (see the quotes above). Some, like Peterson (2004: 129), simply note that 'governance by network maybe becoming a steadily *more* important feature of the EU' (emphasis added). Others claim it is 'the *only* real' means of coordinating such a dynamic, multisector, multi-actor, multilevel political system such as the EU (Peters 2003: 28) (emphasis added).

In this book we have sought to examine empirically the potential of new modes of EU governance, specifically those that seek to harness the coordinating power of networks. Our empirical testing ground has been one particularly complex horizontal policy challenge, namely EPI. We have assessed whether the necessary networks have emerged in response to this challenge, and if so, in what form. This necessitated a two-level network audit, which looked at the coordinating capacities within the network and the participating actors. In this concluding chapter, we return to the three questions posed in Chapter 1. Thus, in the next section we assess the extent to which the coordination *tasks* identified in Chapter 1 are satisfactorily performed. In Section 3, we examine the *capacities at network level* and assess their fitness for purpose. In Section 4, we review the *capacities of the actors* within the network or networks. For reasons explained in Chapter 1, here we distinguish between inter- and intradepartmental coordination, paying particular attention to the cross-sectoral coordinating units in the five environmental departments. In Section 5 we respond to Peterson's (2004: 133) recent call for 'normative propositions' about how EU policy networks *should* be structured to serve the European good. After all, as interest in complementary modes of governing grows, the EU *should* be more aware of what networks can—and, perhaps, just as importantly, cannot—offer by way of delivering policy objectives. The concluding section returns to consider some of the broader governance-related themes raised towards the end of Chapter 1.

What coordination tasks need to be fulfilled?

As discussed in Chapter 1, there a number of basic coordination tasks that have to be discharged to facilitate greater cross-sectoral policy coordination. Drawing on the empirical findings of Chapters 6–10, this section assesses how well they are currently being fulfilled.

Identify the environmental implications of new policies

The empirical chapters show that this is not systematically occurring in any of the five actors. Some (i.e. the Commission, the UK, and the Netherlands) have developed environmental policy appraisal systems, but in spite of repeated requests, the other two have not. Clearly it is impossible for one or even all these actors to discharge this task for the whole of the EU, due to the workloads involved. The EEA could conceivably be given some kind of role in producing or even auditing the appraisals that are produced, but for various reasons has not yet been invited to do this. There is some evidence that more actors in the EU (specifically the Parliament) are coming around to the idea that policy appraisal needs to be formally coordinated (see Chapter 3), but this has not yet been adequately embedded in the right combination of coordination capacities.

Share information

One of the obvious corollaries of not appraising policies is that information on the environmental implications of new policies is not shared freely or sufficiently early among the actors. Consequently, environmentally damaging proposals continue to be adopted by the sectors, which undermine the long-term targets set out in broader strategies such as the Cardiff process and the SDS. If information is not shared sufficiently well between actors, then it is even more important that it is shared *within* them. Despite some recent progress, this is not routinely occurring either, even in the more actively coordinated actors such as the UK. Many of the reasons are specific to particular actors. In Germany and the Netherlands, it has a lot to do with their continuing reliance on passive information. In the UK, it has more to do with the low political salience of environmental issues across the board but especially in the sectoral ministries. That said, we have uncovered a much more systematic aversion in all the actors to using policy appraisal procedures to coordinate across sectors. The problem is that appraisal is commonly regarded as being too constraining, too costly, and too time consuming (Russel and Jordan 2005). It is significant in this respect that three of the five actors (namely, the Netherlands, the UK, and the Commission) have recently sought to overcome this aversion by consolidating their appraisal procedures and making them more mandatory, with the apex playing more of an oversight role (i.e. the Cabinet Office in the UK and the

Secretariat General in the Commission). The jury is still out on the impact of these changes.

Set medium- to long-term priorities

Long-term targets have been set in the Cardiff and Lisbon processes, but these tend to be too sectorized to have much of a steering role. They are also not adequately rooted in (i.e. they do not directly inform) daily policymaking. One obvious way in which the actors could address this is to monitor future policy agendas and identify priorities. Individually, Germany, the Netherlands, and the Commission have not really explored how this might be achieved in a more systematic fashion. Some actors (e.g. the Commission, the Netherlands, and the UK) have set their own targets, but these tend to be too loose, too limited in number, and generally insufficiently coordinated within and across sectors and actors, to have much effect.

Share workloads

No single actor can possibly monitor the environmental impact of all policies in all jurisdictions and arrive at truly integrated policy decisions. Sharing workloads is one obvious way in which this could be addressed. Interestingly, the new Rules of Procedure in the Council (Council of the European Union 2004) encourage this. However, our research suggests that this is not being done in relation to environmental coordination, not even amongst three of the more pro-environment member states in the EU. More specifically, the Commission makes little use of national appraisal capacities; member states do not combine their resources to assist the Commission prepare its IAs, or to update them during the Council phase. But we have detected a growing appreciation of the need more fully to involve member states in the preparation of Commission IAs. In other words, the actors are beginning to appreciate their vertical and horizontal interdependence, at least as regards policy appraisal.

Maintain a focus on coordination throughout the policy process

This is not systematically and comprehensively achieved, because the sector officials are not adequately motivated by the existing coordination capacities to support EPI throughout the full cycle of policy development. We see this, for example, in relation to environmental policy appraisal, which continues to be regarded as a 'one-off' affair, dominated by the Commission. Because of this weak focus, environmental coordination tends to occur only when a particular actor (or coalition of actors) is sufficiently motivated to track issues across the various sectoral Councils. More often than not, external crises and political pressures provide the trigger to think and act horizontally (see Chapter 3). Without these, many environmentally damaging proposals are not adequately picked up and amended.

Identify priorities and resolve conflicts proactively

High workloads are beginning to force more and more actors to identify priorities, but at present this is not necessarily being done in a particularly coordinated manner. Agendas, therefore, have to be used in more strategic ways to support environmental coordination. However, with the exception of the UK, this is not being systematically achieved by any of the actors. Much appears to depend on the vagaries of political attention, which in turn depends on pressure arising from a binding international commitment (e.g. on climate change) or internationally driven process (e.g. world trade reforms), a crisis situation (e.g. the collapse of North Sea fish stocks), or an internal reform programme (e.g. the Common Agricultural Policy) (Hinterberger and Zacherl 2003: 24; CEC 2004b: 32; EEA 2003: 274). Without these, many intersectoral conflicts are not picked up early enough in the EU policy process. When proposals are picked up, it is often because of personal links (e.g. in the Parliament) or the campaigning efforts made by a particular actor, neither of which provide a particularly sturdy or reliable basis for pursuing cross-sectoral policy coordination, hence the OECD's push for the deeper institutionalization of the EPI principle.

Act efficiently

The political and administrative systems in all the actors are not responding adequately enough to the double challenge of 'thinking European' and 'thinking horizontally' (i.e. EPI). Horizontal interdependence is too demanding for everyone to be able to follow everything. Active information is a must. But passive information continues to be the order of the day in all the actors, apart from the UK. The inefficiencies thus created place an especially large burden on the shoulders of the respective environment departments, which, in spite of their pleas for 'common

255

ownership', have to hunt around for information on environmental spill-overs before they can identify targets for EU-EPI.

Summary

Our overall finding is that none of the basic coordination tasks that we identified in Chapter 1 is currently being satisfactorily discharged. Worse still, several of them are barely being addressed at all. In view of the high-level political commitment to achieve EU-EPI at the heads of state level (see Chapter 1), we first examine what type(s) of network(s) have (or have not) formed around the problem of EPI. Second, we explore the internal capacities of the participating actors, to see where the roots of these failures might lie.

Coordination capacities at the network level

Coordination via networks: a brief reprise

The EU is replete with policy networks. What most concerns us, however, are those networks that seek to achieve greater coordination across sectors. The existing literature on networks is, as we showed in Chapter 1, very much divided on the question of how these emerge and function. We noted the claim made by some scholars that *all* networks are essentially self-organizing, this being *the* defining feature of governance. Then there are others, who are a lot less sanguine insofar as they foresee some need for network management. The next part of this section therefore reviews the different *types* of networks that have (or have not) emerged around the problem of EPI. We look at how they were formed. Are they primarily sectoral in nature, or are they genuinely cross-sectoral? Do they exist purely at EU level, or are they adequately supported by coordination capacities at national level? What kinds of leadership or secretarial structures do they have—that is, to what extent are they *managed*?

What kinds of networks are there?

Chapters 3 and 4 revealed that there are at least three EU-level networks that are potentially relevant to EU-EPI: the *Cardiff process network;* the *network of national environmental coordinators;* and the *Environment Policy Review Group* (EPRG). Importantly, these three have very different objectives, different origins, and function in very different ways. The *Cardiff process network* comprises a very loosely connected set of sectoral bodies (primarily located in the Council and the Commission), without a strong overall manager (see below). Formed in response to demands made concurrently by the Commission and the European Council, it seeks to grapple simultaneously with vertical and horizontal interdependence. But its links into daily policy and politics are weak and recently the backing it receives from political leaders has waned quite significantly. In fact, grave concerns have been aired about its long-term survival (see Chapter 3).

By contrast, the *network of national environmental coordinators* was successfully 'self-organized' by member state environment departments, without any central network management. It comprises middle-ranking bureaucrats from the member state environment departments. However, it primarily addresses vertical rather than horizontal interdependence. Meanwhile, the *Environment Policy Review Group* is also a kind of high-level *team* which tries to steer the strategic, long-term direction of EU environmental policy (i.e. it also primarily addresses vertical rather than horizontal interdependence). Crucially, these two networks are *sectoral*; they do not seek to work horizontally.

These preliminary observations about the structure and remit of the three networks strongly suggest that sectoral networks *are*, as Chapter 2 suggested, much more likely to self-organize (and endure) than cross-sectoral ones. In the next section, we start to explore them in a little more detail.

What coordination capacities do they possess?

In Chapter 1 we noted that when adequate coordination networks do not spontaneously 'self-organize', a central coordinator may have to step in to create the necessary incentives. We differentiated between two different forms that network management might take: *weak*—essentially a supportive *secretary*, which mainly works within a given network to improve the efficiency of decisionmaking; and *strong*—a *manager* which seeks to alter the underlying structure and composition of the network.

In some respects, the *Cardiff process network* exhibits some characteristics of strong management. It has, for example, been able to draw upon the backing of heads of state to bring in more sectors (i.e. from three to ten—see Box 3.1). Since 1998, both the quantity and the quality of the primary outputs—the Cardiff integration strategies with their targets and timetables—increased quite substantially, although not nearly as far or as fast as DG Environment had originally hoped. With hindsight, however, more could have been achieved with stronger and more consistent network management. It is significant that the network lacks a strong manager. For a Council-focused process, it is somewhat strange that the management tasks are shared between the Commission (which is bureaucratic, indirect, and hence quite weak) or individual Presidencies (which have more force, but are politically driven and hence quite episodic). Crucially, both of them have shied away from more politically sensitive tasks such as 'naming and shaming' to put pressure on the laggard sectors.

The other two relevant networks—the *national environmental coordinators* and the *EPRG*—can be dealt with relatively quickly as neither seeks simultaneously to manage horizontal and vertical interdependence. In both, the management capacities are of a relatively weak and secretarial nature. More importantly, there is no sustained focus either on EU-EPI or on finding a balance between sectoral priorities in daily policymaking.

Summary: weak network management?

Our main finding, therefore, is that contrary to the predictions made by some governance theorists, no formal EU-EPI has spontaneously self-organized. Instead, at least three different networks have emerged, some of which tackle EPI more directly and with more energy than others. Moreover, the three are not linked together in any logical way and do not benefit from consistent leadership. Hence, the EU's attempt to implement Article 6 via networked governance appears to lack an effective implementing network. Moreover, the heads of state have routinely given Cardiff their broad political backing, but this is not a proper substitute for high-level leadership and management. Some states have championed EPI during their Presidencies but many others have not, so the overall thrust has been quite diffuse and intermittent (the evidence is displayed in Table 3.2). The collective action problem of network leadership discussed in Chapter 2 is painfully apparent. Everyone with environmental responsibilities seems to want to focus on the work of the Environment Council, because this is a tried and tested route, and it offers external visibility especially to the more environmental constituencies of interest. By contrast, interfering in cognate sectors is very time consuming and provokes resistance (and thus tends to be unpleasant). Not surprisingly, everyone expects someone else to take the lead. This includes DG Environment, which wants everyone to be responsible for EU-EPI.

In recent years, DG Environment has visibly backtracked from the (limited) leadership role it assumed in the late 1990s. It has, for example, moved on to establish new coordinating networks (i.e. the thematic strategies associated with the Sixth EAP); it has also been forced by critics to retreat back to the older governing approach (the Community Method) of developing more politically acceptable forms of environmental legislation. Under Barroso, it has even been forced to defend the existing environmental *acquis* from attacks from those pushing a pro-industry line. It is symptomatic of these changing political fortunes, that the first Cardiff stocktake produced by the sustainability unit in DG Environment contained only one genuinely new proposal—to create an interactive internet portal to share ideas not on EPI, but sustainability (CEC 2004*b*: 36). This amounts to a very weak form of network management (EEA 2005*a*: 34).[1]

To conclude, with only weak forms of networked governance, limited market-based mechanisms, and a continuing failure to scrutinize or influence policies in other areas, it is hardly surprising that the EU has struggled to implement Article 6. In effect, it has set itself a political target, then failed to put in place sufficient implementing (or, to be more precise, *coordinating*) mechanisms to deliver it. Insofar as networks have spontaneously emerged, they have tended to be relatively inward looking (i.e. they lack a sufficiently strong horizontal focus).

Coordination capacities at the actor level

Observing that there are no cross-sectoral networks is not necessarily a sufficient explanation for poor coordination. If all the actors have sufficient capacities to monitor relevant developments and formulate adequate responses, a loosely coupled network (in the sense suggested by Weick (1976)) could still lead to effective integration (cf. Landau 1969). To put this more concretely, if all the member states arrive at the various expert meetings and negotiation tables with sufficiently coordinated policy positions, EU-EPI could still be achieved without an EU-level network. But to do this, the member states need the coordination capacities (and bilateral links) to integrate the environment into the early stages of sectoral policymaking. Hence, we do need to drill down to the level of individual actors to ascertain whether sufficient coordination capacities exist for integration, from the bottom up (i.e. Level II in Table 1.1). This is a different way of making the same point made by Metcalfe (2000: 832), who suggested that if the coordination capacities of the participating actors are weak, then any overarching network will be prone to break down, and vice versa.

What sort of coordination capacities do the actors require? Based on our summary of the coordination literature, each actor should at least be able to: (1) *work proactively*—that is, achieve a high level of coordination in the early Commission phases; (2) *resolve differences* as early as possible to avoid logjamming the already overloaded EU decisionmaking system (Level 7 on the scale is therefore the minimum that is needed); (3) *coordinate efficiently*[2] in situations of complex interdependence; (4) *avoid being overloaded* by having the capacity to reach high levels of coordination as and when necessary (i.e. administrative subsidiarity).

The performance of the actors (output)

This subsection summarizes the performance (output) of the actors using the coordination scale outlined in Chapter 2. The first part assesses the coordination capacities of each actor (i.e. input) in terms of interdepartmental policymaking. The next looks at why the environmental coordinators in the environmental departments (and, in particular, their EU coordinators) have such a key part to play in driving EU-EPI forward. In so doing, we fit together the inter- and intradepartmental dimensions of coordination identified in the opening chapters of this book.

THE COMMISSION PHASES

The empirical chapters show that the member states only haphazardly monitor the Commission phases and hardly use them to find preliminary agreement on negotiating positions. Only White Papers and other strategic documents acquire (increasing) attention. Moreover, our interviews indicate that the tremendous workload associated with daily EU decisionmaking prevents any real progress in this area. This should serve as a strong warning to states like Germany and the Netherlands that their current coordination capacities are seriously deficient with respect to wicked issues. After all, monitoring the 'wrong' proposals at a very early stage can create extra workloads that persist for years. The Parliament is generally limited in its capacity and incentives to monitor the early Commission phases, as its Environment Committee tends to look no further than DG Environment. In summary, therefore, none of the actors has fully adapted itself to consider upcoming EU policy agendas.

THE COUNCIL PHASES

Much greater differences are apparent in the way in which the five actors coordinate the Council phases. The UK starts quickly, whereas Germany and the Netherlands move slowly from light coordination (gathering views and trying to keep everyone informed), towards nailing down instructions for the COREPER. The Parliament's committees work very independently. Consultation between them is light and the advantage generally lies with the lead committee. A lot depends on its willingness to share information with the environment committee. The Environment Committee tries to influence outcomes by writing opinions, but coordination is heavily reliant on cooperation within political groups.

The other notable feature about these three actors and the Commission is that they are all highly 'event' related. Interestingly, each one focuses on slightly different events (the Netherlands on instructions for COREPER and Council; Germany almost exclusively on COREPER instructions; the Commission on Hebdo and College meetings). With the advent of co-decision, the Parliament is now active in all the phases, but the coordination across its committees tends to be highly uncertain, depending on the activities of the *rapporteurs*, the chairmen, and the political groupings. By contrast, the UK system persistently deals with issues (i.e. problems) early in the Commission phases, but also after the proposal has been formally issued.

Summary

We therefore conclude that Germany is at a huge disadvantage in Brussels because of its failure to manage internal disagreements. On the one hand, the continuing struggle between departments means that there is always *an* opportunity to pursue EPI. However, exploiting it requires an awful lot from the environment department, when information flows so passively in the German system. The Dutch system on the other hand seems to function better, but it is also relatively inefficient. Of the five actors, the UK appears to have the best administrative system. However, two major qualifications emerged in relation to its handling of EU-EPI. First, the environment department has not invested to make the 'Rolls Royce' system work to its advantage (see Chapter 8). This combination is actually quite dangerous for EPI, because if environment slips out at an early phase, then it is very difficult to reintegrate it later on.[3] Second, the Commission stages are not as well coordinated, so the advantages of the UK system are not uniformly spread.

The coordination capacities of the actors (coordination input)

HIERARCHICAL MECHANISMS

Hierarchical mechanisms are those controlled directly by the apex, be that the prime minister of a member state, or the president of the Parliament or Commission. In spite of the strong political support expressed by the hierarchies of all five actors, none is directly involved in pursuing EU-EPI or, it has to be said, even monitoring performance. Moreover (and with the obvious exception of the UK), the other actors have college structures,[4] which would dramatically reduce the effectiveness of hierarchical coordination—were it ever attempted.

BUREAUCRATIC PROCEDURES

Bureaucratic procedures seek to standardize behaviour (e.g. in relation to who to inform, and when and how to apply impact assessments). An important distinction that we introduced in Chapter 2 was between an active and a more passive exchange of information. The Commission has made huge strides in terms of coordinating itself better (see also the 2005 Transparency Initiative), through procedures such as IA, roadmaps, and SPP. Consequently, information has started to flow more actively. The work of the Parliament is also governed by procedures. These start with the one governing the allocation of dossiers to lead committees and for problem-solving. These mechanisms do not, however, function very well due in large part to the dominance of the lead committees.

Of the three states, Germany has the most unregulated coordination system. There are *bureaucratic procedures* governing how to behave but the lack of *hierarchical* capacities means there are effectively no penalties for disobeying them. Therefore, information flows very passively and coordination only really occurs when it has to; that is, when proposals arrive at the COREPER. In the Netherlands, EU policy coordination is highly routinized and supported by rules on how to behave. However, they are not supported by higher level mechanisms (cf. the Cabinet Office and UKREP in the UK) and there are no punishments for withholding information. Therefore, information continues to flow quite passively. By contrast, the UK has many rules and procedures which facilitate active information. Over time, a strong culture of informal cooperation has emerged, backed up by the *watchdog* roles of the Cabinet Office and foreign affairs. Only strong ministers are brave enough selectively to disseminate information or 'go beyond their brief' in Brussels. Finally, the Netherlands, the Commission, and the UK do have environmental policy appraisal procedures in place, but we identified weaknesses in all of them. They are also not very well interconnected. Consequently, there is plenty of scope for coordinated Commission proposals to be unpicked by subsequent interventions from national governments.

SKILLS DEVELOPMENT AND TRAINING

Some of the actors provide their staff with training in relation to procedures such as environmental policy appraisal, but its overall contribution tends to be quite limited in a world full of multiple policy objectives and cripplingly high workloads. We therefore remain convinced that this particular coordination capacity is best used to support other coordination capacities such as *bureaucratic procedures* and various *horizontal mechanisms*.

SPECIFICATION OF OUTPUT ('MANAGEMENT BY OBJECTIVES')

In general terms, the Commission has accepted the need to implement EPI, but has struggled to get the EU to adopt more specific EPI objectives than Article 6. We found that most officials working outside—and sometimes even within—the environmental departments in Germany, the Netherlands, and the UK are not very familiar with the Cardiff process. The same applies to the sectoral committees in the Parliament. Hence, those targets and objectives that do exist, tend to be sector specific and/or mainly of a symbolic nature.

HORIZONTAL COORDINATION MECHANISMS

Informal relations between officials in the Netherlands have increased in recent years, but they are often unreliable. Moreover, the workload that everyone is under often stymies the informal exchange of information. *Liaison roles* for EU-EPI hardly exist. Most environment departments at national level do have European units, but they tend to be internally facing (i.e. monitoring policymaking activities in DG Environment and the Environment Council), and as such do not pursue EPI in their host department. The Netherlands recently created a new coordinating *team* but, as discussed in Chapter 7, it is very small and makes relatively little contribution to EPI. Germany, too, relies heavily on *informal relations*. These are, however, more diverse and unreliable compared to the Netherlands. Moreover, they are very defensive; the prevalence of passive coordination means that environment officials have to go to extraordinary lengths to monitor policy developments in cognate sectors.

More *liaison roles* are planned in Germany, but whether they will actually work is unclear given the debilitating effect of passive information. The most notorious features of the German system include the number of coordinating committees (*teams*) at different levels and the large 'control trips' organized to monitor negotiations directly in Brussels. Given the collegial nature of the German system, many conflicts are quickly transmitted up to the cabinet or state secretaries to resolve. This is a recipe for inefficient and potentially highly ineffective coordination.

In terms of *informal relations*, the active exchange of information in the UK ensures a high level of coordination. Active information and subsidiarity decisionmaking mean that *liaison roles* hardly exist in the UK. Committees (*teams*) are only convened to solve specific problems (cf. the Netherlands, where each department is present for the coordination of each and every Council).

In the Commission, *informal relations* have been advocated, but the workload as well as the inherently fragmented structure of the organization, makes them unreliable. Moreover, little has been done to formalize them. The Commission is full of general *teams* at different levels (e.g. directors meetings, the Hebdo, and the weekly meetings of the college of Commissioners). These are important, but require DG Environment to put in a lot of work (note, the debilitating effect of passive information). *Strong integrating roles* do exist but they are not robust enough to rein in strong DGs and Commissioners.

In the *Parliament,* the relations between committees and between the relevant chairmen shape the horizontal exchange of information. If these relationships are bad, the lead committee can reduce the information flow to a trickle. Very often, the most effective cross-committee cooperation involves informal contacts between members of the same political groups. The official *teams* (i.e. the Conference of Committee Chairmen) seldom play a role in finding compromises on the content of dossiers. The plenary vote is very much an instrument for ratifying the final decision, not coordinating its production. This underlines the fact that there is still precious little continuous exchange—and hence little mutual learning—about overlapping policy objectives between parliamentary committees. This stands in sharp contrast to the four other (and much more administrative) actors in our study, which at least have the possibility to interact with cognate departments throughout all the phases of policymaking.

MISSION STATEMENTS ('SPECIFICATION OF OWNERSHIP')

The Commission, the UK, and the Netherlands have mission statements that support the general principle of EPI in the EU. But—and this counts for all the actors—these ideals are all too readily sacrificed in the ebb and flow of daily politics.

SUMMARY

To conclude, none of the five actors scores highly against the four minimum requirements identified above. This makes the lack of strong leadership at the network level (see above) all the more telling. Germany and the Netherlands are easily overloaded because they do not move information around actively enough and do not devolve work to the lowest effective level. By contrast, the UK is more efficient because it operates a subsidiarity-based system. Moreover, instead of increasing the number of coordination capacities like the other actors, they have taken steps to lighten coordination by merging coordination teams and stressing the subsidiarity nature of the meetings (see Chapter 8). However, because EU-EPI is a collective action problem, it cannot possibly be solved by one very well-coordinated state (or even a small number of coordinated states).

Finally, there are the two EU institutions. In recent years, the Commission has made a concerted effort to improve its reputation for internal coordination, via the use of internal programming and IAs, etc. However, the jury is still out on whether they lead to genuine improvements. By contrast, the Parliament is very poor in terms of horizontal coordination. Worse still, it appears to be doing relatively little to improve the situation. Its basic structure and the expansiveness of decisionmaking (co-decision alone can last up to two years) militate against quick and simple solutions.

To conclude, none of the five actors has adapted itself fully in terms of either its outlook and/or its coordination capacities. In the absence of weak central management, it is conceivable that progress could still be achieved in building (i.e. self-organizing) coordination capacities at actor level. But this would require one actor or a small group of powerful actors to take the lead. Currently, however, no one apparently has the incentive to stand back and perform management tasks such as undertaking network or actor audits, building support, or generally displaying leadership. Instead of facing up to and engaging with this, the environmental actors continue to put their faith in the ideology of 'shared ownership', which of course conveniently assumes away the problem.

We did not set out to explore the level convergence (or otherwise) amongst the five. The existing literature paints a mixed picture of 'limited similarity combined with considerable divergence' (Kassim 2003*b*: 102). Our more detailed analysis suggests that the overall pattern is actually one of pronounced *divergence*. For example, Germany and the Netherlands have tried to make their system less passive by adopting more and more committees, but this has had the perverse effect of making their systems more inefficient and event-driven. By contrast, the UK and the Commission have tried to make their systems more actively coordinated. The Commission's move towards active coordination, greater internal and external transparency, and IAs is all the more remarkable given its poor reputation (see Chapter 9). Finally, the Parliament is particularly note-worthy, because it is one of the more obvious sources of political pressure on the other actors. Yet, it remains almost blithely fragmented in a world of growing policy interdependence. Despite several internal reports, it is very difficult to identify much internal pressure for reform, let alone a clear reform agenda (Chapter 10). These are large differences to bridge if EU-EPI is going to be addressed through peer review and benchmarking activities organized under the OMC. Crucially, there does not even appear to be an obvious example of 'best practice' for the rest to try and emulate.

Strengthening actors and managing networks

What are the policy options?

Having noted these deficiencies, what additional coordination capacities could be developed at both levels of our study—that is, at network level and within the actors (see Table 1.1)—to compensate? At the moment, the discussion about new capacities is framed mainly in terms of what can be done at EU level (e.g. witness the debate about whether or not to resuscitate the Cardiff process, or the viability of creating new sustainable development committees in the Council) (see Chapter 3). However, there are a number of political and administrative obstacles to what can be achieved solely by acting at EU level. For example, none of the member states in our sample has shown much appetite for introducing new *hierarchical mechanisms* (i.e. the direct involvement of the apex in policy delivery—see Chapter 2) at national level, so it seems most unlikely that they will countenance their use at EU level (e.g. via the direct involvement of the European Council or a nominated team of integration Commissioners). Similarly, more forceful and/or more specific *mission statements* at EU level are unlikely to do much either. Our research reveals that statements like Article 6 help to raise the political profile of coordination challenges like EPI (i.e. they emphasize what needs to be done), but in and of themselves do not really do much to translate them into the nitty-gritty of daily policymaking in the sectors.

More importantly, our bottom-up and cumulative understanding of coordination suggests that it is as, if not more, important to ensure that steps taken at EU level are solidly rooted in the sublevel capacities of actors. That is, in order to be effective, coordinating networks need adequately resourced and incentivized actors. We have shown that the two levels are actually interdependent—improving actor capacities needs to be undertaken in network settings to ensure an adequate degree of inter-actor coordination. Interestingly, this was very much the same point made by the Kok report on the operation of the Lisbon process (High Level Group 2004: 7). Therefore, in this section we start by looking at the actors and then move up to networks at EU level.

New capacities at actor level

After myriad frustrations had been expressed with the traditional Community Method of legislating, the EU started to experiment with new modes such as Cardiff. But as they are also proving to be problematic, the search has begun for even newer instruments (e.g. witness the recent shift from environmental policy appraisal to integrated appraisal). As this shift gathers pace, it is worth noting the absence of any solid diagnostic work at national or European levels. Our interviews suggest that the Commission pushed for a partnership (or networked) approach in 1997–8, because it suited the preferences of the member states at the time. Analyzing and addressing the underlying capacity problems has never been a particularly popular activity, especially among member states; our interviews suggest that national and EU officials are not very well trained to think in terms of (let alone audit) multilevel administrative systems.

In view of the lack of strong central management, the most obvious place to start is by looking at the five environment departments who—and this bears repeating—have done the most to popularize the concept of EPI at EU level. Even though EPI would appear to require a sea change in thinking (from seeing environment as a 'stand-alone' policy to a more cross-cutting challenge), all five remain more preoccupied with policies flowing into and out of the Environment Council. They simply do not see the scrutiny of cognate agendas as their priority, but something for everyone to own. The problem is that in a world of multiple objectives and scare resources, when everyone is in charge of something, in practice no one is. Due to their implicit belief in the ideology of wider 'ownership', the roles and the resources of their respective EU coordinating and national sustainable development units have not evolved to fit the demands of EU-EPI (Schout and Jordan 2005). One obvious thing that the environmental departments could do is bolster the size of their respective EU-coordinating units, by giving them the task of pursuing EPI across both levels of our multilevel study.

Second, actors that coordinate very passively (in our sample, Germany and the Netherlands) need to develop radically different ways of working. With increasing horizontal and vertical interdependence, the limits of passive coordination are close to being reached. However, far from improving the situation, recent reforms initiated by Germany and the Netherlands (e.g. the proliferation of monitoring units in Germany), seem to have made things worse. Instead of overhauling their systems, they have simply created more committees and more meetings. As a result, their systems threaten to become less, not more, efficient. Interestingly, the Commission already appears to have responded before reaching this point.

Coordinating capacities at network level

Thinking about better multilevel coordination forces us to consider the design of networks. At the EU level, we have shown that the political discussion about strengthening coordination networks is often rather superficial. For example, the debate at EU level is currently focused on how best to resuscitate the Cardiff process network and/or prevent it from being completely eclipsed by the networks evolving around the Lisbon process. This could, as some of the more pro-environment states like Sweden have recently suggested, involve a renewed push to develop new integration strategies, embodying more specific targets and firmer time-tables. It could also incorporate stronger review processes, league tables of performance, and the public 'naming and shaming' of the worst perform-ing sectors. Or, even more ambitiously, it could be extended to include auditing potentially sensitive topics such as individual and collective administrative strengths. Interestingly, Chapter 3 noted that very similar suggestions have been made in relation to the emerging networks around the Sixth EAP and the SDS.

Amid this competition between different types of networks, one vital aspect still does not gain the attention that it desperately needs: network *management*. Here, the EU must confront a very serious dilemma, because it is not a government (in the sense used in many existing studies of network management), but a system of multilevel governance. The prevailing literature does not resolve the matter of who manages networks in such settings. Klijn et al. (1995: 441–2), for example, argue that the manager 'may' be a governmental actor, 'but it may also be an actor from outside government'. At the national level, the situation is somewhat clearer—normally, central government is the preferred network manager.[5] As well as being the most obvious choice (Kickert et al. 1997b: 168), among other things, it enjoys political legitimacy and is the guardian of certain core democratic values. However, none of the environment departments in our sample of three states seems willing or able to the lead on this task.[6] Nor do the core executives of the three states, or the Presidents of the Commission and the Parliament. In short, what we see is a classic collective action problem. If we also bring the other twenty-two member states into the equation, the scale of the coordination challenge confronting the EU is potentially awesome.

As argued above, the most obvious candidate for this job is, of course, the Commission.[7] It has a formal policy initiating role, good access to information (it is the focal point of many sectoral networks), and a broader responsibility to ensure that EU policy is designed and carried out effectively. The need for it to perform more network management tasks was a strong theme of the recent High Level Group (Kok) report on the Lisbon process (High Level Group 2004: 43). 'The Commission must', it argued:

be prepared to name and shame those that fail as well as 'fame' those that succeed. Too much is at stake to respect the sensibilities of those who hinder the pursuit of the common European good. (High Level Group 2004: 17)

But giving the Commission these and other sensitive management tasks would be seriously inconsistent with the dominant *realpolitik* in the EU today, in spite of the rhetorical commitment to employ more networked governance. First, during 2005 the EU moved into a period of deep introspection regarding such core issues as the economic competitiveness of Europe and even the viability of the entire European political project. Following the failure of the French and Dutch governments to ratify the draft Constitution, EU-EPI has dropped even further down the Commission's list of priorities. Second, the Commission is already seriously overworked and underresourced, hence the appeal of new modes of governance which *appear* to provide the EU with an opportunity to do 'more with the same'. Our research suggests that this assumption is rather misguided; new modes like Cardiff need to be properly nurtured and managed. Any network management tasks will, of course, need to be harmonized with the multiplicity of other roles which the Commission currently fulfils—policy initiation; policy management and implementation; mediation; power brokering; and external representation. Third, the Commission is internally fragmented and hence not in an ideal position to manage cross-sectoral networks (cf. also Pollitt and Bouckaert 2004: 236). Fourth, Commission officials have little training in network audits or network management (for a list of what this might entail, see Kickert et al. 1997*b*: 175–7). Finally, network management has the potential to trespass on some very politically sensitive ground. To see why, one need only look at the superficial network audit produced by the Council Secretariat in 2001. The opening sentence of its report made it abundantly clear that 'internal coordination in the Member States *is, and must remain, the exclusive preserve of each government*' (Council of the European Union 2001: 1) (emphasis added). The idea that national administrations are sacrosanct is strongly at odds with the idea of strong network management, hence the interest in newer modes of governing that rely on benchmarking and the bilateral sharing of best practices.

One obvious actor that could do more is DG Environment, through its role in the EPRG network. The EPRG is important because while it is supposed to guide EU environmental policy, it generally has not taken a synoptic overview of EPI (see Chapter 3). The EU does not necessarily need to create an entirely new network; the EPRG could pick up a number of new tasks to give a stronger push to EU-EPI, possibly with the support of a more junior group. First of all, it could examine the Commission and Presidency agendas in other policy fields. It could also usefully pick up the Cardiff strategies (or similar) and use them as navigating devices to shape the future direction of EU policies. It could also try to assess the extent to which national EPI/sustainability targets support the attainment of similar goals set at EU level. One possibility (which is heavily trailed in the Kok report (High Level Group 2004: 40–1)) is to develop national EPI programmes (or Cardiff-like strategies),[8] whose content could be benchmarked by the Commission. Crucially, this would shift the focus from *intersectoral* learning (where the coordination capacities of the Council formations are relatively weak) to *interstate* learning (where they are stronger and better developed). Much more radically, the EPRG could also explore new ways to encourage greater cooperation between national environment departments across the EU. This could be achieved by identifying common agendas and then allocating certain key tasks to particular groups of environment departments (e.g. tracking a particularly environmentally damaging proposal as it moves through the EU decisionmaking system and reporting back to the rest of the network). For the time being, the EU is not thinking or acting in this way; everyone seems to be fixated with writing different more and more high-level strategies, rather than the nitty-gritty aspects of policymaking in the sectors. That three of the greener member states in the EU (namely, the Netherlands, the UK, and Germany) are far from being fully prepared for this challenge, should be a matter of concern for DG Environment.

The coordination of the EU

Exploring the capacities of networked governance

The EU is confronted by a number of complex policy problems where horizontal and vertical interdependence collide. In response, it has seized on new and more 'open' methods of coordination, which rely upon 'networked' forms of governance (Stubb, Wallace, and Peterson 2003: 148). We have shown that these very often complement 'older' modes of governing such as regulation. Having now looked at how the EU employs networks to address one, admittedly very challenging, coordination problem, are we in a better position to understand their strengths and weaknesses vis-à-vis other modes of coordination? Furthermore, what does our study contribute to the rapidly developing academic debate about different modes of governance?

Although we have focused on the gradual emergence of a European administrative system and the importance of good network building and management, we do not wish to downplay the importance of *political* will (Peters 1998b: 52). Ultimately, coordination capacities at network and actor level need political pressure. Network managers need to have the political support to engage in what are very often complex and sensitive tasks such as building trust between actors or reframing problems. Within particular actors, if officials believe that 'our minister is not interested', then no administrative system—however well endowed with coordination capacities—will work. Having said that, we have also shown that the coordination capacities which guide policies through the various policy phases are important, too. We have shown how they help to identify and resolve sectoral differences, which can then be raised at an appropriately high level in order to foster the necessary political interest in coordination. Politics and administration are therefore like the proverbial chicken and egg.

What is strikingly similar about the Cardiff and the Lisbon processes (High Level Group 2004: 39) is the absence of sustained political leadership. Heads of state have repeatedly given both their blessings. But on a more day-to-day basis, clear and firm political leadership has depended on a particular Presidency or state taking the lead. This is simply not enough in a complex multilevel governance system such as the EU. The European Parliament is still not politically mature or internally coordinated enough to fill this gap in political leadership, so the political incentives needed to make networks function effectively have to come from elsewhere. Whether one sees this as a failure of political leadership or of network management is largely irrelevant, because the two are, we would argue, intimately interconnected.

This study has revealed that policy coordination goals require more than high-level political support to have an effect on the ground. Our analysis reveals that many of the basic political and institutional features of the EU strongly inhibit cross-sectoral coordination. These include:[9]

- *The absence of a network manager*: when it comes to managing EU networks, there is no obvious candidate for this job;
- *The unremitting speed of the EU policy process*: tight deadlines and high workloads seriously frustrate holistic policymaking;
- *The vertical separation between the EU's administration*: national servants believe their main allegiance is to 'their' member states and that the Commission will take care of the EU's policies. Rather than cooperating with one another to tackle shared coordination problems, they tend to see problems in national terms. This severely inhibits the scope for achieving simultaneous vertical and horizontal coordination;
- *The large number of actors, with different preferences and coordination capacities*: to make matters worse, some of the actors in our sample are altering their coordination systems in rather perverse ways;
- *Passive coordination systems*: The Netherlands, Germany, and—for the time being—the Commission, all rely on reactive coordination mechanisms that require a lot of effort from departments that are not in the lead. Better coordination requires much more proactive and efficient problem-solving;

- *Adapting roles to horizontal objectives*: despite major shifts in policy discourse, the environment departments have not adapted the roles and resources of their EU-coordinating units to pick up the cross-sectoral challenges posed by EPI and sustainability.

Some analysts believe that the underlying problem is the deep and enduring sectorization of the EU into functional sectors and networks (Peters and Wright 2001). However, our much more cumulative view of coordination suggests that differentiation per se is not the problem (it could even be viewed as the first step on the road to effective coordination) (Lawrence and Lorsch 1967). Rather, the key challenge is to find ways to *manage* differentiation. If this is to be achieved using networked governance, one inherent weakness will need to be addressed, which is that networks flourish where there are relatively small numbers of actors who interact regularly, share common values, and trust one another (Thompson et al. 1995: 15; Thompson 2003: 30). Unfortunately, these are not typical features of many cross-cutting policy problems in the EU.

Consequently, what we find in relation to environmental coordination (and, we suspect, many other similar coordination challenges in the EU) is a 'policy mess' (Rhodes 1985: 11; 1997a: 13), which arises when policy problems cut across a set of relatively discrete sectoral policy networks. In these situations, adequate coordination networks do not spontaneously 'self-organize' because the testing conditions for self-management specified by Ostrom in Chapter 2 are not satisfied. To make matters worse, the EU has not yet invested in sufficient coordination capacities at network or actor level to overcome this situation. Our research therefore suggests that some of the more extreme claims made about the self-coordinating abilities of networks need to be questioned and, perhaps, heavily qualified.[10]

Learning lessons and looking to the future

In this final section, we will endeavour to draw out and explore a number of more general lessons about the governance of the EU that emerge from our analysis. The first is that coordination is often wrongly presented as if it was either the EU's responsibility or the member states'. On the contrary, coordination requires a *system-wide* response from the various parts of the EU. Currently, this is simply not happening: each actor continues to look at problems from its own perspective. What our study powerfully confirms is that the EU's administrative 'system' (if, indeed, that does not overplay the coherence of the organizational links between EU institutions and member states) is still struggling hard, to catch up with the ambitious political promises to make the EU 'more coordinated'.

Second, new and networked forms of governance are undoubtedly in vogue, but they are by no means a panacea. Having witnessed the difficulties of using networks to tackle coordination challenges, EU decisionmakers may well decide to revisit some of the more hierarchical and market-based modes of coordinating. There is certainly evidence that this is occurring in relation to EPI. For example, 'new approaches' to legislating are appearing via the Community Method, as are non-legislative tools such as voluntary agreements and environmental management standards. But as Chapter 3 revealed, market-based environmental instruments are still conspicuous by their virtual absence from EU environmental policymaking. In fact, our analysis reveals many opportunities where the three main modes of coordination can be fruitfully combined, bearing in mind that some 'mix like oil and water' (Rhodes 1997a: 53). Mintzberg's typology helpfully reveals a number of opportunities to combine different coordinating devices. For example, *teams* and other *integrating roles* can help to resolve conflicts that emerge from the use of more *hierarchical* mechanisms, and so on. By proceeding in this way, decisionmakers can, as Jessop (2002: 10) suggests, begin to identify the best 'repertoire of responses'—this being the essence of meta-governance.[11]

Third, if decisionmakers are genuinely committed to using networks to deliver greater coordination,[12] they need to reflect critically upon some of the dilemmas associated with 'network management' (Kickert et al. 1997c)—which is itself an exercise in hierarchy (Héritier 2001: 18). Currently, the EU is simply not building sufficient coordination capacities either at actor or at network levels to support the use of new modes like Cardiff and Lisbon. One reason is that such interventions are implicitly 'written out of the script by new governance advocates' (Peters 2000: 45), as well, one suspects, as the apexes of the Commission and the member states (Schout and Jordan 2005). Moreover, the tasks performed by network managers in the EU may have to extend well beyond the relatively minimal role envisaged by Kickert et al. (1997a: 10) (i.e. of 'coordinating strategies of actors with different goals and preferences... *within an existing network* of inter-organizational relations') (emphasis added), to include much more politically sensitive tasks such as network creation, network auditing, and 'naming and shaming'. Indeed, we suspect that the challenge may often go well beyond ensuring that existing networks function effectively; entirely new networks may, on occasions, have to be constructed from scratch. Moreover, even if, as in our case, a weak network does emerge at EU level, it may mask (and be incapable of addressing) significant weaknesses at the level of the participating actors. In the rush to explore new modes, EU policymakers should be careful not to forget that they do not entirely absolve them of the need to work hierarchically.

Therefore, the main message which emerges from our analysis is that the EU should be much more sceptical about the long-term coordinating potential of networks (Héritier 2001: 19). Decisionmakers should, in a word, be more reflexive in the way they go about employing networked governance than is currently the case. They must much more carefully select the right *kind* of coordinating mechanisms for the coordination problems they wish to tackle. The potential for more comparative work in this area is vast.[13] Particularly careful thought is needed into how to ensure that the coordinating capacities at the level of the network and the participating actors complement one another. These things are not nearly as immediate or as eye-catching in their impact as amending the Treaties, publishing grand strategies, creating coordination czars, or establishing high-level task forces (although these do help). We would go as far as to suggest that the EU puts its faith too easily in these things, without undertaking a fuller and more detailed investigation of the coordinating capacities at national and EU level. The Cardiff process provides a sobering reminder of what happens when a simple network is established, but insufficiently endowed with coordinating capacities. Effective networked governance demands patience, tact, and diplomacy.

If all this sounds too much for EU decisionmakers to stomach and coordination failure is, as some governance theorists suggest, the rule rather than the exception,[14] then perhaps they should be more honest about what they can and cannot deliver. By setting ambitious policy coordination and then not achieving it, the EU is in danger of exacerbating the vicious circle of declining public distrust in EU institutions that the governance White Paper set out to respond to in the first place. A similar note of caution was sounded by Pressman and Wildavsky (1984) in their classic study of interorganizational coordination. There, they urged policymakers to set more achievable goals and generally 'keep things simple'. The whole policy discourse surrounding the appearance of new modes of governance is about finding new ways to meet the EU's objectives. Identifying and better understanding what these new modes are *not* capable of achieving in their current form, may be the hardest lesson of all for EU policymakers to learn.

Notes

1. There has, however, been some discussion about the need for administrative networks linking different DGs and (possibly) the Parliament to coordinate the more technical task of preparing impact assessments.
2. It is very striking that the existing literature on EU coordination completely skirts this point.
3. However, in contrast to its opposite numbers in Germany and the Netherlands, the UK environment department at least has the potential to influence other Whitehall departments very early in a policy negotiation.
4. In its own way, the Parliament functions in the same way as a college system with the meeting of chairs of the committees being the central body for cross-committee coordination. But, crucially, this body does not solve sectoral conflicts—that is done through votes in the plenary (see Chapter 10).
5. Other branches of the network management literature suggest that the management powers enjoyed by central government are significantly less than that implied by the 'Dutch school'. Rhodes (1997a: 57), for example, believes that UK central government has had to acquire a new management style to cope with its declining hierarchical power, which is based on 'facilitation, accommodation and bargaining'.
6. Other states have admittedly tried to take on certain tasks. For example, the Austrian environment department has funded several independent studies of the Cardiff and Lisbon processes (Görlach et al. 1999; Hinterberger and Zacherl 2003), and hosted a number of workshops to discuss the administrative dimensions of EU-EPI.
7. Metcalfe gives the strong impression that the Commission is the *only* realistic candidate for this job.
8. Akin to the national economic reform programmes that member states submitted to the Commission for review in late 2005.
9. Compare with Ostrom's conditions in Chapter 2.
10. On closer reading, it is apparent that Rhodes is actually more concerned with *sectoral* policy networks, rather than the more specialized cross-sectoral coordination networks that we explore in this volume. Moreover, he argues that the term network 'describes the several interdependent actors involved in *delivering services'* (Rhodes 1997b: xii).
11. He actually seems to imply that the more types of coordinating mechanism that can be deployed, the better ('requisite variety') (Jessop 2002: 8).
12. And not engage in symbolic politics by deliberately putting in place ineffectual coordinating instruments (Edelman 1973).
13. A start has been made by Hoornbeek and Peters (2005).
14. Jessop (2002: 5), for example, argues that success is indeed the exception not the rule, especially when (as in the EU) one is juggling 'multiple objectives over extended spatial and temporal horizons'.

BIBLIOGRAPHY

Abélè, M., Bellier, I., and McDonald, M. (1993). *Approche Anthroplogique de la Commission Européenne*. Report prepared for the European Commission. Brussels: Commission of the European Communities.

Adelle, C., Hertin, J., and Jordan, A. (2006). 'Sustainable Development "Outside" Europe: What Role for Impact Assessment?'; *European Environment* 16: 57–72.

Algemene Rekenkamer (Audit Office) (2004). *Aandacht Voor Financiële Gevolgen van Europees Beleid*. Internal Report: 9 September 2004. Den Haag: Algemene Rekenkamer.

Allison, G. T. (1971). *Essence of Decision*. Boston, MA: HarperCollins.

—— and Zelikow, P. (1999). *Essence of Decision: Explaining the Cuban Missile Crisis*. Boston, MA: HarperCollins.

Alter, C. and Hage, J. (1993). *Organizations Working Together*. San Francisco, CA: Sage.

Arp, H. (1992). *The European Parliament in European Community Environmental Policy*. EUI (European University Institute) Working Paper. Florence: European University Institute.

Auel, K. and Benz, A. (2004). *National Parliaments in EU Multilevel Governance: Dilemmas and Strategies of Adaptation*. Institute for Political Science Working Paper, Number 60. University in Hagen: Institute of Political Science.

Backes, C. W. and Ozinga, J. C. (2002). *Externe Iintegratie Milieurechtelijke Beginselen: Inventarisatie van Milieurelevante Wetgeving Waarop de in de Wet Milieubeheer te Codificeren Beginselen van Toepassing Zouden Kunnen Worden Verklaard*. Centrum voor Omgevingsrecht en Beleid/NILOS. Utrecht: Universiteit Utrecht.

Bache I. and A. Jordan (eds.) (2006). *The Europeanization of British Politics Palgrave: London*.

Beach, D. (2004). 'The Role and Influence of the Council Secretariat', *Journal of European Public Policy*, 11/3: 408–39.

Bendor, J. and Hammond, T. H. (1992). 'Rethinking Allison's Models', *American Political Science Review*, 86/2: 301–22.

Benz, A. and Eberlein, B. (1999). 'The Europeanization of Regional Policies: Patterns of Multi-level Governance', *Journal of European Public Policy*, 6/2: 329–48.

Beuermann, C. (2000). 'Germany: Regulation and the Precautionary Principle', in W. Lafferty and J. Meadowcroft (eds.), *Implementing Sustainable Development*. Oxford: Oxford University Press.

Beuermann, C. and Burdick, B. (1997). 'The Sustainability Transition in Germany', *Environmental Politics*, 6/1: 83–107.

Bevir, M. and Rhodes, R. (2003). *Interpreting British Governance*. London: Routledge.

BMU (Bundesministerium für Umwelt, Naturschutz und Reaktorsicherheit) (2004). *Info zum Thema Umweltgesetzbuch*. Available on the homepage of the Federal Ministry of the Environment, Nature, and Nuclear Safety (BMU): http://www.bmu.de/de/txt/sachthemen/gesetz/umweltgesetz.

Börzel, T. (1998). 'Organizing Babylon: On the Different Conceptions of Policy Networks', *Public Administration*, 76: 253–73.

Bos, J. N. M. van den (1995). 'De Coördinatie van Nederlandse EU-standpunten: Het Algemene Kader', in J. N. M. van den Bos, E. Derksen, S. Pellegrom, T. Teunissen, T. van Toor, and M. Wolters (eds.), *De Vierde Macht in de Vierde Bestuurslaag*. Den Haag: Parlementaire Documentatie.

Boyce, B. (1995). 'The June 1994 Elections and the Politics of the European Parliament', *Parliamentary Affairs*, 1: 141–56.

Bressers, H. Th. A. and Plettenburg, L. A. (1997). 'The Netherlands', in M. Janicke and H. Weidner (eds.), *National Environmental Policies: A Comparative Study of Capacity Building*. Berlin: Springer-Verlag.

Bulmer, S. and Burch, M. (1998). 'Organizing for Europe: Whitehall, the British State and the EU', *Public Administration*, 76/4: 601–29.

—— —— (2000). 'The Europeanization of British Central Government', in R. A. W. Rhodes (ed.), *Transforming British Government*. Basingstoke: Macmillan.

—— —— (2006). 'Central Government', in I. Bache and A. Jordan (eds.), *The Europeanization of British Politics*. London: Palgrave/Macmillan.

Bundesministerium der Finanzen (Federal Ministry of Finance) (2004). *EU-Handbuch: Koordinierung and Unterrichtungsaufgaben der Bundesregierung*. Berlin: Bundesministerium der Finanzen.

Burns, C. (2005). 'The European Parliament: Environmental Champion or Political Opportunist?', in A. Jordan (ed.), *Environmental Policy in the European Union*, 2nd edn. London: Earthscan.

Cabinet Office (2003). *Regulatory Impact Assessment Guidance*. London: Cabinet Office. For the latest version, see: http://www.cabinetoffice.gov.uk/regulation/ria/index.asp.

Calster, G. and. Deketelaere, K. (1998). 'Amsterdam, the IGC and Greening the Treaty', *European Environmental Law Review*, January: 12–25.

Carter, N., Day, P., and Klein, R. (1992). *How Organisations Measure Success*. London: Routledge.

CEC (Commission of the European Communities) (1993). *Integration by the Commission of the Environment into other Policies*. SEC (93) 785/5, 28 May. Brussels: CEC.

—— (1995). *Progress Report on the Implementation of the European Community Programme of Policy and Action in Relation to the Environment and Sustainable Development: Towards Sustainability*. COM (95) 624, January 1996. Brussels: CEC.

—— (1998). *Communication from the Commission to the European Council: Partnership for Integration: A Strategy for Integrating Environment into EU Policies.* COM (98) 333 final, June. Brussels: CEC.

—— (1999a). *Conclusion of the Global Assessment Stakeholder Consultation, 9–10 February 1999.* European Commission Working Paper. Brussels: CEC.

—— (1999b). *Commission Working Document: From Cardiff to Helsinki and Beyond— Report to the European Council on Integrating Environmental Concerns and Sustainable Development into Community Policies.* SEC (99) 1941 final, 24 November. Brussels: CEC.

—— (2000a). *Reforming the Commission—Background Document.* COM (2000) 200 final. Brussels: CEC.

—— (2000b). *Rules of Procedure.* COM (2000) 3614. Brussels: CEC.

—— (2000c). *White Paper on Environmental Liability.* COM (2000) 66, 12 February. Brussels: CEC.

—— (2000d). *Global Assessment: Europe's Environment—What Directions for the Future?* Brussels: CEC.

—— (2001a). *European Governance: A White Paper.* COM (2001) 428, final, 25 July. Brussels: CEC.

—— (2001b). *Commission Staff Working Paper: Consultation Paper for the Preparation of a EU Strategy for Sustainable Development.* SEC (2001) 517 final, 27 March. Brussels: CEC.

—— (2002a). *European Governance: Better Lawmaking.* COM (2002) 275 final, 5 June. Brussels: CEC.

—— (2002b). *Communication from the Commission on Impact Assessment.* COM (2002) 276 final. Brussels: CEC.

—— (2003a). *Report from the Commission: Better Lawmaking 2003.* COM (2003) 770 final, 12 December. Brussels: CEC.

—— (2003b). *Communication From the Commission to the Council and the European Parliament: 2003 Environmental Policy Review.* COM (2003) 745 final. Brussels: CEC.

—— (2004a). *Fonctionnement de la Commission et Coordination Interne.* SEC (2004) 1617/4. Brussels: CEC.

—— (2004b). *Integrating Environmental Considerations into Other Policy Areas: A Stocktaking of the Cardiff Process.* COM (2004) 394 final, 1 June. Brussels: CEC.

—— (2004c). *Communication from the Commission to the Council and the European Parliament: 2004 Environmental Policy Review.* COM (2005) 17 final, 27 January. Brussels: CEC.

—— (2004d) *Communication From the Commission to the European Parliament and the Economic and Social Committee: Integration of Environmental Aspects into European Standardization.* SEC (2004) 206, 25 February. Brussels: CEC.

—— (2004e). *Impact Assessment: Next Steps in Support of Competitiveness and Sustainable Development.* SEC (2004)1377. Brussels: CEC.

CEC (Commission of the European Communities) (2004*f*) *National Sustainable Development Strategies in the EU: A First Analysis by the European Commission.* Commission Staff Working Document, April. Brussels: CEC.

—— (2005*a*). *The 2005 Review of the EU Sustainable Development Strategy: Initial Stocktaking and Future Orientations.* SEC (2005) 37 final. Brussels: CEC.

—— (2005*b*) *Working Together for Growth and Jobs: A New Start for the Lisbon Strategy.* COM (2005) 24, 2 February. Brussels: CEC.

—— (2005*c*). *Impact Assessment Guide.* SEC (2005) 791, 15 June. Brussels: CEC.

—— (2005*d*). *Report from the Commission: Better Lawmaking 2004: 12th Report.* SEC (2005) 364, 21 March. Brussels: CEC.

—— (2005*e*) *Commission Work Programme for 2005L Communication from the President in Agreement with V-P Wallström.* COM (2005) 15 final, 26 January. Brussels: CEC.

—— (2005*f*). *Groups of Members of the Commission.* Available at the Commission's website: www.europa.eu.int/comm (1 June). Brussels: CEC.

—— (2005*g*). *Implementing the Community Lisbon Programme: A Policy Framework to Strengthen EU Manufacturing.* COM (2005) 474 final. Brussels: CEC.

—— (2005*h*). *Communication from the Commission to the Council and the European Parliament: Draft Declaration on Guiding Principles for Sustainable Development.* COM (2005) 218 final, 25 May. Brussels: CEC.

—— (2005*i*). *Commission Working Document: Better Regulation and the Thematic Strategies.* COM (2005) 466 final, 28 September. Brussels: CEC.

Challis, L., Fuller, S., Henwood, M., Klein, P., Plowden, W., Webb, A., and Whittingham, P. (1988). *Joint Approaches to Social Policy: Rationality and Practice.* Cambridge: Cambridge University Press.

Chisholm, D. (1989). *Coordination Without Hierarchy: Informal Structures in Multi-Organizational Systems.* Berkeley: University of California Press.

Cini, M. (1996). *The European Commission: Leadership, Organization and Culture in the EU Administration.* Manchester: Manchester University Press.

—— (2005). *Pragmatism Prevails: Barroso's European Commission.* RIIA Briefing Paper, 05.01. London: Chatham House.

Coffey, C. (1999). *Sustainable Development and the EC Fisheries Sector.* London: Institute for European Environmental Policy.

—— (2003). *The Draft Constitution for Europe: Maintaining Progress Towards a Green Constitution.* London: Institute for European Environmental Policy.

Collier, U. (1997). *Energy and Environment in the EU.* Aldershot: Ashgate.

Consultative Forum (on the Environment and Sustainable Development) (1999). *Sustainable Governance.* Brussels: Commission of the European Communities.

Corbett, R., Jacobs, F., and Shackleton, M. (2005). *The European Parliament,* 6th edn. London: John Harper.

Council of the European Union (1999). *Operation of the Council with an Enlarged Union in Prospect ('The Trumpf–Pirris Report').* Report by the Working Party set up by the Secretary-General of the Council. Brussels: General Secretariat of the Council.

—— (2001). *Preparing the Council for Enlargement, Part I: Overall Assessment; Part II: Evaluation of Implementation of the Helsinki Recommendations, Part III*. 19 June, 9518/01. Brussels: General Secretariat of the Council.

—— (2004). *Council Decision Adopting the Council's Rules of Produre*. 5163/04, 21 January. Brussels: General Secretariat of the Council.

Court of Auditors (1992). 'Special Report No. 3/92 Concerning the Environment'. *Official Journal*, C245, 23 September: 1–30.

Cram, L. (1997). *Policy Making in the EU*. London: Routledge.

de Búrca, G. and Scott, J. (eds.) (2006). *Law and the New Governance in the EU and the US*. Oxford: Hart Publishing.

De la Porte, C. (2002) 'Is the Open Method of Coordination Appropriate for Organising Activities at EU Level in Sensitive Policy Areas?', *European Law Review*, 8/1: 38–58.

DEFRA (Department for Environment, Food, and Rural Affairs) (1998). *Policy Appraisal and the Environment: Policy Guidance*. London: Department for Environment, Food, and Rural Affairs.

—— (2004). *Regulation Taskforce Report*. March 2004. London: Department for Environment, Food, and Rural Affairs.

Derlien, H.-U. (2000). 'Co-ordinating German EU Policy: Failing Successfully?', in H. Kassim, G. B. Peters, and V. Wright (eds.), *National Co-ordination of EU Policy-making*. Oxford: Oxford University Press.

DETR (Department of the Environment Transport and the Regions) (1999). *A Better Quality of Life: A Strategy for Sustainable Development in the UK*. London: Stationery Office.

Deubner, C. and Huppertz C. (2003). *Die Koordinierung der Deutschen Europapolitik. Kritische Analyse und Perspektiven*. Working Paper. Paris: Commissariat du Plan.

Devuyst, Y. (2004). *EU Decision Making after the Treaty Establishing a Constitution for Europe*. European Union Centre Working Paper No 9. Pittsburgh: University of Pittsburgh.

Di Maggio, P. J. and Powell, W. W. (1983). 'The Iron Cage Revisited: Institutional Isomorphism and Collective Rationality in Organizational Fields', *American Sociological Review*, 48: 147–60.

Dimitrakapoulos, D. and Richardson, J. J. (2001). 'Implementing EU Public Policy', in J. J. Richardson (ed.), *European Union: Power and Policy Making*. London: Routledge.

Dinan, D. (1999). *Ever Closer Union: An Introduction to European Integration*, 2nd edn. Basingstoke: Macmillan.

Dobson, A. (2000). *Green Political Thought*, 3rd edn. London: Routledge.

Dobson, L. and Weale, A. (2003). 'Governance and Legitimacy', in E. Bomberg and A. Stubb (eds.), *The European Union: How Does it Work?* Oxford: Oxford University Press.

DoE (Department of the Environment) (1993). *The Links Between the DoE and the Institutions of the EC*. London: Department of the Environment.

Dunsire, A. (1993). 'Modes of Governance', in J. Kooiman (ed.), *Modern Governance: New Government–Society Interaction*. London: Sage.

Eales, R., Smith, S., Twigger-Ross, C., Sheate, W. et al. (2005). 'Emerging Approaches to Integrated Appraisal in the UK', *Impact Assessment and Project Appraisal*, 23/2: 113–23.

Eberlein, B. and Kerwer, D. (2004). 'New Governance in the EU: A Theoretical Perspective', *Journal of Common Market Studies*, 42/1: 121–42.

Ecologic (1999). *Best Practice for Integrating Environmental Protection Requirements into Other Sector Policies*. Proceedings of a Workshop, 25–6 May. Bonn: Ecologic.

Edelman, M. (1971). *Politics as Symbolic Action*. Chicago, IL: Markham.

EEA (European Environment Agency) (2003). *Europe's Environment: The Third Assessment (Full report)*. Copenhagen: European Environment Agency.

—— (2005*a*). *Environmental Policy Integration in Europe: State of Play and an Evaluation Framework*. EEA technical report, No 2/2005. Copenhagen: European Environment Agency.

—— (2005*b*). *Environmental Policy Integration in Europe: Administrative Culture and Practices*. EEA technical report, No 5/2005. Copenhagen: European Environment Agency.

—— (2005*c*). *European Environment Outlook*. EEA report 4/2005. Copenhagen: European Environment Agency.

EEB (European Environment Bureau) (1999). *Do Sector Strategies Work?* Brussels: European Environment Bureau. Available at: http://www.eeb.org/publication.

—— (2003). *Environmental Policy Integration: EEB Article 6 Watch Project*. July 2003–June 2004. Brussels: European Environment Bureau.

Egeberg, M. (1987). 'Managing Public Organizations', in K. Eliassen and J. Kooiman (eds.), *Managing Public Organizations*. London: Sage.

Eising, R. and Kohler-Koch, B. (1999). 'Introduction: Network Governance in the EU', in B. Kohler-Koch and R. Eising (eds.) *The Transformation of Governance in the EU*. London: Routledge.

ENDS (Environmental Data Services) Ltd., *Environmental Data Services (ENDS) Report* (various years).

—— Daily Ltd., *Environmental Data Services (ENDS) Daily Report* (various years).

European Parliament (1997). *Report on Alleged Contraventions or Maladministration in the Implementation of Community Law in Relation to BSE, Without Prejudice to the Jurisdiction of the Community and National Courts: Temporary Committee of inquiry Into BSE*. Rapporteur: Mr Manuel Medina Ortega, A4-0020/97. Brussels: European Parliament.

—— (1998). *Resolution on the Commission Communication 'Partnership for Integration'*. B4-0981/98, 5 November. Brussels: European Parliament.

—— (2001*a*). *European Parliament Resolution on Environment Policy and Sustainable Development: Preparing for the Gothenburg European Council*. (2000/2322(INI)), A5-0171/2001, 31 May. Brussels: European Parliament.

—— (2001*b*). *Draft Report on Environment Policy and Sustainable Development: Preparing for the Gothenburg European Council.* Committee on the Environment, Public Health and Consumer Policy, Rapporteur: Anneli Hulthén, 5 April. Brussels: European Parliament.

—— (2001*c*). *Draft Report on the Commission Communication to the Council and the European Parliament on Bringing our Needs and Responsibilities Together: Integrating Environmental Issues with Economic Policy.* Committee on the Environment, Public Health and Consumer Policy. Rapporteur: Hans Blokland, 23 March. Brussels: European Parliament.

—— (2002*a*). *Activity Report, 1 August 2001 to 31 July 2002 of the Delegations to the Conciliation Committee.* Brussels: European Parliament.

—— (2002*b*). *Assisting the European Parliament and its Members: Raising the Game.* Note for the Members of the Bureau, 02-0419, Brussels, 25 June. Brussels: European Parliament.

—— (2004). *Activity Report 1 May 1999 to 30 April (5th Parliamentary term) of the Delegations to the Conciliation Committee.* PE 287.644. Brussels: European Parliament.

—— (2005). *'Raising the Game' Review—Has the Game Been Raised?* Note for the Members of the Bureau, D (2005) 10590. Brussels: European Parliament.

Everson, M., Majone, G., Metcalfe, L., and Schout, A. (2000). *The Role of Specialised Agencies in Decentralising EU Governance.* Background report to the Commission White Paper on Governance. Maastricht: European Institute of Public Administration.

Faas, T. (2002). 'Why do MEPs Defect? An Analysis of Party Group Cohesion in the 5th European Parliament', *European Union Online Papers (EioP)*, 6/2. Available at: http://eiop.or.at/eiop/texte/2002-002a.htm.

Fergusson, M. et al. (2001). *The Effectiveness of EU Council Integration Strategies and Options for Carrying Forward the 'Cardiff Process'.* London: Institute of European Environmental Policy.

Flinders, M. (2002). 'Governance in Whitehall', *Public Administration*, 80/1: 51–76.

—— (2004). 'Distributed Public Governance in the EU', *Journal of European Public Policy*, 11/3: 520–45.

Fransman, M. (1990) *The Market and Beyond: Cooperation and Competition in Information Technology in the Japanese System.* Cambridge: Cambridge University Press.

Galbraith, J. R. (1973). *Designing Complex Organizations.* Reading, MA: Addison-Wesley.

Gemengde Commissie (2005) *Sturing EU-aangelegenheden.* Eindrapport, Programma Andere Overheid. Rijksbrede takenanalyse, 7 juni. Den Haag: Gemengde Commissie.

German Council of Environmental Advisors (*Der Rat von Sachverständigen für Umweltfragen*) (2000). *Beginning the Next Millennium, February 2000.* Summary available at: www.umweltrat.de.

German Council of Environmental Advisors (*Der Rat von Sachverständigen für Umweltfragen*) (2002). *Environmental Report 2002 (Für eine neue Vorreiterrolle)*, March 2002. Summary available at: www. umweltrat.de.

—— (*Der Rat von Sachverständigen für Umweltfragen*) (2004). *Environmental Report, 2004*. Summary available at: www.umweltrat.de.

Goldsmith, S. and Eggers, W. D. (2004). *Governing by Network: The New Shape of the Public Sector*. Washington, DC: Brookings Institution Press.

Gomez, R. and Peterson, J. (2001). 'The EU's Impossibly Busy Foreign Ministers: "No One is in Control"', *European Foreign Affairs Review*, 6/1: 53–74.

Görlach, B., Hinterberger, F., Schepelmann, P. et al. (1999). *From Vienna to Helsinki: The Process of Integration of Environmental Concerns in all Policies of the EU*. Germany: Wuppertal Institut.

Haagsma, A. (1989). 'The European Community's Environmental Policy: A Case Study in Federalism?', *Fordham International Law Journal*, 12: 311–59.

Haas, P. M. (1992). 'Introduction: Epistemic Communities and International Policy Coordination', *International Organisation*, 46/1: 1–35.

Haersolte, J. C. van and Oosterkamp, J. S. van de (2003). 'De Coördinatie van Nederlandse Standpunten over Europees Recht en Europees Beleid in de Haagse Praktijk', *SEW (Tidschrift voor Europees en Economisch Recht)*, 5: 129–39.

Haigh, N. (ed.) (2002). *Manual of Environmental Policy: The EU and Britain*. Oxford: Elsevier.

—— (ed.) (2005). *Manual of Environmental Policy: The EU and Britain*. Leeds: Maney.

Hanf, K. (1978). 'Introduction', in K. Hanf and F. Scharpf (eds.), *Inter-organizational Policy Making: Limits to Coordination and Central Control*. Beverly Hills, CA: Sage.

—— and de Gronden, E. (1998). 'The Netherlands', in K. Hanf and A.-I. Jansen (eds.), *Governance and Environment in Western Europe*. Harmondsworth: Longman.

Hayes-Renshaw, F. (2002). 'The Council of Ministers', in J. Peterson and M. Shackleton (eds.), *The Institutions of the European Union*. Oxford: Oxford University Press.

Hayward, J. (ed.) (2006). *Leaderless Europe*. Oxford: Oxford University Press.

Hennessey, P. (1989). *Whitehall*. London: Fontana.

Héritier, A. et al. (1994). *Die Veränderung von Staatlichkeit in Europa: Ein Regulativer Wettbewerb*. Frankreich: Opladen.

—— (2001). *New Modes of Governance in Europe: Policy Making Without Legislating?* Max Planck Project Group, Preprints, 2001/14. Bonn: Max-Planck Institute.

—— (2003). 'New Modes of Governance in Europe: Increasing Political Capacity and Policy Effectiveness?', in T. Börzel and R. Cichowski (eds.), *The State of the European Union: Law, Politics and Society*, vol. 6. Oxford: Oxford University Press.

Hertin, J., Jacob, K. and Volkery, A. (2007). 'Policy Appraisal', in A. Jordan and A. Lenshow (eds.), *Innovation in Environmental Policy? Integrating Environment for Sustainability*. Norwich: CSERGE, University of East Anglia.

Hey, C. (1998). *Nachhaltige Mobilität in Europa Akteure*. Wiesbaden: Institutionen und Politische Strategien.

—— (2002). 'Why Does Environmental Policy Integration Fail?', in A. Lenschow (ed.), *Environmental Policy Integration: Greening Sectoral Policies in Europe*. London: Earthscan.

Heywood, A. (2000). *Key Concepts in Politics*. Basingstoke: Palgrave/Macmillan.

High Level Group (chaired by Wim Kok) (2004). *Facing the Challenge: The Lisbon Strategy for Growth and Employment*. November. Luxembourg: Office for Official Publications of the European Communities.

Hill, J. and Jordan, A. (1993). 'The Greening of Government: Lessons from the White Paper Process', *ECOS*, 14, 3/4: 3–9.

—— —— (1995). 'Memorandum from the Green Alliance', in House of Lords Select Committee on Sustainable Development, *Report from the Select Committee, Volume II*. London: HMSO.

Hinterberger, F. and Zacherl, R. (2003). *Ways Towards Sustainability in the European Union: Beyond the European Spring Summit in 2003*. Vienna: SERI Institute.

Hix, S., Raunio, T., and Scully, H. (1999). *An Institutional Theory of Behaviour in the European Parliament*. Paper prepared for presentation at the Joint Sessions of the European Consortium for Political Research, 26–31 March, Mannheim.

H. M. Treasury (1998). *Modern Public Services for Britain: Investing in Reform*. Cmnd 4011. London: Stationery Office.

—— (2002). *2002 Spending Review: Public Service Agreements 2003–2006*. Cmnd 571. London: The Stationery Office.

Hocking, B. (1999). *Foreign Ministries: Change and Adaptation*. Basingstoke: Macmillan.

Hodson, D. and Maher, I. (2001). 'The Open Method as a New Mode of Governance: The Case of Soft Economic Policy Coordination', *Journal of Common Market Studies*, 39/4: 719–46.

Homeyer, I., Klasing, A,. and Kraemer, A. (2004). *Exploiting the EU Open Method of Coordination*. Paper for a workshop 'The Open Method of Co-ordination—Risks and Chances for European Environmental Policy', 22 March, Brussels.

Hooghe, L. (ed.) (1996). *Cohesion Policy and European Integration: Building Multi-level Governance*. Oxford: Oxford University Press.

Hoornbeek, J. and Peters, B. G. (2005). *The Problem of Policy Problems*. Mimeograph, Department of Political Science. Pittsburgh: University of Pittsburgh.

Hult, K. and Walcott, C. (1990). *Governing Public Organization: Politics, Structure and Institutional Design*. Pacific Grove, CA: Brooks.

Humphrey, M. (2003). 'Environmental Policy', in P. Dunleavy, A. Gamble, R. Heffernan, and G. Peele (eds.), *Developments in British Politics 7*. Basingstoke: Palgrave.

Humphreys, J. (1996). *A Way Through the Woods: Negotiating in the EU*. EPSED, Department of the Environment. London: Department of the Environment.

IEEP (Institute for European Environmental Policy) (1992). *The Integration of Environmental Protection Requirements into the Definition and Implementation of Other Policies*. London: Institute for European Environmental Policy.

IEEP (Institute for European Environmental Policy) (1995). *Integrating the Environment into Other EU Policies: Developments Since 1992*. London: Institute for European Environmental Policy.

Jachtenfuchs, M. (2001). 'The Governance Approach to European Integration', *Journal of Common Market Studies*, 39/2: 245–64.

—— and Kohler-Koch, B. (2004). 'Governance and Institutional Development', in A. Wiener and T. Diez (eds.), *European Integration Theory*. Oxford: Oxford University Press.

Jacob, K. and Volkery, A. (2004). 'Institutions and Instruments for Government Self-Regulation: Environmental Policy Integration in a Cross-Country Perspective', *Journal of Comparative Policy Analysis*, 6/3: 291–309.

—— —— (2006). 'Institutions and Instruments for Government Self-Regulation', in M. Jänicke and K. Jacob (eds.) *Environmental Governance in Global Perspective*. Berlin: Freie Universität, Berlin.

Jacobs, F. and Best, E. (2004). 'Ready for the Future? The Impact of Enlargement on the European Parliament', *EIPASCOPE*, 3: 14–19.

James, O. (2004). 'The UK Core Executive's Use of Public Service Agreements as a Tool of Governance', *Public Administration*, 82/2: 397–420.

Jänicke, M. et al. (2002). 'Germany', in OECD (ed.), *Governance for Sustainability: Five Case Studies*. Paris: OECD.

Jans, J. (2000). *European Environmental Law*, 2nd edn. Groningen: Europa Law.

Jansen, A.-I., Osland, O., and Hanf, K. (1998). 'Environmental Challenges and Institutional Changes', in K. Hanf and A.-I. Jansen (eds.), *Governance and Environment in Western Europe*. Harlow: Longman.

Jessop, B. (2002). *Governance and Meta-Governance*. Lancaster: Department of Sociology, University of Lancaster. Available at: http://www.comp.lancs.ac.uk/sociology/papers/jessop-governance-and-metagovernance.pdf.

—— (2003). 'Governance and Meta-Governance', in H. Bang (ed.), *Governance as Social and Political Communication*. Manchester: Manchester University Press.

Jordan, A. J. (2000). 'Environmental Policy', in P. Dunleavy, A. Gamble, I. Holliday, and G. Peele (eds.), *Developments in British Politics 6*. Basingstoke: Macmillan.

—— (2001). 'National Environmental Ministries: Managers or Ciphers of European Environmental Policy?', *Public Administration*, 79/3: 643–63.

—— (2002a). *The Europeanization of British Environmental Policy*. Basingstoke: Palgrave.

—— (2002b). 'The Implementation of EU Environmental Policy: A Policy Problem Without a Political Solution?', in A. J. Jordan (ed.), *Environmental Policy in the European Union*. London: Earthscan.

—— (2002c). 'Efficient Hardware and Light Green Software: Environmental Policy Integration in the UK', in A. Lenschow (ed.), *Environmental Policy Integration*. London: Earthscan.

—— (2002d). 'Introduction', in A. J. Jordan (ed.), *Environmental Policy in the European Union*. London: Earthscan.

—— (2003). 'The Europeanization of National Government and Policy: A Departmental Perspective', *British Journal of Political Science*, 33/2: 261–82.

—— (2004). 'The UK: From Policy "Taking" to Policy "Shaping"?', in A. Jordan and D. Liefferink (eds.), *Environment Policy in Europe: The Europeanization of National Environmental Policy*. London: Routledge.

—— (2005). 'Introduction: EU Environmental Policy', in A. Jordan (ed.), *Environmental Policy in the European Union*, 2nd edn. London: Earthscan.

Jordan, A., and Lenschow, A. (2000). 'Greening the European Union: What Can Be Learned from the Leaders of EU Environmental Policy?', *European Environment*, 10/3: 109–20.

—— and Liefferink, D. (eds.) (2004). *Environment Policy in Europe: The Europeanization of National Environmental Policy*. London: Routledge.

—— Russel, D., Schout, A., and Unfried, M. (2003). 'Written Memorandum by Dr. Andrew Jordan and Others', in House of Lords, European Union Committee, *European Union Waste Management Policy*, Session 2002–3, 47th report, HL Paper 194. London: Stationery Office.

—— Schout, A., Unfried, M., and Zito, A. (2007). 'Environmental Policy: Shifting From Passive to Active Coordination?', in H. Kassim et al. (eds.), *Coordinating the European Union*. Lanham, MD: Rowman and Littlefield.

—— Wurzel, R., and Zito, A. (eds.) (2003). *New Instruments of Environmental Governance? National Experiences and Prospects*. London: Frank Cass.

—— —— —— and Breuckner, L. (2003*a*). 'European Governance and the Transfer of "New" Environmental Policy Instruments', *Public Administration*, 81/3: 555–74.

—— —— —— —— (2003*b*). 'Consumer Responsibility-taking and Eco-labelling Schemes in Europe', in M. Micheletti, A. Follesdal, and D. Stolle (eds.), *The Politics Behind Products*. Somerset, NJ: Transaction.

—— Wurzel, R., and A. Zito (2005). 'The Rise of 'New' Policy Instruments in Comparative Perspective: Has Governance Eclipsed Government?', *Political Studies*, 53/3: 477–96.

Judge, D. (1995). 'The Failure of National Parliaments?', *West European Politics*, 18/3: 79–100.

—— (2002). 'Predestined to Save the Earth? The Environment Committee of the European Parliament', in A. J. Jordan (ed.), *Environmental Policy in the European Union*. London: Earthscan.

—— and Earnshaw, D. (2006). 'The European Parliament: Leadership and "Followship"', in J. Hayward (ed.), *Leaderless Europe*. Oxford: Oxford University Press.

Kassim, H. (2000). 'The UK', in H. Kassim et al. (eds.), *The National Co-ordination of EU Policy: The Domestic Level*. Oxford: Oxford University Press.

—— (2001). 'Representing the UK in Brussels', in H. Kassim et al. (eds.), *The National Co-ordination of EU Policy: The European Level*. Oxford: Oxford University Press.

—— (2003*a*). 'The European Administration: Between Europeanization and Domestication', in J. Hayward and A. Menon (eds.), *Governing Europe*. Oxford: Oxford University Press.

Kassim, H. (2003*b*). 'Meeting the Demands of EU Membership: The Europeanization of National Administrative Systems', in K. Featherstone and C. Radaelli
(eds.), *The Politics of Europeanization*. Oxford: Oxford University Press.

—— et al. (ed.) (2000). *The National Coordination of EU Policy: The Domestic Level*.
Oxford: Oxford University Press.

—— et al. (eds.) (2001). *The National Co-ordination of EU Policy: The European Level*.
Oxford: Oxford University Press.

Kaufman, F. X., Majone, G., and Ostrom, E. (eds.) (1985). *Guidance, Control and
Evaluation in the Public Sector*. Berlin: De Gruyter.

Kersbergen, K. van, and Waarden, F. van (2004). 'Governance as a Bridge Between
Disciplines', *European Journal of Political Research*, 43: 143–71.

Keohane, R. O. and Ostrom, E. (eds.) (1995). *Local Commons and Global Interdependence: Heterogeneity and Cooperation in Two Domains*. London: Sage.

Kickert, W. J. M. (1993). 'Autopoiesis and the Science of (Public) Administration:
Essence, Sense and Nonsense', *Organization Studies*, 14: 261–78.

Kickert, W. J. M. (1997*a*). 'Introduction: A Management Perspective on Policy Networks', in W. J. M. Kickert et al. (eds.), *Managing Complex Networks*. London: Sage.

—— Klijn, E.-H., and Koppenjan, J. (1997*b*). 'Managing Networks in the Public
Sector: Findings and Reflections', in W. J. M. Kickert et al. (eds.), *Managing
Complex Networks*. London: Sage.

—— —— —— (eds.) (1997*c*). *Managing Complex Networks*. London: Sage.

Kinnock, N. (2004). *Progress Review of Reform*. SPEECH/04/65, Press Conference,
9 February. Brussels: CEC.

Kjær, A. M. (2004). *Governance*. Cambridge: Polity.

Klijn, E.-H. et al. (1995). 'Managing Networks in the Public Sector', *Public Administration*, 73/3: 437–54.

—— and Koppenjan, J. (2000). 'Public Management and Policy Networks: Foundations of a Network Approach to Governance', *Public Management*, 2/2: 135–58.

Knill, C. and Lenschow, A. (2000). *Implementing EU Environmental Policy*. Manchester: Manchester University Press.

Koenig-Archibugi, G. and Zürn, M. (eds.) (2006). *New Modes of Governance in the
Global System*. Basingstoke: Palgrave.

Kooiman, J. (ed.) (2003). *Governing as Governance*. London: Sage.

Koppenjan, J. and Klijn, E.-H. (2004). *Managing Uncertainties in Networks*. London:
Routledge.

Kraemer, A. et al. (2001). *Results of the Cardiff Process: Assessing the State of Development and Charting the Way Ahead*. Report to the Federal German Environmental
Agency and the Federal Environment Ministry. Berlin: Ecologic.

Kraemer, R., Klassing, A., Wilkinson, D., and von Homeyer, I. (2002). *EU Environmental Governance: A Benchmark of Policy Instruments, Final Report*. Berlin:
Ecologic.

Kronsell, A. (1997). 'Policy Innovation in the Garbage Can: The EU's Fifth Environmental Action Programme', in D. Liefferink and M. Skou Andersen (eds.), *The Innovation of EU Environmental Policy*. Oslo: Scandinavian University Press.

Lafferty, W. and Hovden, E. (2003). 'Environmental Policy Integration: Towards an Analytical Framework', *Environmental Politics*, 12/3: 1–22.

Landau, M. (1969). 'Redundancy, Rationality and the Problem of Duplication and Overlap', *Public Administration Review*, July/August: 346–58.

Lawrence, P. and Lorsch, J. (1967). *Organization and Environment*. Boston, MA: Harvard Business School Press.

Lenschow, A. (1999). 'The Greening of the EU: The Common Agricultural Policy and the Structural Funds', *Environment and Planning C*, 17: 91–108.

—— (2002a). *Environmental Policy Integration*. London: Earthscan.

—— (2002b). 'Dynamics in A Multi-level Polity: Greening the Regional and Cohesion Funds', in A. Lenschow (ed.), *Environmental Policy Integration*. London: Earthscan.

—— (2002c). 'Conclusion', in A. Lenschow (ed.), *Environmental Policy Integration*. London: Earthscan.

—— (2005). '"New" Regulatory Approaches in "Greening" EU Policies', in A. Jordan (ed.), *Environmental Policy in the European Union*, 2nd edn. London: Earthscan.

Liefferink, D. (1995). *Environmental Policy in the Netherlands: National Profile*. Paper prepared for the Workshop on 'New Nordic member states and the impact on EC environmental policy in the framework of the European Community, RTD Programme Environment'. Final draft.

—— (1996). *Environment and the Nation State: The Netherlands, the EU and Acid rain*. Manchester: Manchester University Press.

—— (1997). 'The Netherlands: A Next Exporter of Environmental Policy Concepts', in M. S. Skou Andersen and D. Liefferink (eds.), *European Environmental Policy: The Pioneers*. Manchester: Manchester University Press.

—— (1999). 'The Dutch National Plan for Sustainable Society', in N. Vig and R. Axelrod (eds.), *The Global Environment*. Washington, DC: Congress Quarterly Press.

—— and van der Zouwen, M. (2004). 'The Netherlands: The Advantage of Being Mr Average', in A. Jordan and D. Liefferink (eds.), *Environment Policy in Europe: The Europeanization of National Environmental Policy*. London: Routledge.

Lodge, M. (2005). *Comparing Non-Hierarchical Governance in Action: The Open Method of Cooperation in Pensions and Information Society*. Paper presented at the biennial EUSA Conference, 31 March–2 April, Austin, Texas.

Lyall, C. and Tait, J. (eds.) (2005). *New Modes of Governance: Developing an Integrated Policy Approach to Science, Technology, Risk and the Environment*. Aldershot: Ashgate.

McCormick, J. (2001). *Environmental Policy in the European Union*. Basingstoke: Palgrave.

McDonagh, B. (1998). *Original Sin in a Brave New World*. Dublin: Institute of European Affairs.

Majone, G. (1996). *Regulating Europe*. London: Routledge.

Mandell, M. P. (1990). 'Network Management: Strategic Behavior in the Public Sector', in R. W. Gage and M. P. Mandell (eds.), *Strategies for Managing Intergovernmental Policies and Networks*. New York: Praeger.

March, J. G. and Simon, H. A. (1958). *Organizations*. New York: Wiley.

Marks, G. (1993). 'Structural Policy and Multi-level Governance in the EC', in A. Cafruny and G. Rosenthal (eds.), *The State of the European Community*. London: Longman.

—— Hooghe, L., and Blank, K. (1996). 'European Integration From the 1980s: State-Centric v. Multi-level Governance', *Journal of Common Market Studies*, 34/3: 341–78.

Marsden, S. (1999). 'Legislative EA in the Netherlands: The E-Test as a Strategic Integrative Instrument', *European Environment*, 9: 90–100.

Marsh, D. and Rhodes, R. (eds.) (1992). *Policy Networks in British Government*. Oxford: Clarendon Press.

Maurer, A. (2002). 'Das Europäische Parlament', in W. Weidenfeld and W. Wessels (eds.), *Jahrbuch der Europäischen Integration*. Berlin: Institut für Europäische Politik.

—— (2003). 'Fragmented Structures in a Complex World', in W. Wessels et al. (eds.), *Fifteen into One?* Manchester: Manchester University Press.

—— and Wessels, W. (2001). 'The German Case: A Key Moderator in a Competitive Multilevel Environment?', in H. Kassim et al. (eds.), *The National Coordination of EU Policy: The European Level*. Oxford: Oxford University Press.

Meltsner, A. J. and Bellavita, C. (1983). *The Policy Organization*. London: Sage.

Metcalfe, L. M. (1993). 'Public Management: From Imitation to Innovation', in J. Kooiman (ed.), *Modern Governance: New Government–Society Interaction*. London: Sage.

Metcalfe, L. (1994). 'International Policy Coordination and Public Management Reform', *International Review of Administrative Sciences*, 60: 271–90.

—— (1996). 'Building Capacities for Integration: The Future Role of the Commission', *EIPASCOPE*, 1996/2: 2–8.

—— (2000). 'Reforming the Commission: Will Organizational Efficiency Produce Effective Governance?', *Journal of Common Market Studies*, 38/5: 817–41.

Meyer, C. (2004). 'The Hard Side of Soft Policy Coordination', *Journal of European Public Policy*, 11/5: 814–31.

Ministerie van Algemene Zaken (1993). *De Organisatie en Werkwijze van de Rijksdienst*. Report of the Secretaries-General. Den Haag: Ministerie van Algemene Zaken.

Ministerie van Financiën (1989). *Gevolgen EG-beleid voor het Bestaande Nationale Beleid*. Rapport van de Heroverwegingswerkgroep. Den Haag: Ministerie van Financiën.

Mintzberg, H. (1979). *The Structuring of Organizations: A Synthesis of the Research*. Englewood Cliffs, NJ: Prentice Hall.

—— (1983). *Designing Effective Organizations: Structure in Fives.* Englewood Cliffs, NJ: Prentice Hall.

—— (1989). *Mintzberg on Management: Inside Our Strange World of Organizations.* New York: Free Press.

Moravcsik, A. (1998). *The Choice For Europe.* Ithaca, NY: Cornell University Press.

—— (2005). 'The European Constitutional Compromise and the Neo-functionalist Legacy', *Journal of European Public Policy,* 12/2: 349–86.

Mosher, P. and Trubek, D. (2003). 'EU Governance, EU Employment Policy and the European Social Model', *Journal of Common Market Studies,* 41/1: 63–88.

Muijen, M.-L. van (2000). 'The Netherlands: Ambitious Goals, Ambivalent on Action', in W. Lafferty and J. Meadowcroft (eds.), *Implementing Sustainable Development.* Oxford: Oxford University Press.

Mulford, C. L. and Rogers, D. L. (1982). 'Definitions and Models', in D. L. Rogers and D. A. Whetten (eds.), *Inter-organizational Coordination: Theory, Research and Implications.* Ames: Iowa State University Press.

Müller E. (2002). 'Environmental Policy Integration as a Political Principle: The German Case and the Implications of European Policy', in A. Lenschow (ed.), *Environmental Policy Integration: Greening Sectoral Policies in Europe.* London: Earthscan.

National Audit Office (2005). *Lost in Translation: Responding to the Challenges of European Law.* 26 May. London: Stationery Office.

Neuhold, C. (2001). 'The "Legislative Backbone" Keeping the Institution Upright? The Role of European Parliament Committees in the EU Policy-Making Process'. *European Union Online Papers (EioP),* 5/10. Available at: http://eiop.or.at/eiop/texte/2001-010a.htm.

Nolkaemper, A. (2002). 'Three Conceptions of the Integration Principle in International Environmental Law', in A. Lenschow (ed.), *Environmental Policy Integration.* London: Earthscan.

Nooteboom, S. (2002). *Dutch Thoughts about Sustainability Impact Assessment.* Presentation given at a conference on 'Sustainability Impact Assessment', organized by the Institute of European Environmental Policy (IEEP), Brussels, 25 May.

North, D. (1990). *Institutions, Institutional Change and Economic Performance.* Cambridge: Cambridge University Press.

Norton, P. (ed.) (1996). *National Parliaments and the European Union.* London: Frank Cass.

Nugent, N. (2000). *At the Heart of the Union: Studies of the European Commission,* 2nd edn. Basingstoke: Macmillan.

—— (2001). *The European Commission.* Basingstoke: Palgrave/Macmillan.

—— (2002). 'The Commission's Services', in J. Peterson and M. Shackleton (eds.), *The Institutions of the European Union.* Oxford: Oxford University Press.

OECD (Organization for Economic Cooperation and Development) (1993). *Environmental Performance Reviews: Germany.* Paris: OECD.

—— (1995). *Planning for Sustainable Development: Country Experiences.* Paris: OECD.

OECD (Organization for Economic Cooperation and Development) (2001). *Environmental Performance Reviews: Germany*. Paris: OECD.

—— (2002*a*). *Governance for Sustainable Development: Five OECD Case Studies*. Paris: OECD.

—— (2002*b*). *Environmental Performance Reviews: The United Kingdom*. Paris: OECD.

—— (2002*c*). *Improving Policy Coherence and Integration for Sustainable Development: A Checklist*. Paris: OECD.

—— (2003). *Environmental Performance Reviews: The Netherlands*. Paris: OECD.

Olsen, J. P. (2005). *Maybe its Time to Re-discover Bureaucracy?* ARENA Working Paper, 10/2005. Oslo: ARENA (Centre for European Studies), University of Oslo.

Ostrom, E. (1990). *Governing the Commons: The Evolution of Institutions for Collective Action*. Cambridge: Cambridge University Press.

—— Gardner, R., and Walker, J. (1994). *Rules, Games, and Common-Pool Resources*. Ann Arbor: University of Michigan Press.

O'Toole, L. (1988). 'Strategies for Inter-governmental Management: Implementing Mechanisms in Inter-Organisational Networks', *Journal of Public Administration*, 25/1: 43–57.

Palumbo, D. J. (1975). 'Organization Theory and Political Science', in F. I. Greenstein and N. W. Polsby (eds.), *Handbook of Political Science, Volume 2: Micro-Political Theory*. Reading, MA: Addison-Wesley.

Parsons, W. (1995). *Public Policy*. Aldershot: Edward Elgar.

Pearce, D. W. (1998). 'Cost-Benefit Analysis and Environmental Policy', *Oxford Review of Economic Policy*, 14/4: 84–100.

Pehle, H. (1997*a*). 'Germany', in M. S. Andersen and D. Liefferink (eds.), *European Environmental Policy: The Pioneers*. Manchester: Manchester University Press.

—— (1997*b*). *Das Bundesministerium für Umwelt, Naturschutz und Reaktorsicherheit: Ausgegrenzt Statt Integriert: Eine Analyse des Institutionellen Fundaments der Deutschen Umweltpolitik*. Habilschrift, University of Erlangen-Nürnburg. Nürnburg: University of Erlangen-Nürnburg.

—— and Jansen, A. (1998). 'Germany', in K. Hanf and A.-I. Jansen (eds.), *Governance and Environment in Western Europe*. Harlow: Longman.

Perri 6, Leat, D., Seltzer, K., and Stoker, G. (2002). *Towards Holistic Governance*. Basingstoke: Palgrave/Macmillan.

Peters, B. G. (1998*a*). 'Managing Horizontal Government', *Public Administration*, 76: 295–311.

—— (1998*b*). *Managing Horizontal Governance: The Politics of Coordination*. Canadian Centre for Management Development, Research Paper 21. Ottawa: Canada School of Public Service.

—— (2000). 'Government and Comparative Politics', in J. Pierre (ed.), *Debating Governance*. Oxford: Oxford University Press.

—— (2003). *The Capacity to Coordinate*. Paper presented at workshop on 'Coordinating the EU: Constructing Policy Coordination and Coherent Action in a Multi-Level System', Birkbeck College, University of London, 28–9 November.

—— and Wright, V. (2001). 'The National Coordination of European Policy-Making', in J. Richardson (ed.), *European Union: Power and Policy-Making*. London: Routledge.

Peterson, J. (1995). 'Decision Making in the EU: Towards a Framework for Analysis', *Journal of European Public Policy*, 2/1: 69–93.

—— (1997). 'States, Societies and the EU', *West European Politics*, 20/4: 1–23.

—— (1999). 'The Santer Era: The European Commission in Normative, Historical and Theoretical Perspective', *Journal of European Public Policy*, 6/1: 46–65.

—— (2002). 'The College of Commissioners', in J. Peterson and M. Shackleton (eds.), *The Institutions of the European Union*. Oxford: Oxford University Press.

—— (2004). 'Policy Networks', in A. Wiener and T. Diez (eds.), *European Integration Theory*. Oxford: Oxford University Press.

—— and Bomberg, E. (1999). *Decision-Making in the European Union*. Basingstoke: Palgrave Macmillan.

—— and Sjursen, H. (eds.) (1998). *A Common Foreign Policy for Europe?* London: Routledge.

Pfeffer, J. and Salancik, G. R. (1978). *The External Control of Organizations: A Resource Dependence Perspective*. New York: Harper and Row.

Pierre, J. and Peters, B. G. (2000). *Governance Politics and the State*. Basingstoke: Macmillan.

Pollitt, C. (2003). 'Joined up Government: A Survey', *Political Studies Review*, 1: 34–49.

—— and Bouckaert, G. (2004). *Public Management Reform: A Comparative Analysis*, 2nd edn. Oxford: Oxford University Press.

Powell, W. W. (1990). 'Neither Market Nor Hierarchy: Network Forms of Organisation', *Organizational Behavior*, 12: 295–336.

Pressman, J. and Wildavsky, A. (1984). *Implementation: How Great Expectations in Washington are Dashed in Oakland*, 2nd edn. Berkeley: University of California Press.

Rein, M. and Schön, D. (1996). 'Frame Critical Policy Analysis and Frame Reflective Policy Practice', *Knowledge and Policy*, 9/1: 88–90

Rhodes, R. A. W. (1985). 'Power-dependence, Policy Communities and Intergovernmental Networks', *Public Administration Bulletin*, 49: 4–29.

—— 'The New Governance: Governing Without Government', *Political Studies*, 44: 652–67.

—— (1997a). *Understanding Governance*. Milton Keynes: Open University Press.

—— (1997b). 'Foreword', in W. J. M. Kickert et al. (eds.), *Managing Complex Networks*. London: Sage.

—— (2000a). 'Governance and Public Administration', in J. Pierre (ed.), *Debating Governance*. Oxford: Oxford University Press.

—— (2000b). 'The Governance Narrative: Key Findings and Lessons From the ESRC's Whitehall Programme', *Public Administration*, 78/2: 345–63.

Bibliography

Rhodes, R. A. W. (2003). 'What is New About Governance and Why Does it Matter?', in J. Hayward and A. Menon (eds.), *Governing Europe*. Oxford: Oxford University Press.

—— Bache, I., and George, S. (1996). 'Policy Networks and Policy Making in the European Union: A Critical Appraisal', in L. Hooghe (ed.), *Cohesion Policy and European Integration*. Oxford: Oxford University Press.

Richards, D. and Smith, M. (2002). *Governance and Public Policy*. Oxford: Oxford University Press.

Rittel, H. and Weber, M. (1973). 'Dilemmas in a General Theory of Planning', *Policy Sciences*, 4/3: 155–69.

RIVM (*Rijksinstituut voor Volksgezondheid en Milieu*) (2003). *The Netherlands: National Inventory Report, 2003*. Bilthoven: Rijksinstituut voor Volksgezondheid en Milieu.

ROB (Raad voor het Openbaar Bestuur) (2004). *Nationale Coördinatie van EU-beleid: een Politiek en Proactief Proces*. Den Haag: Raad voor het Openbaar Bestuur.

Rosenau, J. and Czempiel, E. O. (eds.) (1992). *Governance Without Government: Order and Change in World Politics*. Cambridge, MA: Cambridge University Press.

Rosenthal, U. (1988). *Bureaupolitiek en Bureaupolitisme: Om het Behoud van een Competitief Overheidsbestel*. Alphen a/d Rijn: Samsom H. D. Tjeenk Willink.

Ruiten, P. van (2002). *Lessons Learned with Environmental Assessment of Legislation in the Netherlands*. Paper presented at the International Association for Impact Assessment Annual Conference, 15–21 June, Den Haag.

Russel, D. (2004). *Environmental Policy Appraisal in UK Central Government: A Political Analysis*. Ph.D. Thesis, School of Environmental Sciences, UEA, Norwich.

—— (2004). *Gearing up Governance for Sustainable Development: Patterns of Environmental Policy Appraisal*. Paper for the Association of American Geographers Annual Conference, Philadelphia, 14–19 March.

—— and Jordan, A. (2005). *Gearing up Governance for Sustainable Development: Patterns of Environmental Policy Appraisal in UK Central Government*. CSERGE Working Paper, University of East Anglia.

Sbragia, A. (2000). 'The EU as Coxswain', in J. Pierre (ed.), *Debating Governance*. Oxford: Oxford University Press.

—— (2002). *The Dilemma of Governance with Government*. Jean Monnet Working Paper 3/02, New York University School of Law.

Scharpf, F. (1994). 'Games Real Actors Could Play: Positive and Negative Coordination in Embedded Negotiations', *Journal of Theoretical Politics*, 6/1: 27–53.

—— (1999). *Governing in Europe: Effective and Democratic?* Oxford: Oxford University Press.

Schein, E. H. (1985). *Organizational Culture and Leadership*. San Francisco, CA: Jossey-Bass.

Schendelen, M. van (1995). *Gelijk Hebben of Winnen: De Nederlandse Belangenbehartiging in de Europese Unie*. Amsterdam: Amsterdam University Press.

Schendelen, R. van (2004). *Machiavelli in Brussels: The Art of Lobbying the EU*. Amsterdam: Amsterdam University Press.

Schout, A. (1996). *VROM en EU: Halverwege een Overgangsproces?* Den Haag: Ministry of Environment, Housing, and Spatial Planning (VROM).

—— (1999a). *The Internal Management of External Relations.* Maastricht: European Institute of Public Administration.

—— (1999b). 'The European Network for the Implementation and Enforcement of Environmental law (IMPEL): The Strengths and Weaknesses of an Informal Network', in M. Everson et al. (eds.), *The Role of Specialised Agencies in Decentralising EU Governance—Report for the European Commission.* Florence/Maastricht: EIPA/EUI.

—— (2000). 'Europese Sturingsuitdaging: Van Creëren Naar Beheren van de Interne markt', *Bestuurskunde*, 4: 152–63.

—— (2004). 'De Nederlandse EU Coördinatie: Het Actieve Coördinatie Alternatief', in *Raad voor het Openbaar Bestuur* (ed.), *Nationale coördinatie van EU-beleid: een politiek en proactief proces.* Den Haag: Raad voor het Openbaar Bestuur.

—— (2006). 'Beyond the Rotating Presidency', in J. Hayward (ed.), *Leaderless Europe.* Oxford: Oxford University Press.

—— and Bastmeijer, C. J. (2003). 'The Next Phase in the Europeanisation of National Ministries: Preparing EU Dialogues', *EIPASCOPE*, 1: 1–10.1.

—— and Jordan, A. J. (2004). 'The Specificity of Governance: Can the EU Rise to the Challenge of Environmental Integration?', in E. Bohne, C. F. Bonser, and K. Spencer (eds.), *Transatlantic Perspectives on Liberalization and Democratic Governance.* Piscataway, NJ: Transaction.

—— and Metcalfe, L. (1999). *Integratie van het Milieubeleid in de Europese Vakraden: Interministeriële Afstemming van 'Event' naar 'Issue' coördinatie?* Mimeograph. Maastricht: European Institute of Public Administration.

—— —— (2005). 'Coordinating European Governance: Self-Organising or Centrally Steered?', *Public Administration*, 83/1: 201–20.

—— and Nomden, K. (2000). 'Het Europeaniserings debat in Nederland 1990–2000', *Bestuurswetenschappen*, 54: 5–6.

Scott, C. (2002). 'The Governance of the European Union: The Potential for Multi-Level Control', *European Law Journal*, 8/1: 59–79.

Scott, J. and Trubek, D. (2002). 'Mind the Gap: Law and New Approaches to Governance in the European Union', *European Law Journal*, 8/1: 1–18.

Scott, W. R. (1995). *Institutions and Organizations.* London: Sage.

Seidman, H. (1970). *Politics, Position and Power.* New York: Oxford University Press.

Selznick, P. (1957). *Leadership in Administration: A Sociological Interpretation.* Berkeley: University of California Press.

Sharp, R. (1998). 'British Environmental Diplomacy in Europe', in P. Lowe and S. Ward (eds.), *British Environmental Policy and Europe.* London: Routledge.

Sheate, W., Dagg, S., Richardson, J., Aschemann, R., Palerm, J., and Steen, U. (2001). *SEA and Integration of the Environment into Strategic Decision Making: Volume 1 (Main Report).* London: Imperial College Consultants (ICON).

Simon, H. A. (1976). *Administrative Behaviour: A Study of Decision-making Processes in Administrative Organizations.* New York: Free Press.

Siwert-Probst, J. (1998). 'Die Klassischen Aussenpolitischen Institutionen', in W.-D. Eberwein and K. Kaiser (eds.), *Deutschlands neue Aussenbpolitiek*. München: Oldenbourg.

Smith, M. (1993). *Pressure, Power and Policy*. London: Harvester Wheatsheaf.

Soetendorp, B. (1991). 'Een Institutionele Herstructurering van het Nederlands Buitenland Beleid', *International Spectator*, 45/5: 270–8.

SPD–Bündnis 90/Die Grünen (1998). *Aufbruch und Erneuerung: Deutschlands Weg ins 21. Jahrundert*. Koalitionsvereinbarung zwischen der Sozialdemokratischen Partei Deutschlands und Bündnis '90/Die Grünen, 20 October, Bonn.

Spence, D. (1993). 'The Role of the National Civil Service in European Lobbying', in S. Mazey and J. Richardson (eds.), *Lobbying in the EU*. Oxford: Oxford University Press.

—— (1994). 'Structure, Functions and Procedures in the Commission', in G. Edwards and D. Spence (eds.), *The European Commission*. Harlow: Longman.

—— (1995). 'The Coordination of European Policy by Member States', in M. Westlake (ed.), *The Council of the European Union*. London: Cartermill.

—— (2000). 'Plus ça Change, Plus C'est la Meme Chose: Attempting to Reform the European Commission', *Journal of European Public Policy*, 7/1: 1–25.

Stevens, A. and Stevens, H. (2001). *Brussels Bureaucrats: The Administration of the European Union*. Basingstoke: Palgrave/Macmillan.

Stichting Natuur en Milieu (2001). *Stichting Natuur en Milieu Positief Over Beleidsvernieuwing in NMP4*. Press Release, 13 July. Amsterdam: Stichting Natuur en Milieu.

Strauss-Kahn, D. (2004). *Building a Political Europe*. Brussels: CEC.

Stubb, A., Wallace, H., and Peterson, J. (2003). 'The Policy Making Process', in E. Bomberg and A. Stubb (eds.), *The European Union: How Does it Work?* Oxford: Oxford University Press.

Sustainable Development Commission (2004). *Shows Promise, But Must Try Harder: An Assessment by the Sustainable Development Commission of the Government's Report Programme on Sustainable Development over the Past 5 Years*. London: UK Sustainable Development Commission.

Tenbensel, T. (2005). 'Multiple Modes of Governance: Disentangling the Alternatives to Hierarchies and Markets', *Public Management Review*, 7/2: 267–88.

Teulings, A. W. M. (1992). *Sturing op Afstand: Resultaatverantwoordelijkheid als Coördinatiewijze van Organisaties*. Wassenaar: Netherlands Institute for Advanced Studies.

Thatcher, M. (1998). 'The Development of Policy Network Analyses', *Journal of Theoretical Politics*, 10/4: 389–416.

Thompson, G., F., Frances, R., Levacic, S., and Mitchells, J. (eds.) (1995). *Markets, Hierarchies and Networks*. London: Sage.

—— (2003). *Between Hierarchies and Markets: The Logic and Limits of Network Forms of Organization*. Oxford: Oxford University Press.

Toonen, T. (1983). 'Administrative Plurality in a Unitary State: The Analysis of Public Organisational Pluralism', *Policy and Politics*, 11/3: 247–71.

Trubek, D. M. and Trubek, L. G. (2005). 'Hard and Soft Law in the Construction of Social Europe: The Role of the Open Method of Co-ordination', *European Law Journal*, 11/3: 343–64.

Tweede Kamer der Staten-Generaal (2002). *Op tijd is te laat*. Vergaderjaar 2002–3, 28 632, Nr. 1. Den Haag: Tweede Kamer.

Underdal, A. (1980). 'Integrated Marine Policy: What? Why? How?', *Marine Policy*, 4/3: 159–69.

Unfried, M. (2000). 'The Cardiff Process: The Institutional and Political Challenge of Environmental Integration in the EU, *RECIEL*, 9/2: 112–19.

—— (2004). *Environmental Integration and the Coordination of EU Affairs: The Case of Germany*. Mimeograph. Maastricht: European Institute of Public Administration.

—— and Blau, S. (2003). *The European Parliament and Environmental Policy Integration: Internal Problems with Cross-sector Policy Making*. Mimeograph. Maastricht: European Institute of Public Administration.

Verheem, R. A. A (2004). *The Evolution of the Dutch E-Test*. The Netherlands: Commission for Environmental Impact Assessment.

—— and Tonk, J. A. M. N. (2000). 'SEA: One Concept, Multiple Forms', *Impact Assessment and Project Appraisal*, 18/3: 177–82.

Verschuuren, J. M. (2004). 'Implementatie Milieurichtlijnen: Nederland Raakt Achterop', *Nederlands Tijdschrift voor Europees Recht*, 10/2: 348–51.

VROM (Ministerie van Volkshuisvesting, Ruimtelijke Ordening en Milieubeleid) (2001). *Met Recht Verantwoordelijk: Discussienota Over de Toekomst van een op Duurzame Ontwikkeling Gerichte Milieuwetgeving in een Verantwoordelijke Samenleving*. Den Haag: Ministerie van Volkshuisvesting, Ruimtelijke Ordening en Milieubeleid.

—— (2003). *Assessment of Proposed Regulation: A Manual*. Den Haag: Ministerie van Volkshuisvesting, Ruimtelijke Ordening en Milieubeleid.

VWS (Ministerie van Volksgezondheid, Welzijn en Sport) (2003). *Rapportage BrusselProof. Onderzoek Naar de Kwaliteit van het Europa-beleid van het Ministerie van Volksgezondheid, Welzijn en Sport*. Den Haag: Ministerie van Volksgezondheid, Welzijn en Sport.

Wallace, H. (1996). 'Relations Between the EU and the British Administration', in Y. Mény et al. (eds.), *Adjusting to Europe*. London: Routledge.

—— (1997). 'At Odds with Europe', *Political Studies*, 45: 677–88.

Warleigh, A. (2000). 'The Hustle: Citizenship Practice, NGOs and "Policy Coalitions" in the European Union', *Journal of European Public Policy*, 7/2: 229–43.

WCED (World Commission on Environment and Development) (1987). *Our Common Future*. Oxford: Oxford University Press.

Weale, A. (1992). 'Implementation Failure: A Suitable Case For Review?', in E. Lykke (ed.), *Achieving Environmental Goals*. London: Belhaven Press.

Weale, A. (1993). 'Ecological Modernisation and the Integration of European Environmental Policy', in D. Liefferink, P. Lowe, and A. Mol (eds.), *European Integration and Environmental Policy*. Chichester: Wiley.

—— and Williams, A. (1992). 'Between Economy and Ecology? The Single Market and the Integration of Environmental Policy', *Environmental Politics*, 1/4: 45–64.

—— et al. (2000). *European Environmental Governance*. Oxford: Oxford University Press.

Weick, K. E. (1976). 'Educational Organizations as Loosely Coupled Systems', *Administrative Science Quarterly*, 21: 1–19.

Weller, P., Bakvis, H., and Rhodes, R. A. W (eds.) (1997). *The Hollow Crown: Countervailing Trends in Core Executives*. Basingstoke: Macmillan.

Whetten, D. A. (1977). 'Toward a Contingency Model for Designing Inter-organizational Service Delivery Systems', *Organizations and Administration Sciences*, 8: 77–96.

Wildavsky, A. (1996). *Speaking Truth to Power: The Art and Craft of Policy Analysis*. London: Transaction.

Wilkinson, D. (1995). *Approaches to Integrating the Environment into other Sectoral Policies: An Interim Evaluation of Experience in the European Commission and Parliament*. London: Institute for European Environmental Policy.

—— (1997). 'Towards Sustainability in the European Union? Steps Within the European Commission Towards Integrating the Environment into other European Union Policy Sectors', *Environmental Politics*, 6/1: 153–73.

—— (1998). 'Steps Towards Integrating the Environment into other EU policy Sectors', in T. O'Riordan and H. Voisey (eds.), *The Transition to Sustainability*. London: Earthscan.

—— Skinner, I., and Ferguson, M. (2002). *The Future of the Cardiff Process: A Report for the Danish Ministry of the Environment*. London: Institute for European Environmental Policy.

—— Monkhouse, C., and Baldock, D. (2004a). *The Future of EU Environment Policy: Challenges and Opportunities*. A Special report for the All-Party Parliamentary Environment Group, December. London: Institute for European Environmental Policy.

—— Fergusson, M., Bowyer, C. et al. (2004b). *Sustainable Development in the European Commission's Integrated Impact Assessments for 2003: Final Report*. London: Institute for European Environmental Policy.

Wise Men Report (I) (1999). *Allegations Regarding Fraud, Mismanagement and Nepotism in the European Commission*. Brussels: CEC.

Wise Men Report (II) (1999). *Analysis of Current Practice and Proposals for Tackling Mismanagement, Irregularities and Fraud*. Brussels: CEC.

Wollman, H. (2003). 'Coordination in the inter-governmental Setting', in B. G. Peters and J. Pierre (eds.), *Handbook of Public Administration*. London: Sage.

Wright, V. (1996). 'The National Co-ordination of European Policy-making: Negotiating the Quagmire', in J. Richardson (ed.), *European Union: Power and Policy-Making*. London: Routledge.

Wurzel, R. (2001). 'Integrating Environmental Requirements into Other Policy Sectors: The Role of the EU Presidency', *European Environmental Law Review*, 19/1: 5–15.

—— Jordan, A., Zito, A., and Bruckner, L. (2003). 'From High Regulatory State to Social and Ecological market Economy? "New" Environmental Policy Instruments in Germany', *Environmental Politics*, 12/1: 115–36.

—— (2004*a*). 'Germany: From Environmental Leadership to Partial Mismatch', in A. Jordan and D. Liefferink (eds.), *Environment Policy in Europe: The Europeanization of National Environmental Policy*. London: Routledge.

—— (2004*b*). *The EU Presidency: "Honest Broker" or Driving Seat? An Anglo-German Comparison in the Environmental Policy Field*. London: Anglo-German Foundation.

Yukl, G. (1998). *Leadership in Organizations*, 4th edn. Upper Saddle River, NJ: Prentice Hall.

Zito, A. (2000). *Creating Environmental Policy in the European Union*. Basingstoke: Palgrave Macmillan.

—— Jordan, A., Wurzel, R., and Bruckner, L. (2003). 'Instrument Innovation in an Environmental Lead State: "New" Environmental Policy Instruments in the Netherlands', *Environmental Politics*, 12/1: 157–78.

Index